The Most Dangerous Art

The Most Dangerous Art

Poetry, Politics, and Autobiography after the Russian Revolution

Donald Loewen

LEXINGTON BOOKS

A division of
ROWMAN & LITTLEFIELD PUBLISHERS, INC.
Lanham • Boulder • New York • Toronto • Plymouth, UK

LEXINGTON BOOKS

A division of Rowman & Littlefield Publishers, Inc.
A wholly owned subsidiary of The Rowman & Littlefield Publishing Group, Inc.
4501 Forbes Boulevard, Suite 200
Lanham, MD 20706

Estover Road
Plymouth PL6 7PY
United Kingdom

Copyright © 2008 by Lexington Books

All rights reserved. No part of this publication may be reproduced, stored in a retrieval system, or transmitted in any form or by any means, electronic, mechanical, photocopying, recording, or otherwise, without the prior permission of the publisher.

British Library Cataloguing in Publication Information Available

Library of Congress Cataloging-in-Publication Data

Loewen, Donald, 1962–
 The most dangerous art : poetry, politics, and autobiography after the Russian revolution / Donald Loewen.
   p. cm.
 Includes bibliographical references and index.
 ISBN-13: 978-0-7391-2083-5 (cloth : alk. paper)
 ISBN-10: 0-7391-2083-2 (cloth : alk. paper)
 1. Russian poetry—20th century—History and criticism. 2. Mandel'shtam, Osip, 1891–1938—Criticism and interpretation. 3. Tsvetaeva, Marina, 1892–1941—Criticism and interpretation. 4. Pasternak, Boris Leonidovich, 1890–1960—Criticism and interpretation. 5. Politics and literature—Soviet Union. 6. Soviet Union—Politics and government—1917–1936. I. Title.
 PG3056.L59 2008
 891.71'409—dc22   2007030531

Printed in the United States of America

∞™ The paper used in this publication meets the minimum requirements of American National Standard for Information Sciences—Permanence of Paper for Printed Library Materials, ANSI/NISO Z39.48–1992.

For Evelyn

Contents

Acknowledgments	ix
A Note on Transliteration and Abbreviations	xi
Introduction	1
1 Endangered Genre, Endangered Artist	15
2 Early Warning Signs	29
3 The Search for Safe Passage	59
4 Fighting for Breath	91
5 The Poet's Birthright	121
6 A Survivor's Story	157
Conclusion	179
Endnotes	185
Bibliography	211
Index	219
About the Author	225

Acknowledgments

This book would not be possible without the support, advice and encouragement provided by many individuals and organizations throughout the many stages of its development. I would like to thank the Social Sciences and Humanities Research Council of Canada and the Graduate School of the University of Wisconsin-Madison for Fellowship assistance in the earliest stages, when some of the ideas found here were being formed and tested as part of my dissertation research. I am also very grateful to Jean-Pierre Mileur, the Dean of Harpur College at Binghamton University (SUNY), for the provision of a Dean's Research Semester to develop those ideas further. For their willing assistance in locating and providing access to materials, I would like to thank the staff at the Russian State Library and Binghamton University's Glenn G. Bartle Library. T. J. MacDuff Stewart, Patrick Dillon and the rest of the staff at Lexington Books have been unfailingly generous with their time and advice.

I am grateful to Peter France and Jon Stallworthy for permission to quote from their translation of Boris Pasternak's "Marburg," from *Selected Poems* (Penguin). Thanks to Clarence Brown for permission to quote from his translations of Osip Mandelstam's *The Noise of Time* and "Fourth Prose." Extracts from *The Voice of Prose* by Boris Pasternak, edited by Christopher Barnes, are reproduced by permission of Birlinn Ltd. (www.birlinn.co.uk).

One of the best things about participating in a scholarly community is the opportunity to benefit from the advice and wisdom of colleagues in a variety of fields. For their encouragement and willingness to read and share their knowledge with me at various stages of this project, I am deeply grateful to Jeanne Eichelberger, Judith Deutsch Kornblatt, Ingeborg Majer O'Sickey, David McDonald, Luiza Franco Moreira, Rosmarie Morewedge, Neil Christian Pages, Andrew Reynolds, Gary Rosenshield, and David Stahl. David Bethea provided both inspiration and a wealth of generous feedback for me. Nancy Tittler's generosity with her time, her careful reading, and her support for the project was an encouragement throughout. And I benefited more than I can say from Martin Bidney's breadth of knowledge, his ability to read carefully, and his concise, well-considered advice.

I am also grateful to Victor and Marian Loewen and Hans and Frieda Kasdorf for their encouragement and support. Finally, for their patience, interest and understanding, my deepest thanks to Evelyn, Talia and David.

A Note on Transliteration and Abbreviations

For Russian names and words that appear in the body of the text, I have used a modified version of the Library of Congress transliteration system to make them easier to recognize and pronounce for nonspecialists. In all other instances (including the bibliography and the parenthetical references to a work's Russian title) I have used the standard Library of Congress system.

The following is a list of abbreviations used in the notes:

BP, PP	Boris Pasternak, *People and Propositions* in *People and Propositions*. Vol. 2 of *The Voice of Prose*. Edited and translated by Christopher Barnes. Edinburgh: Polygon, 1990.
BP, SC	Boris Pasternak, *Safe Conduct* in *The Voice of Prose: Early Prose and Autobiography*. Vol. 1. Edited and translated by Christopher Barnes. Edinburgh: Polygon, 1986.
BP, Ss	Boris Pasternak, *Sobranie sochinenii v piati tomakh*. 5 vols. Moscow: Khudozhestvennaia literatura, 1991.
MTs, CS	Marina Tsvetaeva, *A Captive Spirit: Selected Prose*. Edited and translated by J. Marin King. Ann Arbor, MI: Ardis, 1994.
MTs, Ss	Marina Tsvetaeva, *v Sobranie sochinenii v semi tomakh*. Edited, compiled, and annotated by Anna Saakiants and Lev Mnukhin. Moscow: Terra, 1997.
OM, CCPL	Osip Mandelstam, *The Complete Critical Prose and Letters*. Edited by Jane Gary Harris. Translated by Jane Gary Harris and Constance Link. Ann Arbor, MI: Ardis, 1979.

OM, "FP"	Osip Mandelstam, "Fourth Prose," in *The Noise of Time and Other Prose Pieces*. Translated by Clarence Brown. London: Quartet Books, 1988.
OM, *NT*	Osip Mandelstam, *The Noise of Time* in *The Noise of Time and Other Prose Pieces*. Translated by Clarence Brown. London: Quartet Books, 1988.
OM, *Ss*	Osip Mandel'shtam, *Sobranie sochinenii v chetyrekh tomakh*. 4 vols. Moscow: Terra, 1991; New York: Mezhdunarodnoe Literaturnoe Sodruzhestvo, 1969.

Introduction

Could the act of writing poetry, or of identifying oneself as a poet, be a courageous or even heroic act? Could a poet deserve a place in the national mythology usually reserved for larger than life legends like Davy Crockett at the Alamo, or Joan of Arc at Orleans? For many readers the words "poet" and "courage" (let alone "hero") just don't fit together. An anonymous 1899 letter to the editor of the American magazine *The Dial* provides eye-opening—and extreme—testimony to the poet's ignominious stature in many eyes. The letter writer predicts that soon all poetry will be written by women, because "men (manly men, I mean) are growing more and more shy of writing poetry, or at least of letting people know they do it, because they feel that a man making verses is more or less of a ridiculous object. So if they do make verses it is usually . . . with every precaution against being caught red-handed in the act."[1] The letter-writer's casual chauvinism is rooted in the assurance that public opinion supports his (if we can take the writer to be a man) convictions. Poetry was for wimps and women. Real heroes were found elsewhere.

This book is about three twentieth-century Russian poets who show that writing poetry and defending one's right to be a poet can stand as profoundly courageous acts in their own right. They used pen and voice, not sword and gun, but in their own way these poets stood for freedom and fairness at a time when it was not just risky, but potentially fatal to take such a stance. They openly proclaimed themselves to be poets when life would have been easier—or longer—if they had chosen to compromise, if they had given up some of their fierce loyalty to poetry and the idea of being a poet. In the end, their acts of courage cost them dearly.

Osip Mandelstam was the first to go, perishing in Stalin's gulag for a poem that he wrote. Marina Tsvetaeva was next, hounded to the point of suicide after her return to the Soviet Union from abroad. Boris Pasternak carried on through these and many other poets' deaths, eventually winning recognition in the west but never succumbing to the demand that he become the new State Poet, a designation that would have ensured an even greater adulation at home.

Contemporary western readers may have a hard time imagining an environment where literary convictions carry such a price. We are not accustomed to thinking of literary endeavors as serious enough to threaten the author with anything other than financial or professional embarrassment, so the notion that literature, and especially poetry, could be part of such a high-stakes world seems almost impossible. Perhaps this is one reason why the separation of authorial agency from literary text has been resisted more by Slavists than by those who focus on western literary traditions. In too many places and in too many eras, the literary text's real world implications in Russia, the Soviet Union, and beyond have led to tragedy.

This linkage between text, author and society became especially critical in the years after the 1917 revolutions that led to the establishment of the Soviet Union. And it wasn't just poets who felt the strain. Prose writers, painters, photographers, filmmakers: all found themselves in an increasingly confusing environment where the notions of success and failure were constantly in flux. In the official sphere, success came from the ability to understand and support the Communist Party's ideological line; failure resulted from an inability to adapt to shifting ideological positions, or from resistance to the dominant ideology. The appetites of the public became virtually irrelevant, since a central authority began to dictate supply while simultaneously defining "demand." When poetry came to be seen as a less useful genre, and when Russian poets started to face suspicion and rejection instead of the respect they had enjoyed for years, poets faced difficult choices. To succeed, they could abandon poetry for another form of writing, or they could try to continue as poets by sticking carefully to the Party program.

For Mandelstam, Tsvetaeva, and Pasternak, success on these terms ultimately required concessions that they couldn't make. They couldn't conceive of poetry as a pastime that could be taken up or abandoned by choice. They were poets in their very essence; indeed, they carried the conviction of having been chosen to be poets by something beyond themselves. But they also shared the conviction that a true poet could never be coerced into blindly supporting the party line, whether it was the line of the Communist Party in Moscow or of the Russian exile community in Paris. A poet must remain committed to an ultimate and personal vision of truth and must resist becoming simply a hired pen, someone who produces verse on demand for the current Party plan. Within the highly charged political climate of the time, their decision to resist the advance of state-controlled ideology into culture was itself a political choice and statement. Mandelstam and Pasternak lived in the Soviet Union and faced these choices more immediately than Tsvetaeva, who lived in exile abroad from 1922 to 1939. But Tsvetaeva also learned that living according to her convictions carried a price. Poems became harder and harder to publish, and she found herself isolated from the Russian exile community in Paris. Facing such daunting challenges, each of these poets turned to autobiographical prose to formulate a powerful defense of poetry and the poet. Their efforts resulted in some of the most passionate prose ever written, with each one constructing a personal narrative that identifies the author as a poet above all else.

It was while reading one of these narratives that I gained a fundamentally different and much deeper appreciation for poetry, and the idea for this book was born. The prose was Osip Mandelstam's short autobiographical "Fourth Prose" (*Chetvertaia proza*), where he presents a defense of poetry so personal and even savage that my mind filled with questions. The biggest one was simply, How could anyone be so passionate about poetry? After all, I liked poetry as much as the next former English major. I could remember being captivated by Robert Frost, marveling at E. E. Cummings, and recognizing genius when I first came across the opening lines of T. S. Eliot's "The Love Song of J. Alfred Prufrock." But I also remembered the sense of detachment I found in Eliot's elegant essays about poetry and compared that to the raw immediacy of Mandelstam's writing. What might lie behind this difference, I wondered, since I couldn't imagine that Eliot loved poetry any less than Mandelstam did.

From that first question, I found myself drawn as much into questions about the political and social environments in which poets wrote as I was into the world of their poetry. The beauty of the Russian sounds in Mandelstam's poem "Running out onto the square, free" (*Na ploshchad' vybezhav, svoboden*) are just as much the inspiration for this book as his essays defending the poet's need for artistic independence. It was the linkages between cultural politics and the poet's life, poetry, and prose that became more and more engrossing, especially as I learned about the tragedy of Mandelstam's own life and then death in the Stalinist prison camp system.

More important for Mandelstam than the question of his own survival or death, however, was the question of whether poetry and the cultural status of the Poet would survive in Russian literature. In the increasingly gloomy literary climate that characterized the first decades of the Soviet Union, with politics replacing aesthetics as the arbiter of value, this question was more than just academic. Nadezhda Mandelstam recalls her husband's pointed observation that "Poetry is respected only in this country—people are killed for it. There's no place where more people are killed for it."[2]

It was precisely this fatal respect that made poetry the most dangerous art, threatening poets with death and poetry itself with extinction. In a country where poets had long been considered prophetic figures and where poetry was known for its ability to both inspire and incite, giving poets too much freedom was a risk that the state did not want to take. Stephen Spender once suggested that writing poetry is one of the least revolutionary of human activities, and thought it a "remote possibility" that a poem might generate as much passion as a propagandist film. But he also recognized poetry's potential for idealism, and suggested that there is an implicit and sometimes powerful counterrevolutionary thread in poetry that stems from its universal compassion for human beings "regardless of class or race."[3] Spender may have underestimated poetry's role in urging revolutionary change (at least in Russia's case), but he did identify one of the most compelling reasons for poetry's perceived "counterrevolutionary" threat to the Soviet system. Idealism fit into the emerging Soviet aesthetic only when it remained within a closely guarded channel that praised the new state's accomplishments and objectives.

There are indications that Bolshevik leaders recognized poetry's counterrevolutionary threat and fought against it from the earliest days of the new state, considering the poet's character to be essentially irreconcilable with the demands of a power-hungry state. When Alexander Blok, the country's most widely celebrated poet, wanted to go to Finland for medical reasons in the summer of 1921, Vladimir Lenin asked one of his colleagues whether the request should be granted. V. R. Menzhinsky responded to Lenin on July 11, 1921 with the observation that "Blok is a poet by nature. If some event produces a bad impression on him, he will quite naturally write poetry against us. In my opinion it's not worth letting him out; let's rather set him up [here] somewhere in a nice sanatorium." The next day, Blok's request was turned down at a session of the Politburo. He died the following month, having finally received permission to leave after his health had deteriorated to the extent that he was no longer able to travel.[4]

I mention this recently uncovered evidence about Blok's final months not because of the tragedy that resulted from the Politburo's callous decision, since Blok's medical complications had likely passed the point where he could have been helped by treatment available to him at the time. Instead, the real significance here is that influential figures within the Bolshevik hierarchy saw Blok as an inevitable and dangerous foe simply *because he was a poet* and had a true poet's nature. The real poet, they realized, will not remain silent. A poet with a sense of independence, someone whose ideals and sense of compassion reach beyond a narrowly focused and politically expedient range, will inevitably stray beyond the acceptable bounds and—even more dangerous—invite readers and listeners to follow. If poetry had the potential to lead people away from the new ideological path, it eventually would have to be contained or eliminated. And the same applied to poets.

"Eliminated" is an extreme term and may seem hyperbolic to some. After all, poetry has been pronounced dead so frequently in the past two centuries that American Poet Laureate Donald Hall's exasperated response is evident even in the title of his 1994 book, *Death to the Death of Poetry*. Hall looks primarily at American poetry to show that accounts of poetry's death are premature, to say the least. Poetry's fortunes have oscillated dramatically, but poetry has always survived. Does that mean that talk of poetry's "death" becomes irrelevant? Perhaps it does, at least in America, Britain, or France. But what if the threat originates elsewhere, in a place where the literary and political environments have little in common with the western literary marketplace?

That was the situation faced by Russian poets in the early decades after the 1917 Bolshevik Revolution. At first poetry actually seemed to gain stature as a literary genre because it featured elements that made it useful to the new state. But when circumstances changed and poetry no longer seemed a reliable means of transmitting ideological messages, poetry's fortunes changed rapidly and even the cultural figure of the poet came under direct attack.

My decision to examine these three poets, and especially the way their prose autobiographies defend poetry, cannot produce a comprehensive depiction of the era, of course. Resistance to the increasingly dominant ideology was certainly not limited to these poets, or to those poets who shared their convictions. Resistance could be found in every part of the cultural community and throughout society. Novelists, journalists, factory workers, peasants, doctors, teachers: Every segment of society offers its own examples of courageous resistance to the state's increasing demands. So while this study will focus on the resistance of three poets, I am not suggesting that they provide the only—or the most unequivocal—examples of those who stood for artistic integrity during these difficult decades.

It is equally important to note that although these poets in many ways have taken a hero's place in the national psyche, the complexity of the world in which they lived makes a linkage between "poet" and "hero" necessarily subject to careful clarification. I have tried not to depict these poets as unambiguously heroic in an idealized, triumphal understanding of the term. In the first place, they did not see themselves as heroes, especially not in the caricatured mold of fantasy figures supremely confident in their ability to triumph over all obstacles, immune to self-doubt. Above all, they were human. They were forced to balance very human concerns—about safety, about providing for themselves and their loved ones, about survival in a hostile environment—against other concerns like justice, art, and freedom.

It is not surprising, then, to find decisions and actions (or inaction) that counter a depiction of these poets as heroes. We find suicide attempts that grow out of depression and despair—not just Tsvetaeva's fatal suicide attempt, but also the suicide attempts that Pasternak and Mandelstam survived. We find Mandelstam writing an ode to Stalin, or Pasternak translating a rapturous hymn to Stalin for a prominent place in the pages of *Pravda*, or writing his own poems in praise of Stalin in *The Banner* (*Znamia*). These are acts that complicate a monolithic portrait and prevent us from slipping these poets seamlessly into the mold of the comic book hero. Their "inconvenience" does not mean that they should be politely ignored or casually explained away.

Instead, I find these actions to be signs of humanity that make the poets' fundamental loyalty to poetry even more impressive—more courageous, even heroic, to return to the admittedly risky framework that I introduced at the outset. I would characterize these poets as heroes because, when it came to poetry, they struggled through profound human weakness and conveyed their ultimate loyalty to poetry in courageous ways, including some of the prose autobiographies that form the basis of my study.[5] It is in that quiet and often unassuming sense that these poets deserve to be considered heroes; a grander depiction that conforms to the romantic notion of poet as hero just doesn't fit, and would be sure to make the poets themselves cringe, even flinch.

I have decided to focus particularly on what these poets say about poetry in their autobiographical prose because until now, little has been done to juxtapose these autobiographies with each other and against the larger sociopolitical and cultural trends that they engage so directly. Also, narrative prose offers a very different vantage point from which to address the broad cultural and political currents that were flowing across the still loosely formed Soviet state. Besides the pragmatic advantage of writing in a mode that was less threatening to authorities increasingly wary of more "imaginative" (and thus potentially troublesome) genres like poetry, the autobiographical mode offers a reflective scope that is hard to implement in poetry, even in longer narrative poems.

I have not attempted to combine this focus on autobiography with a comprehensive study of the way these (or other) poets address similar issues in lyric form. Nor have I provided a thorough and comprehensive biography for each poet. Instead, I identify several of the poems that I consider most relevant and I provide biographical context that relates most directly to the autobiographical prose. Fortunately, the gaps that remain are filled by numerous comprehensive biographies and critical studies of these poets and their poetry; references to many of these excellent materials are included in notes and the bibliography so that interested readers have suggestions for further study.

The three poets who receive most attention here—Osip Mandelstam, Marina Tsvetaeva, and Boris Pasternak—are not the only poets to suffer in the Soviet era. Indeed, the list of poets who died for their poetry, or who endured exile and imprisonment, or who were forced into silence, is extensive. Even those who initially supported the Revolution were at tremendous risk. Nikolai Klyuev offers only one example of a poet who went so far as to join the Party and then suffered for daring to challenge the lasting human costs that accompanied the Revolution. Klyuev's name is rarely mentioned today, but at the peak of his popularity he was noticed, praised and even sought out by some of Russia's greatest poets, including Alexander Blok and Sergei Esenin.

Klyuev left the Party in the early 1920s and by the end of the decade was writing poems that were increasingly critical of what he saw emerging in the Soviet state. After the publication of "The Village" (*Derevnia*) he was no longer able to publish his poems and in 1934 he was arrested and then interrogated by the same man who would soon be Osip Mandelstam's chief interrogator. The arrest was carried out by officers of the state security apparatus, of course, but Klyuev's file in the KGB archives suggests that it was high-ranking figures in the literary world who provided the impetus for the charges. Indeed, the interrogation record notes explicitly that the accusation of "anti-Soviet agitation" was based on ideas that Klyuev had allegedly propagated "through dissemination of . . . counterrevolutionary literary works."[6] Later, after his sentence of hard labor had been commuted to exile in Siberia, Klyuev described in letters to friends how his poetry had provided the impetus for the arrest warrant. Accounts of which specific poems provoked the arrest vary,[7] but even a brief look at some of Klyuev's poetry from the early 1930s shows why it caused such a forceful reaction: His efforts to link the state to images of suffering, desolation, and restriction could not be allowed to continue. In June 1937, Klyuev was arrested a second time and accused of plotting against the government. He was executed four months later.[8]

It is Anna Akhmatova, though, whose absence from this trio of poets is most conspicuous. By any standards she deserves a place with them among the truly great Russian poets of the twentieth century and she certainly experienced the effects of a cultural policy that squeezed and then silenced many lyric poets. Akhmatova's case was particularly difficult, for she was among the very first poets to be declared unpublishable. After gaining extraordinary popularity in the early 1920s, when by

Akhmatova's own account her works sold more than 15,000 copies and went through multiple editions, she was prohibited from publishing by a secret state decree in 1925. It was only fifteen years later that Akhmatova was again able to see her work in print, and then only because the government was desperate to rally support for the fight against the invading German armies.

Like many others who had suffered various forms of state persecution in the past, Akhmatova responded to the wartime call for assistance by throwing her support behind the national effort to expel a foreign invader, much like in the nineteenth century the country rose up against the armies of Napoleon. She wrote poems that exhorted her country's men and women to stand firm, to show the indomitable will of the Russian people. It was poems like "Courage" (*Muzhestvo*) that epitomized this call: "The hour of courage has sounded. / And courage will not desert us." But it was not a defense of the Soviet state that she envisioned. Instead, as the poem's continuation makes clear, Akhmatova was defending her culture and its essence, the sacred word: "And we will save you, Russian speech, / Mighty Russian word. / Free and pure we will pronounce you / Saving you from captivity and passing you on / Forever!"⁹

"Courage" appeared in *Pravda* on March 8, 1942 and became an immediate focal point for a nation searching for a symbol of national pride. Akhmatova found herself once again a "permitted" poet and for a period of just over four years she was a celebrated figure. Poetry readings were arranged during and immediately after the war and in the first part of 1946 it seemed that she would once again be permitted to resume a normal literary life. Publication contracts were signed, her readings were greeted with intense applause: It was thus an even greater shock when on August 14, 1946 a new campaign against Akhmatova was launched with a Central Committee decree denouncing her. This was followed by a bitter personal attack in a speech by Politburo member Andrei Zhdanov. Akhmatova was not imprisoned (or worse), but her life became a struggle for survival because all legal means for supporting herself were gone.

The immediate consequences of Zhdanov's attack were the cancellation of all Akhmatova's publishing contracts and the seizure of an entire print run that was already awaiting distribution. She was expelled from the Writers' Union and, had it not been for the generosity of friends who collected money for her support, Akhmatova's position could quickly have become life-threatening. At the same time, the psychological and physical effects of the campaign against her were counterbalanced by a growing realization that the opposition she faced was a confirmation of her identity and importance as a poet. Indeed, according to the report that an informer filed at the time, Akhmatova was inspired by the signs of support that made their way to her, telling friends that the Party's resolution and

Zhdanov's attack had actually increased her readership and her credibility as a poet. Had the Party taken the opposite approach and tried to tame her with favors and the perks of exalted status, Akhmatova realized, she would have been dismissed by the still considerable number of people who valued poets for providing prophetic symbols of resistance.[10]

All of this stands as powerful confirmation of Akhmatova's relevance and value as a suitable counterpart for Tsvetaeva, Pasternak, and Mandelstam. Indeed, Akhmatova herself recognized the affinity and linked herself to the autobiographical projects of Pasternak and Mandelstam at one point, referring to their early autobiographies when she noted that "a cousin to *Safe Conduct* and *The Noise of Time* should appear." But then she immediately distanced herself from the project, saying "I am afraid that in comparison to its sumptuous cousins it will seem a slob, a simpleton" as she went on to observe that both Mandelstam and Pasternak wrote their autobiographies when all that they were describing was still recent and fresh in their minds; for her to remember the events of her childhood "without vertigo" seemed impossible to her.[11]

And although the idea of an autobiography in prose stayed with Akhmatova through the 1950s and lingered until her death in 1966, it never materialized. Various references to it exist in notes and isolated references in Akhmatova's notebooks, and a number of fragments have been identified as entries that were likely to have been included in the autobiography if it had materialized. But somehow it never became a project to which she dedicated herself with full concentration and energy and it was left to later generations to search through archival materials and attempt a compilation of these entries for publication in various forms in the decades after Akhmatova's death. As a result, Akhmatova's own most significant autobiographical statements came in the more concentrated form of powerful narrative poems like *Requiem* (*Rekviem*) and *Poem Without a Hero* (*Poema bez geroia*). The more discursive mode of autobiographical prose was never one that she pursued to fruition. Thus despite her undoubted stature as a poetic equal of the poets examined closely here, Akhmatova will play a lesser role because of my focus on the poets' prose.

The following chapters will examine the literary turmoil that erupted in the post-Revolutionary decades and then examine the ways that Mandelstam, Pasternak, and Tsvetaeva responded to poetry's declining fortunes by offering a personal defense of poetry in autobiographical prose. I will begin in chapter 1 by tracing Russian poetry's cycles of rising and falling popularity from the nineteenth into the early twentieth centuries and then look closely at the rapid transitions in the cultural politics of the 1920s. Here we find that the Bolshevik Party's initial hands-off policy in cultural affairs started to shift by the middle of the decade when Party leaders issued a directive that still expressed support for cultural diversity but also provided clear indications that Party tolerance only existed within a narrowly defined ideological space. As various literary groups struggled to dominate the literary debate, the most aggressively class-conscious proletarian literary groups fought their way to the top and argued that a new state needed new literary forms to supercede the bourgeois forms of the past; lyric poetry was the most immediate victim of the new stance that eventually found its strongest expression in the 1934 decree that socialist realism should be considered the best and most useful approach to art.

Not everyone went along with the increasing pressure to curtail the writing and publication of poetry. Chapter 2 looks at Osip Mandelstam's *The Noise of Time* (*Shum vremeni*), written between 1923 and 1925 when the struggle between the radical "proletariat-first" literary groups and the more tolerant groups had started to gain intensity. Those who favored less micromanagement of the literary scene were already starting to give ground to their more aggressive foes. Mandelstam's text resonates with the times since his obvious alarm in the last section of the work (written in 1925) does not turn into the fierce invective that characterizes his next autobiographical work only a few years later. Instead, *The Noise of Time* arrests the reader with the power of Mandelstam's observations about his place and time. Poetry—and especially Mandelstam's love for language—finds an important place in the work, but the understated way that Mandelstam traces his poetic path seems to reflect his ethos. The poet exists in a world of turmoil and violence, but feels himself constrained rather than condemned.

The next chapter examines Boris Pasternak's *Safe Conduct* (*Okhrannaia gramota*), published in three installments from 1929 to 1931. By then the atmosphere for poets had become much more ominous, with a growing demand for a "literature of fact" starting to crowd out the literary imagination. Pasternak's autobiography responds to these developments with a subversive rebellion against "facts" and an attempt to find a safe personal space. Pasternak already recognizes that his destiny is rooted in poetry, and *Safe Conduct* describes the journey of discovery that taught him to accept this reality. But Pasternak also recognizes that living as a poet has grown increasingly treacherous in the Soviet Union, and *Safe Conduct* describes his struggle to find out what kind of poet can actually live and write in Soviet reality. The importance of this question came home to Pasternak with terrible finality after he had published the first installment, when he heard that fellow poet Vladimir Mayakovsky had shot himself. Pasternak knew Mayakovsky quite well, and the spectral figure of Mayakovsky haunts the concluding sections of *Safe Conduct*. In light of Mayakovsky's death and the growing opposition to the notion of "poet," could there be any alternative besides Mayakovsky's? Pasternak hoped to find one on the pages of the wistfully named *Safe Conduct*.

Mandelstam turned to autobiographical prose again at the very end of the 1920s, not long after Pasternak started to write *Safe Conduct*. In chapter 4 I will look at Mandelstam's "Fourth Prose," a short piece of autobiographical prose that ranks as one of the most passionate works ever written. Much more than Pasternak, Mandelstam had developed a hypersensitivity to the political currents bearing down on poetry, since Mandelstam had already felt the ominous weight of the literary establishment's wrath in a way that Pasternak had not. The conflict erupted when Mandelstam revised a book translation for republication and the original translator accused him of plagiarism. Soon the affair took on a menacing character out of all proportion to its real significance. Mandelstam responded to this personal nightmare with the literary catharsis that received the name "Fourth Prose," expelling his personal demons and freeing his mind for poetry after a long period of poetic drought. At the very heart of this work lies a bold defense of poetry, and above all the poet. The poet's only chance for survival is to struggle against all odds, Mandelstam writes here, and to remember that the tongue is mightier than the sword. The poet's body may be destroyed and the poet's manuscripts may be confiscated, but the poet's words are a force that nothing can destroy.

It would be hard to imagine another autobiography that could match the type of emotional energy found in "Fourth Prose," but in chapter 5 we find in Marina Tsvetaeva's autobiographical prose a different kind of intensity that may exceed even Mandelstam's prose in its dazzling verbal power. Tsvetaeva's circumstances as an exile in Paris placed her outside the direct control of the Soviet literary establishment, so she did not directly confront the threats faced by Mandelstam and Pasternak. But her unwillingness to enter into the political intrigues of the émigré community, her family connections, and her insistence on artistic control of her work made it harder and harder for her to find an outlet for her poetry. As a result, she felt herself to be a double alien, cut off not only physically from her homeland but also from the local community that could have nourished a sense of cultural belonging. Tsvetaeva's series of short autobiographical prose works features a point of view that is even more personally centered than Mandelstam's, since her writing becomes a powerful defense of her identity as a poet at a time when external circumstances challenged this identity more and more. Tsvetaeva's autobiographical writing presents a defense of poetry and the poet that is just as compelling as Mandelstam's, even though the threat that she faces is less immediate. Ultimately, Tsvetaeva returned to her homeland to find it even less receptive to her genius. After trying unsuccessfully to rejoin the literary community, and after watching family members disappear into the Stalinist gulag, Tsvetaeva eventually took her own life.

The final chapter passes over the remaining literary dark ages of Stalin's Soviet Union and returns to Pasternak, who wrote another autobiography almost thirty years after he began *Safe Conduct*. The zealous ideological fervor that dominated the literary environment in the 1920s has been replaced by institutional torpor, but an underlying ideological constancy means that the fundamental literary politics have not changed much. Pasternak now has an opportunity that neither Mandelstam nor Tsvetaeva had: He can look back at his life with a sense of accomplishment and completeness, since he has survived to a point when death would no longer seem so untimely. As he looks back on his own life, Pasternak reflects on all the poets' lives that were taken too soon, and he takes the opportunity to depict his life the way a poet's life "should" look. In effect, Pasternak uses the compact *People and Propositions* (*Liudi i polozheniia*) as a prose equivalent to the lyric testaments written by Russian poets like Gavrila Derzhavin and Alexander Pushkin more than a century earlier. In these dangerous times a poet's life (and death) needs a broader context, Pasternak suggests. It needs the thread of narrative to show how poetry fits into the broader life context. Could a poet's legacy be shaped by poetry alone? Yes, it could. But perhaps that judgment will take on more universal form if the poetry and the life of the poet are seen together, as part of a whole where the poet stands up for poetry not just in lyric form, but in life form as well. A poet's life beyond the lyric can become its own defense of poetry in every choice that the poet makes, in life and in death.

My approach juxtaposes each text with the milieu in which it arises, including not only the author's own biographical circumstances but also the much larger political and cultural backdrop that frames each work. In this respect my method owes a great deal to Russian scholar Lydia Ginzburg and her emphasis on autobiography's "orientation toward authenticity." Ginzburg steps outside the traditional parameters of the debate about autobiography, since she accepts as a given that autobiography functions as a generic outlaw, something that lies in the uneasy literary borderland between the rigidity of "documentary" literature and the freedom of "artistic" literature. The link that keeps autobiography firmly connected to "documentary" literature, she argues, is the special, intimate relationship between the reader and the author.[12]

This relationship lies at the heart of autobiography because the reader understands that fiction (artistic literature) appropriates reality differently than documentary literature appropriates reality. In fiction, Ginzburg writes, readers assume that reality gives way to art: The factual reliability of the text is aesthetically irrelevant because the reader understands all along that this is a work of fiction. In autobiography the case is different and much more complex, she explains: "Documentary literature . . . thrives on the open correlation of and struggle between these two elements ["reality" and "artistic structure"] . . . The special quality of documentary literature lies in that *orientation toward authenticity* of which the reader never ceases to be aware, but which is far from always being the same thing as factual exactitude."[13]

It is this "orientation toward authenticity" that Ginzburg maintains as the heart of autobiography, and that I take as the starting point for my study of these poets' autobiographies. Ginzburg refuses to eliminate the authorial self entirely, an elimination suggested specifically by writers like Paul de Man and Michael Sprinker and simply assumed by those who follow the lead of Wimsatt, Beardsley and the New Critics in eliminating authors as much as possible from the interpretative process.[14] Instead, Ginzburg looks for the intersection between the documentary and the artistic, that nexus where autobiography oscillates and from which it emerges now in one form, now in another. The author is neither irrelevant nor all-important, since Ginzburg's emphasis on autobiography's "dual orientation" offers a constant reminder that authorial freedom is balanced against the reader's need for "authenticity."

Paul John Eakin is another scholar who argues against the abandonment of extratextual reference points when it comes to autobiography. While many western scholars have emphasized autobiography's artistic (fictive) side and downplayed the documentary (authenticity, real life) side as unknowable or even irrelevant, Eakin joins Ginzburg in arguing for a delicate triangulation in evaluating the relative influence of author, reader and "real life" in the text. Writing in 1992, Eakin argues that "in the age of poststructuralism we have been too ready to assume that the very idea of a referential aesthetic is untenable, but autobiography is nothing if not a referential art." Eakin recognizes that this stance may be controversial because it seems like a step back to the "dark ages of autobiography studies when the presumed model of reading was governed by a simplistic notion of the nature of autobiographical truth. Those were the days when autobiography was ranged with biography and history as one of the artless literatures of fact. Since then . . . the pervasive initiative has been to establish autobiography as an imaginative art."[15]

Certainly Boris Pasternak's *Safe Conduct* and Osip Mandelstam's *The Noise of Time* serve as exceptional examples of autobiography as an imaginative art (and Eakin would not disagree). However, to look at them only as products of the author's imagination, or as an expression of the author's sense of self, impoverishes both the text and the reader. These texts, like each of the other autobiographies examined in this book, are part of a much larger cultural and political canvas. If we ignore this broader context we lose a large part of the text's significance. In this sense I would emphasize the need for a referential aesthetic even more forcefully than Eakin, since these texts deserve the kind of reading that only a recognition of their "authenticity orientation" permits. Each autobiography examined here can profitably be studied as an example of purely aesthetic genius—after all, these are poets who wrote some of the world's best prose. But if we leave these texts exclusively, or even primarily, in the aesthetic realm, we miss one of their most fundamental contributions to literature, and especially to poetry. Without a sense of how these texts stand up to the brutal political environment in which they were created, readers cannot appreciate their lasting significance or the courage it took to compose such statements of poetic commitment.

In the same way, looking at these autobiographies as a group offers insights that remain hidden when each work is examined separately. Only when these texts are juxtaposed both to each other and to their political backdrop does the broader sweep of poetic engagement with the age emerge most clearly. Together, the autobiographies function as a poetic emotional barometer, tracing the intensity with which poets responded to attacks on poetry and the poet. In this way the autobiographies take on a relational, even communal, orientation that goes beyond what Eakin had in mind when he wrote that it is wrong to think of autobiography as an automatically "first person" literature.[16] These autobiographies are relational in the broadest sense, since each poet writes on behalf of all poets when defending poetry; at the same time, an essential core of individuality remains integral to the text, since each poet retains the firm conviction that a true poet must remain free and independent.

1

Endangered Genre, Endangered Artist

The following pages will briefly trace poetry's fortunes in Russia through the nineteenth and into the twentieth century to show why the threat to poetry in the early years of the Soviet Union was radically different from anything seen previously, and why the resistance by poets like Mandelstam, Tsvetaeva and Pasternak was so important. A close examination of Soviet literary trends in the 1920s shows that for the first time, those who feared poetry's extinction had sound justification for their apprehension.

Poetry went into broad decline in Russia long before the 1920s. The precise chronology of poetry's eclipse is difficult to chart, but the process had already started before 1837, when Russia's greatest poet, Alexander Pushkin, was killed in a duel. "Realistic" prose, and especially prose that addressed Russia's social tensions, was called for by a new breed of literary critics and publishers who began to judge writers not just on their aesthetic abilities, but also on their level of social consciousness. Poets, especially those who did not make special attempts to focus on civic themes, found it increasingly difficult to publish their work. Russia's great lyric poet Afanasy Fet published a large number of poems in Russia's influential literary journals in the early 1840s, but the tide turned against him in the middle of the decade and he was unable to publish a single poem in 1848 and 1849. Journals like *Notes of the Fatherland (Otechestvennye zapiski)*, *Library for Reading (Biblioteka dlia chteniia)*, and *The Contemporary (Sovremennik)* went for years without publishing a single poem.[1] In Fet's case, the collapse of poetry led him to limit his literary endeavors for years, and he poured his energy first into a military career and then into the administration of his country estate. Friends like Leo Tolstoy and Ivan Turgenev wrote frequent letters to Fet and urged him not to abandon his muse; Fet responded with a substantial retrospective verse anthology in 1850 that attracted enough readers to prompt a slimmed-down second edition in 1856.

Then in 1863 Fet published a new volume of poetry in what was either a bold step of literary defiance or a case of colossal bad timing. The collection appeared just as the brashest of Russia's radical critics neared the peak of their influence, and Fet soon felt the sting of criticism noteworthy even in that era of widespread *ad hominem* attacks on writers. The journal *The Spark* (*Iskra*) greeted the new poetry anthology with a flurry of satirical parodies of Fet, but the most devastating onslaught came from the journal that had originally been launched by Pushkin himself, *The Contemporary*. Here young Dmitry Pisarev was inspired to write a particularly nasty review. Pisarev, who once wrote that he had been taken in by Fet's lyricism before deciding to "throw all this pure art overboard," described Fet's book as a self-made gravestone that would never leave the booksellers' storage shelves. Then he reconsidered and suggested how Fet's poetry might find wider circulation. Perhaps the book could be broken into pieces, Pisarev wrote, and then sold "by the pood [about 36 pounds] to paper rooms under wallpaper, and to wrap candles, cheese and fish. . . . In this way Fet's works will have some practical use for the first time."[2] No one knows whether anyone followed Pisarev's facetious advice, but it took more than twenty-six years for Fet's anthology of lyrics to sell the last 1,200 copies.

Eventually Russia's long-dormant appetite for poetry returned. Looking back, one of the first signs that change was imminent was Fet's own reemergence with the publication of the anthology *Evening Lights* (*Vechernie ogni*) in 1883; the collection went through four editions before Fet died nearly a decade later in 1892. For the most part, though, the poetry which grew in popularity through the 1890s had a much stronger idealistic base than Fet's lyrics, and soon a group of Symbolist poets emerged as the leading poetic voices. The Symbolists' poetry revealed a yearning for some hidden or higher reality and marked a sharp turn from the decades-long emphasis on socially conscious literature.

In 1899 Russia embarked on an extended centennial celebration to honor the birth of its national poet, Alexander Pushkin. The combined impetus from the Pushkin centennial and the popularity of the early Symbolists propelled poetry back to the place of honor in Russian literature. A new generation of Symbolists began to publish, including the most famous of them all, Alexander Blok. In the first years of the new century the Symbolists were at the center of an astonishingly productive cultural outburst not only in poetry but also in philosophy, painting, prose and more. State censors limited what could be written on theological or political topics, but Russia's poets found themselves caught up in a dynamic, exhilarating decade.

The next decade featured even more poetic ferment as rival groups of poets challenged the dominant Symbolist aesthetic. The most important of these groups were the Futurists and the Acmeists, both of which began to take shape by about 1910. The Acmeists, whose ranks included Anna Akhmatova, Nikolai Gumilyov and Osip Mandelstam, promoted a less abstract poetry that prized clarity over the obscure visions of the Symbolists. A central characteristic of Acmeist poetry was the rejection of mysticism, which they replaced with an emphasis on precision and a "harmonic balance" between content and form, as Gumilyov expressed it in a 1910 review. But while the Symbolists and Acmeists had different views on how poetry could be most relevant in the new twentieth century, they shared an appreciation for poetry's past and a commitment to maintain high artistic standards.

Futurism was very different. Not only was the movement more diffuse, with various groups loosely linked under the Futurist rubric, but even within these smaller groups there was less emphasis on a shared aesthetic. As their name implies, Futurists looked forward rather than back and sought wholly new approaches to poetry. The movement attracted instant attention when one of the Futurist groups issued the scandalous "Slap in the Face of Public Taste" in 1912. Here four poets explicitly denounced most of the leading Symbolists by name, and gained eternal notoriety in Russia by declaring their intention to "throw Pushkin, Dostoevsky, Tolstoy, etc., etc., overboard from the Ship of Modernity." Vladimir Mayakovsky, one of the authors of this manifesto and the poet most associated with Futurism, saw poetry readings as an opportunity to jolt his audience away from Russia's literary past and into the modern age.

All of these groups jostled for poetic space in Russia, but after the 1917 revolutions the literary climate changed almost immediately. While the Symbolists and Acmeists responded cautiously to political developments, some with approval and others with dismay, most of the Futurists exulted in this ultimate triumph of the new over the old. No one knew exactly how the political cataclysm would find its way into literature, but everyone knew that drastic change was inevitable. Poets, like everyone else, would have to find their own way in a world where the past could no longer guide the future.

Ultimately, it was the ideological implications and the practical implementation of the Bolsheviks' scientific, materialistic worldview that threatened poetry with extinction in the Soviet Union. In the early years after the Revolution, though, the danger was still hidden; indeed, judging by the available evidence it would have been natural to conclude that poetry might become the Bolsheviks' favored genre. But within a decade appreciation turned to suspicion and then to a broad rejection of poetry and especially the poet. Tracing this shift shows how growing emphasis on science and technology combined with dramatic shifts in cultural and national politics to directly affect poetry's viability.

One of the key elements in this transformation, and one of the big differences between poetry's struggles in the Soviet Union and other countries like the United States, was the Bolshevik policy of hands-on cultural management that made literature a focal point in the broader political and ideological battles that followed the Revolution. The Bolsheviks had always recognized the tremendous revolutionary value of cultural mechanisms, and they took steps to reform cultural institutions almost immediately after seizing control of the state, even before they had a firm grip on the levers of military and economic control. Leading Bolshevik thinkers Alexander Bogdanov and Anatoly Lunacharsky formed the Proletkult (Proletarian Cultural and Educational Organization), and Bogdanov articulated an activist approach that used literature as a powerful proletariat instrument to organize workers. The first Proletkult meeting confirmed this class-based vision for literature, and the group grew rapidly. Bogdanov ran into trouble, however, when he argued that cultural activities should have relative independence from central Party control. This independent spirit was soon curbed, partially through the intervention of the ultimate authority, Vladimir Lenin himself.[3]

These early developments established a basic pattern for literature that continued until 1932. Literary groups formed and announced their principles, but kept a watchful eye for directives from the Party. Initially, these directives were few: In the early 1920s, Party leaders seemed content to allow vigorous debate about the literary forms and practices that could most effectively advance the revolutionary cause. The literary landscape shifted constantly as groups struggled for ideological dominance in an atmosphere that still had no clear standards to measure success. Later, critics both in the USSR and the west have tended to schematize the era, sometimes dividing the various parties into "the innocent and the guilty, executioners and victims, ardent utopianists and unprincipled politicians," as Evgeny Dobrenko puts it. The reality was more complex, though, and Dobrenko cautions against ignoring the powerful interests that motivated these groups, operating instead under the influence of "ideological magic" which demarcates the era into distinct phases and glosses over ambiguity. Dobrenko's reminder is apt for any discussion of the period and in the short historical summary that follows I have tried to trace the changing fortunes of poetry and poets through actions, pronouncements and policy statements rather than through historical schema.[4]

The jockeying for positions of influence and power began almost immediately after the Revolution. Bogdanov was pushed aside and the Proletkult was fragmented by competing visions. In 1919 a group of poets left the Proletkult to form the Smithy (*Kuznitsa*), which in turn split when its more radical members left to form October, a group that pushed for a rapid shift to a consciously proletarian literature. When the All-Russian Association of Proletarian Writers (widely known as VAPP, after its Russian initials) was formed, members of October successfully maneuvered to gain control of the new association.

All of these literary groups shared certain fundamental assumptions about literature. In the new state, they believed, literature had a responsibility to support and build a new society. "Building" became a dominant theme in much of Soviet literary criticism, and implied fundamental political support for the Revolution and for the subsequent construction of a new Soviet state. "Construction" referred both to the physical construction of cities and factories, and to the social construction of a new Soviet mentality.

The close links between construction, science and technology are clear, and the Smithy poets lived up to their name with enthusiastic support for the program. They devoted entire poems to the importance of work, to the significance of the factory, and to the glories of mechanization and technology. Some expressed their devotion to machines with passionate eloquence, referring to machines as "friends" and celebrating their potential for transformative power. Others, especially those in the October group, focused more on the human challenge. Social construction should be tackled with more urgency, they argued, and poets should place less emphasis on "things" and more emphasis on "the living person." Alexander Bezymensky, one of the most influential of the VAPP poets, challenged Smithy poets to "give us the earth and living people" instead of rhapsodies about machinery.[5]

Bezymensky's challenge to the Smithy poets illustrates the fundamental VAPP conviction that the collective must guide the individual, and the assumption that political objectives should determine poetic practice. It was the first step in a process that eventually threatened to eliminate poets from Russian literature. VAPP leaders believed that they had achieved the purest formulation of Marxist policy for literature, and aggressively tried to extend their influence over individual writers and other literary groups. One observer at the time called the VAPP program unprecedented in its programmatic approach to literature, and in the way poets were called on to subject their individual interests to a common objective.[6] Initially VAPP issued the call to focus on "living people" as an invitation, but VAPP leaders itched for the opportunity to turn this invitation into an injunction. For that to happen, they would need the sponsorship and full authority of the Party.

The Party preferred not to throw its full weight behind aggressive proletariat groups like VAPP—or any other literary group—at this time. The group that came closest to enjoying Party support was the editorial collective at *Red Virgin Soil* (*Krasnaia nov'*), a journal established in 1921 after a meeting in the Kremlin that included Russia's most influential writer, Maxim Gorky, and Lenin himself. *Red Virgin Soil* and its editor, A. K. Voronsky, supported the Revolution and the Party, but adopted policies that directly countered the proletarian writers' groups. While VAPP insisted that proletarians should dominate literature, Voronsky and his colleagues considered this a long-term goal rather than an absolute standard. According to Voronsky, the Revolution could allow some latitude for writers who were not yet fully committed to the new state. These "fellow travelers" would be encouraged to participate and eventually their resistance would disappear through "example and patient persuasion," as Robert Maguire describes it.[7] Besides, Voronsky and his editors noted, there were almost no talented proletarian writers yet. In order to publish the best poetry and prose possible, journals had to include the fellow travelers. Writers and poets should be allowed to find their own way into the socialist state, and *Red Virgin Soil* featured works by many of the writers who had been most successful in pre-Revolutionary literature.

In 1923 two new journals appeared and both took direct aim at Voronsky's relatively tolerant publication policies. *On Guard* (*Na postu*) was launched by the Octobrist core of VAPP, and *LEF* (short for Left Front of the Arts) was started by a literary group of the same name. Both journals argued that all remnants of "bourgeois" literature should be abolished, not allowed to continue deceiving the public on the pages of *Red Virgin Soil*. The debate was taken up vigorously by contributors to *Red Virgin Soil*, and invective flowed freely across the pages of each journal in articles that sometimes turned into spiteful *ad hominem* attacks reminiscent of Russia's nineteenth-century literary debates. The Soviet implementation of a New Economic Policy (NEP) in the 1920s heightened VAPP's sense of urgency and outrage because the NEP appeared to be a retreat from strict communist principles and a slide back toward capitalist and bourgeois values.

Influential Party leaders had their own thoughts on literature in the Soviet state. Leon Trotsky still commanded substantial authority within the Party when he published *Literature and Revolution* (*Literatura i revoliutsiia*) in 1924 and all the competing literary groups examined the book carefully for clues to the Party's position on literature. Aggressive proletarian groups could not have liked much of what they found because Trotsky argued against the possibility of a genuinely proletarian culture. Cultural change takes place slowly, he wrote, and since communist dogma considered the proletarian stage to be a transitional phase on the path to full communism, there would not be time for a proletarian culture to take root. Rather than trying to establish a new and unique culture of the proletariat, literary groups should concentrate on making existing culture accessible to the masses: The proletariat dictatorship should take advantage of its authority by turning quality into quantity.[8]

Trotsky also appeared to support the *Red Virgin Soil* policy of tolerance toward the "old" writers who had not declared absolute allegiance to the Revolution. An entire chapter was devoted to a study of the great Symbolist poet Alexander Blok, whose 1918 poem "The Twelve" (*Dvenadtsat'*) became the most significant poem about the Revolution. "The Twelve" is a complex blend of images and voices that recognizes the wild forces unleashed in the Revolution, and its appearance immediately provoked widely diverging interpretations. Some heralded Blok as the new prophet of Revolution; others argued that Blok might favor the Revolution in principle, but not the way it had been carried out in Russia. Trotsky did not resolve this puzzle when he concluded: "Blok is not one of ours, but he reached out towards us. And in doing so, he broke down. But the result of his impulse is the most significant work of our epoch. His poem, 'The Twelve,' will remain forever."[9]

Such tolerance might suggest that Trotsky had little in common with the absolutism of proletarian groups like VAPP, but other passages reveal Trotsky's fundamental conviction that the proletariat holds the key to the Soviet literary future. Cultural change can't come from groups like Smithy and others who are "trying to be like the proletariat," Trotsky writes. Much more effective than Smithy poetry are the factory newspapers where genuine proletarian voices try to communicate real human achievements. But these proletarians are not yet ready to take up the "higher" literary genres, for as he puts it, "weak and . . . illiterate poems do not make up proletarian poetry because they do not make up poetry at all." Besides this aesthetic standard, Trotsky held poets to an ideological standard that sounded much like VAPP's. He even provided an example for other poets to emulate when he identified Demyan Bedny as a poet who subordinated his personal ego to the larger goals of the Party. The intriguing element in Trotsky's analysis lies in the implicit hierarchy that he establishes, for it is not the aesthetic level of Bedny's poetry that prompts Trotsky's praise, but rather Bedny's willingness to put his poetry to political and ideological use. Bedny writes poetry not just when he "feels inspired," says Trotsky, but day in and day out "as the events and the Central Committee of the Party demand."[10]

When he moves on to discuss the Party's policy toward art, Trotsky's views reflect what had been practiced to that point. The Party should not have to command and direct every development, he writes, but should "protect and help" the proletarian writers instead of participating in every literary argument. At the same time, Trotsky took it for granted that these arguments would occur within an explicitly Marxist framework. A "watchful revolutionary censorship" would ensure that no counterrevolutionary forces entered the fray, and any subversive movements would be eliminated, no matter how aesthetically successful they might be.[11]

Proletarian literary associations like VAPP were not convinced by Trotsky's defense of Party policy on literature. Where Trotsky saw literature as a concern much less urgent than questions about machine guns and transport problems,[12] VAPP saw ideological relativism that threatened to undermine the class that supposedly now functioned as "dictator" in the new state. VAPP leaders began to push for more direct Party involvement in literary politics, especially in censuring the lax editorial policies of *Red Virgin Soil* and other publications that continued to print the works of the fellow travelers.

By July 1925 the Party could no longer stand apart from the increasingly unruly literary disputes and it convened a special hearing where the competing sides could argue their cases. The result was a precedent-setting Party policy statement on literature; the statement did not declare victory for any one side, but it established a clear pattern of direct Party authority over literary practice and policy. Proletarian writers were specifically declared not to have absolute authority in literary affairs, but they were also designated the Party's "future leaders" in literature (points 9, 11). So while the 1925 statement noted explicitly that the Party would not support any particular group or tendency to the exclusion of the rest and that the Party favored "free competition" in the literary arena (points 13, 14), it also contained an implicit promise that this would change in the future. The final declaration made the literary task very concrete: Soviet literature must "work out a proper form understandable to the millions. Only when it has solved this problem will Soviet literature and its proletarian vanguard fulfill its cultural mission" (point 16).[13] The reference to "cultural mission" provided a none-too-subtle reminder of the ideological task that could never be forgotten in the midst of the potentially distracting debates about form and genre. Edward Brown calls this document "almost unique in literary history" in the way a state assumes responsibility and control over literary development, and for the tight link forged between Party politics and literature.[14] The chilling implications of this link between politics and literature did not become completely clear until almost a decade later.

In the midst of all these turbulent theoretical disputes and struggles for power, poets wrote poems. During the early- and mid-1920s, poetry's importance actually rose dramatically, and for very practical reasons. When editors complained about the lack of qualified proletarian writers, literary groups across the country initiated training programs to counter the shortage. Poetry immediately gained prominence because many considered it an easy art form: Poetry's rhythmic base produces an unconscious association with the songs that children learn from infancy, Mikhail Chumandrin argued, and new writers find it easier to express their ideas in short, rhythmic bursts than in the extended discourse of prose.[15]

We find here a curious example of cultural relativism, for while early Soviet literary circles heralded the links between poetry and childhood as a sign of poetry's cultural value, in America only a short time earlier writers like H. E. Warner made this same association but used it to argue for poetry's complete irrelevance. Describing poetry as a normal childish fancy that might continue into the turbulent "emotional development" of youth, Warner argued that it would surely disappear when adulthood leads to concerns "with the practical, the material, the definite."[16] It would be hard to imagine anything more committed to the "practical, material, and definite" than the Soviet literary world of the 1920s, yet these very criteria helped to create more, not less, demand for poetry.

If we look more closely at the way early Soviet attitudes toward poetry relate to a similarly turbulent period for poetry in America between 1890 and 1910, numerous similarities and some crucial differences take shape. It is no surprise to see science and technology's increasing importance in almost every aspect of the Soviet Union's social, economic and even cultural life, just as America witnessed the growth of this influence several decades previously. What comes as a surprise, though, are the occasional references that imply a kind of market mentality in the Soviet literary environment. In America, the market mechanism became the implicit model that both illustrated poetry's predicament, and provided a solution: For poetry to succeed, the product/poem had to regain the interest of the consumer/reader. In the 1920s we find similar suggestions in the USSR. The 1925 Party ruling that the literary environment should include "free competition" and that literature could accommodate a variety of perspectives, suggests a relatively open process. Frequent journal references to readers as "consumers" (*potrebiteli*) suggest that readers are the final arbiters who determine which literary genres and works will be successful. Even the broader economic climate under the New Economic Policy seems to show a retreat from the ideological standards of Marxism and a move back toward the market.

Two fundamental differences more than countered all the apparent similarities. In America, publication options were governed by economic questions: Could a publisher afford to print a particular work? Subsidies or private resources could make publication more feasible, but these were all factored into the basic profit and loss equation. If a journal's combination of subscribers, advertisers and sponsors could support it, publication continued. If not, it disappeared. Ideology became a factor only if it affected a publication's ability to attract readers (positively or negatively), or if it led to legal violations not covered by the right to freedom of speech.

In the Soviet Union, political identity became the single most important factor in literary survival. Economic considerations were subordinated to ideology. Declarations about "free competition" assume a peculiarly circumscribed understanding of "freedom," since competition could take place only among those who had already survived the rigid screening that established their revolutionary credentials, and only within the Party's ideological program. Party objectives became the political litmus test in all discussions about the needs of the consumer/reader. Principles of economic centralization extended to literature and once the Party had defined what the reader "needed," editors and publishing houses ignored this decision at their peril. Noncompliance could lead directly to economic consequences, since the state controlled all the means of production, from the paper supply to the printing presses. Publishers who attempted to publish privately funded journals (still technically possible in the early 1920s) faced almost impossible paper shortages that required them to pay nearly ten times as much as the state-subsidized paper available to journals published through approved organizations.

Within this politically determined literary environment, it becomes easier to see why—initially, at least—the focus on science and industry actually increased poetry's importance in the Soviet Union. If the Revolution instituted the dictatorship of the working class, then any ideologically driven literature had to find a way to communicate with this poorly educated, largely illiterate class. When we factor in the perception that poetry's "simplicity" makes it easy to understand and compose, all the ingredients for active state support of poetry come together. Proletarian poetry could increase the political consciousness of the workers, teach them literacy, and help them to mythologize their own roots and environment. Vigorous "poetry training" workshops across the country started to produce poetry anthologies like the 1924 *Poetry of the Working Class Professions*, or the 1929 *Poetry of the Miners' Blow: First Book of Verses by Miner Worker-Correspondent Poets*.[17] These fledgling poets tended to write about what they knew best, the factories and workplaces where they spent most of their time. For some, poetry offered them an outlet for the passion they felt about their participation in the great construction project that faced the country: "Well, how can I not love, / not pamper the screw-nut?" writes one factory lathe operator. A foundry worker expresses similar devotion as he merges his identity with the factory's production: "With cast iron we are ablaze, / We are happy in labor. / Into machines we transform / The lifeless ore."[18] No one pretended that this poetry was sophisticated or had any intrinsic aesthetic worth; instead, its value lay in its ability to fulfill the "cultural mission" identified in the 1925 Party statement on literature.

In the late 1920s a combination of factors triggered fundamental changes in the Soviet Union's cultural politics, and poetry's fortunes deteriorated sharply. Joseph Stalin's growing dominance in the Party leadership led to the curtailment of the New Economic Policy and then the inauguration of the first Five Year Plan in 1928. This enormous undertaking focused on massive worker mobilization to "overtake and surpass" the industrialized west, but it also emphasized the importance of cultural contributions that would support the national political and production goals. For writers, this meant finding ways to promote the Plan. As Edward Brown puts it, the principle of using literature for Party purposes "was now adopted by the Party in its simplest and crudest form."[19]

The political shifts led to numerous organizational changes in the literary associations and increasingly strict controls on literary expression. Proletarian groups grew stronger, first by dominating a broad Federation of Organizations of Soviet Writers (FOSP) and then by joining forces at a 1928 national congress of proletarian writers where VAPP's name was changed to RAPP. Proletarian groups had effectively become the dominant political force in Soviet literature.

One of the primary factors in this dominance was the proletarians' ability to secure the Party's sponsorship. Three Party members, including the influential Anatoly Lunacharsky, appeared at the 1928 organizational meeting, and all commended RAPP for its zeal in carrying out Party directives. At the same time, the Party did not limit itself to just one plan of attack. While increasing its support for RAPP, the Party also issued a separate literature-related resolution that was addressed directly to publishers. This resolution has been called "one of the most important of all Party directives" in literature, and issued specific instructions on how to select books and writers.[20] The primary emphasis was on utility and political orthodoxy, with no distinction made between *belles lettres*, documentary literature or propaganda.

The new Party directive indicated a significant shift away from toleration, and creative writers were the ones most affected. Literary figures on the extreme left of the ideological spectrum considered the changes long overdue. A new era of literary polemics commenced, and the group known as LEF was delighted to be at the center of the controversy. In the early 1920s LEF had engaged *Red Virgin Soil* in a debate about the wisdom of letting "bourgeois" writers continue to write; now LEF began a series of attacks on the very notion of *belles lettres* in general, and poetry in particular. The new literature promoted by LEF came to be known as a "literature of fact" (*literatura fakta*) and when LEF's theorists revived their journal with the title *New LEF* (*Novyi LEF*) in 1927, the promotion of fact-based art became its dominant theme. "*Belles lettres* is the opium of the people," writes LEFist N. Chuzhak. "We are against the literature of imagination known as *belles lettres*; we favor the primacy of a literature of fact." Poetry was the most immediate and obvious casualty of this approach, but any form of creative prose was suspect. Writers need to get away from the artificial arrangement of material that forms a literary plot, Chuzhak argues. Instead, they should look to genres where the story's "plot" arises spontaneously from life itself. Autobiographies, biographies, travel accounts, administrative records—all of these avoid contrived plot structures and allow reality to speak for itself, he concludes.[21]

This time poetry was not reinvented to survive the emphasis on science, technology and facts. Less than a decade earlier poetry's perceived "simplicity" had allowed it to survive and even given it an edge in the race to build up the poorly educated working class. Now, poetry's future looked grim. Critics considered poetry too highbrow, readers were not interested, and publishers considered it unfeasible, writes Sergei Tretyakov in September, 1928.[22] But although even LEF occasionally used terms like "consumer" and "demand" to explain poetry's decline, the Soviet literary "market" fluctuated only when the Party leadership shifted its ideological and political priorities. Reader "interest" changed by central decree, and most writers hastened to comply with the Party's subtlest hints about shifting literary priorities. Prose moved to the forefront and even though no Party decrees expressed official censure for poetry as a literary genre, literary and political forces appeared ready to relegate poetry, if not to the Soviet literary dustbin, then at least to the dusty shelves of the literary archives.

Another significant element in the cultural changes lay in the attention paid not just to poetry, but to the figure of the poet. In the past, Russian poets had frequently been honored as prophetic figures. Poetry's popularity could rise or fall, but the figure of the poet retained broad overall authority within the culture. Even LEF recognized the ongoing power of this tradition, and in April 1928 warned aspiring writers against being seduced by the title "poet." Not only did this title continue to maintain the ideologically suspect connotation of a "special" person, someone set apart from others, but its ongoing cultural influence set off other alarm bells. A figure that still commanded such popular respect had the potential to become a powerful subversive force, especially if he or she embraced the idealism that Stephen Spender describes as poetry's powerful counterrevolutionary thread.[23] One measure of the persistent lingering of the poet's cultural status can be seen in the frequency and vehemence of LEF's attacks on the figure of the poet. We will never know exactly how many of these emerging proletarian poets found within themselves the spark of poetic genius and were drawn by a sense of cultural destiny toward the traditional prophetic role of the Russian poet—the same role that Bolshevik leaders feared so much, and which they cited as a reason to deny Alexander Blok permission to leave the country. For these new poets, the act of learning to write poetry made them realize that they were *poets*, and that this identity superseded their much more politically acceptable identity as members of the working class.

To counter this threat, ideological watchdogs increased their attacks on individualism. Sergei Tretyakov suggested that "poet," and even the broader notion of "writer," would soon be replaced by the more anonymous and group-oriented "reporter" as the leading representative of contemporaneity.[24] The attack on individual creativity took a much more sinister turn in Osip Brik's article "Against the 'Creative' Personality" (*Protiv "tvorcheskoi" lichnosti*) where Brik confronts not just poets but any artist who considers artistic creation to be an act of personal inspiration. The very notion of a "creative personality" cannot exist in Soviet society, Brik warns, because it invariably implies an individual point of view that contradicts Soviet principles. The path of individualism, he warns, is a "false and fatal" path.[25]

Brik may not have suspected how prophetic—in the literal sense—these words would prove to be, but as the 1920s came to a close and the Five Year Plan tightened its grip on Soviet culture, few ventured to raise voices or pens to defend poetry and the poet. Instead, poets disappeared. Some left poetry for a modified form of prose like the "lyrical feuilleton" promoted by Nikolai Aseev.[26] For too many, though, disappearance was absolute and permanent. Roman Jakobson's very personal lament, "On a Generation that Squandered Its Poets," provides only a partial listing of the poets who were shot, who starved to death, who committed suicide, or who died from other causes between 1921 and 1930: Nikolai Gumilyov, Alexander Blok, Velimir Khlebnikov, Sergei Esenin, and Vladimir Mayakovsky.[27] The next decade added lesser-known figures like proletarian poet Nikolai Kuznetsov, peasant poet Nikolai Klyuev, and more. Who knows how many of them felt the same despair that Mayakovsky expressed in his suicide note, which ends with the cry that "there is no other way out"?

Some poets struggled against Mayakovsky's conclusion. They recognized that the Soviet-era challenge to poetry was unlike poetry's cyclical declines at other times and in other places. The absolutism of Soviet political ideology as it developed in the late 1920s made this an unprecedented situation, and it became clear that poetry could not survive in popular culture if the state decreed it "genre non grata." So when these poets saw that poetry—and especially the cultural value of the Russian poet—might be starting a terminal slide into obsolescence, they decided to resist. Did they know that their efforts might be more symbolic than successful, and did they suspect that their own personal dramas might turn into tragedies with no way out? Perhaps. But for Osip Mandelstam, Boris Pasternak and Marina Tsvetaeva the stakes—and their devotion to poetry—were simply too high for them to accept Mayakovsky's conclusion without a fight.

2

Early Warning Signs

Osip Mandelstam's fame in the west owes more to his life—and especially his death—than to the poetry that secured his reputation in Russia and the Soviet Union. Mandelstam's story emerged when the Cold War still informed much of our reading and thinking about the Soviet Union, and it had all the elements to guarantee a place in the anti-Soviet cultural pantheon: A lone poet takes on Stalin personally, survives one exile, endures terrible mental and physical suffering, and eventually dies in the gulag after a second arrest. The story doesn't have a happy ending, of course—this David only wounds his Goliath, and eventually pays a heavy price for his insolence. But it was not the ultimate price, at least in Mandelstam's personal economy. For him, submission and conformity would have been even worse, and his death as a poetic and political martyr has become a powerful symbol of resistance against overwhelming odds.[1]

Such a powerfully tragic story will naturally gain a readership, especially when told by a storyteller as gifted as the poet's wife, Nadezhda. Her multi-volume memoir provides an inspiring—and chilling—description of human courage (both hers and his) in terrible times. I draw attention to the western fascination with the poet's biography not as an indictment of insensitivity to poetry, but merely to point out a fundamental cultural difference that separates western and Russian readers. In the west, the evocative play of sounds and words in Mandelstam's poems, even when conveyed in an inspired translation, cannot compete in the popular imagination with the chilling romantic tragedy of his biography. In Russia, on the other hand, Mandelstam has always been a gifted poet above all else. His personal tragedy was not ignored, but it never overshadowed the profound awareness of his poetic gift.

It seems ironic, then—to use a term that doesn't begin to capture the agonizing complexity of the times—that in 1923 Mandelstam turned to his biography because it was increasingly difficult to publish his poetry in the Soviet Union. He was commissioned to write his life story by I. G. Lezhnev for the journal *Russia* (*Rossiia*), and Mandelstam took the opportunity to explore not only his own roots, but also the issue of literature's further development in the post-Revolutionary era. His personal story describes his attempt to claim a heritage and eventually shows that his real identity is not biologically but culturally determined. He finds a way into Russian culture, and more specifically into Russian literature, but realizes even as he does so that this new "family" is not completely harmless: A hungry State awaits an inevitable confrontation with literary Russia.

The Noise of Time (*Shum vremeni*), the autobiography that emerged from Mandelstam's efforts during the autumn of 1923, was not what Lezhnev had anticipated. It didn't conform to the pattern set by the other memoirs cascading across the pages of Soviet literary journals and Lezhnev turned it down, calling it "very tame stuff." Other editors must have had a similar response, and the autobiography was only published in 1925.[2] Lezhnev was right in noting that Mandelstam's autobiography did not fit the dominant models of the day. Like everyone else, Mandelstam had lived through the horrors of World War I, the Revolution, the Civil War, and War Communism, but he did not seem to share the popular compulsion to write one's own story into these historic events.

Had Mandelstam wanted to describe his activities during and after the Revolution, his account could have competed with most, for what we know of Mandelstam's life in those years reveals an astonishing range of experience. In 1918 and 1919 he served in a series of official, culturally oriented postings under the new Bolshevik regime, including an appointment to the People's Commissariat for Enlightenment (*Narkompros*) in Moscow that was based on a recommendation given by Commissar Anatoly Lunacharsky himself.[3] Later in 1918 he intervened to prevent a series of arbitrary executions and appealed to the head of the secret police, Felix Dzerzhinsky, for support. In February 1919 Mandelstam left Moscow for Ukraine, where he was almost immediately appointed head of the poetry section of the All-Ukrainian Committee for Literature. The Civil War was still sweeping rival forces back and forth across Ukraine, and when Kiev was taken by the Whites, both Osip and Nadezhda (who were already a couple) had good reason to fear for their lives. Denunciations of Bolsheviks led to numerous lynchings, some within sight of Nadezhda's family home. Later in the year Mandelstam moved on to the Crimea, where he stayed until mid-1920. He was arrested by the Whites, then released. Since it was not possible to get back to Moscow from the Crimea, Mandelstam and his brother Alexander got on a boat bound for Georgia, which at that time was an independent Menshevik state. Their reception was unexpectedly hostile, and both men were arrested by the military authorities three days after arriving in Batum. The prospects were grim, since standard policy in Georgia was to ship unwanted refugees back to their point of departure. For the Mandelstam brothers, this would almost certainly have resulted in execution by White authorities in Crimea. Eventually the brothers were released and made their way back to Moscow by train. After a short time there, Mandelstam moved on to Petrograd.

Mandelstam spent the winter of 1920–1921 in Petrograd's House of Arts, where he had many of the country's leading literary figures as neighbors. His enduring friendship with Viktor Shklovsky and Vasilisa Shklovskaya-Kordi dates to the winter spent in this extraordinary building, the former mansion of the merchant Eliseev. In March 1921, Mandelstam set off once more for Ukraine, where Nadezhda was waiting for him. Together they boarded a train for Georgia, and considered a variety of options for the future: applying for Lithuanian citizenship, settling in Georgia, living in southern Russia. It soon became clear that living in Georgia was not viable for them, and they eventually got on a steamer for the Russian port of Novorossiysk. Slowly they made their way back to Moscow, with Mandelstam working brief stints at a succession of local newspapers along the way. In the spring of 1922 they arrived in Moscow and after two weeks of homelessness were given a room in the city's most prominent refuge for writers, the Herzen House. In 1923 Lezhnev commissioned Mandelstam to write his autobiography and when the Mandelstams were granted passes to a Crimean sanatorium in the autumn of 1923, he used his time there to wander the shores of the Black Sea and compose *The Noise of Time*.

Even this extremely condensed account of Mandelstam's life from 1918 to 1923 shows that he had all the raw materials for a rollicking adventure story set in the turmoil of Revolution. But rather than write this expected account, Mandelstam avoided specifics about his recent experiences and parted company with the traditional chronological narrative of autobiography from the outset. It wasn't that Mandelstam didn't want to bother with history, or that he wanted to ignore the Revolution; indeed, *The Noise of Time* was only the most recent expression of Mandelstam's passionate and ongoing dialogue with his age. But unless we recognize that this dialogue centered on cultural—and more specifically literary—questions, the autobiography loses much of its significance.

The roots of these questions, and of Mandelstam's attempt to engage the new age in dialogue, can be traced back to the earliest days of the post-Revolutionary regime. Already in 1918 the leaders of the *Proletkult*

(Proletarian Cultural and Educational Organization) emphasized that a shift from "bourgeois" to "proletarian" art demanded a shift from a personal lyric voice to a collective voice. "The spirit of individualism, which always stands at the center of the lyric 'I,' is alien to the proletariat," Alexander Bogdanov wrote in an influential article that appeared in the very first issue of *Proletarian Culture* (*Proletarskaia kul'tura*).[4] The proletarian poets answered this call with a torrent of poetry that glorified the Revolution and heralded a complete change in the country's cultural focus. Vladimir Kirillov's popular 1918 poem "We" (*My*) conveys these sentiments unambiguously. "We are the countless, the terrible legions of Labor," he writes, and continues:

> We are under the power of a turbulent, passionate intoxication;
> Let them shout: "You are the executioners of beauty,"
> In the name of our Tomorrow we will burn Raphael,
> We will destroy museums, we will stamp on the flowers of art.
> . . . .
> Tears have dried up in our eyes, tenderness has been killed,
> We have forgotten the smell of grass and spring flowers.
> We have fallen in love with the power of steam and the might of dynamite,
> The song of sirens, the movement of wheels and axles.
>
> O, poet-aesthetes, curse the Great Lout,
> Kiss the fragments of the past under our heel,
> Wash the smashed temple's ruins with your tears.
> We are free, we are brave, we breathe a different beauty.[5]

The poem gained tremendous popularity as an anthem of the new collective spirit, and at the height of its popularity Kirillov and Mandelstam were both working in the bustling halls of Lunacharsky's Narkompros offices, Kirillov in the Literary Department and Mandelstam in the Education Reform Department. It is hard to imagine how Mandelstam could have worked with someone who applauded the burning of Raphael, who longed to destroy museums and smash temples. Some of Mandelstam's best pre-Revolutionary poems concern these same ancient temples. In "Hagia Sophia" (*Aiia-Sofiia*, 1912) he addresses the temple directly, describing it as something "swimming in the world" that shows "the triumph of light." Elsewhere he sings the praises of the Notre Dame cathedral in Paris, and the Kazan Cathedral in St. Petersburg. Characters and places from mythology and the classics fill his lyrics: Homer, Helen of Troy, Rome, Caesar, Phaedra, Hercules, and more. Linking the present with the past, the Russian with the European, was a theme Mandelstam turned to numerous times during these years. In the poem "In the

Discordance of the Maidens' Choir" (*V raznogolositse devicheskogo khora*, 1916), he writes:

> And the five-domed Moscow cathedrals
> With their Italian and Russian soul
> Remind me of the appearance of Aurora,
> But with a Russian name and wearing a fur coat.[6]

Clearly, Mandelstam and Kirillov saw very different paths into the country's cultural future. In 1920–1921, while Kirillov bowed before the apparition of what he termed an "Iron Messiah," "the savior, the lord of the earth, / The master of titanic forces," Mandelstam's elusive vision revealed a vulnerable world where the very nature of "things" had changed significantly.[7] Kirillov's emphatic insistence on an all-powerful machine world collides with Mandelstam's shadowy realm of transparency, subtlety, and a sense that the times are out of joint. In "The Swallow" (*Lastochka*, 1920) Mandelstam introduces a theme of transparency and indeterminacy from the first, troubling words: "I have forgotten the word that I wanted to say."[8] In another poem of 1920, he transfers his beloved classical world into this new uncertainty:

> When Psyche-life, following Persephone,
> Descends into the shadows of a half-transparent forest,
> A blind swallow rushes to her feet
> With Stygian tenderness and a green twig.[9]

In the post-Revolutionary years there were many such odd groupings. It wasn't yet clear who would conform fully to the new ideology; it wasn't even clear what such conformity might require. So Mandelstam found himself working together with poets like Kirillov, assigned to strengthen cultural awareness among the country's undereducated majority. One of Mandelstam's major assignments was to edit a series of booklets on the theme of "Rhythm Education." We do not know whether any of the booklets ever appeared, but Mandelstam did complete his own article for the anthology and his "Government and Rhythm" (*Gosudarstvo i ritm*) makes an intriguing point of comparison to the exuberantly anti-individualist writing of Bogdanov, Kirillov and other proletarian poets who worked alongside Mandelstam in Narkompros. Mandelstam does not argue against the notion of the collective "we," but he does offer a cautious counterpoint: "While organizing society, while raising it from chaos to the harmonious order of social existence, we tend to forget that what must be organized first of all is the individual."[10] Without paying attention to the differences between individuals, Mandelstam observes, the goal of a harmonious collective can't be achieved. The individual remains important.

At the same time, this essay shows Mandelstam's initial support for the transforming force of the Revolution. He expresses a conscious commitment to the educational changes that his department has initiated, and commends those teachers who look to the new state for guidance in "rhythm as an instrument of social education. It seems profoundly instructive to me that these hands are now extended toward the government with hope. They are returning that which rightfully belongs to it. An unerring instinct tells them that rhythmic education must be controlled by the government."[11] Such a positive assessment of the state's role in social construction may surprise those who are more familiar with Mandelstam's later writing, but Nadezhda Mandelstam confirms that "as late as 1919 M. was still trusting, cheerful and light of heart."[12]

Indeed, one can find a variety of responses to the Revolution and its implications in Mandelstam's poetry of the initial post-Revolutionary years. Already in November 1917 Mandelstam was alarmed by the violence that the Revolution had unleashed, writing about the "yoke of violence and wrath" that had been prepared for the people by the "October favorite."[13] But his response was at the very least ambivalent, argues O. P. Smola, who reports never finding the word "revolution" used in a negative context by Mandelstam. The Revolution's fire "burned" Mandelstam, says Smola, and caused him to sing in a voice that wasn't quite his own. Referring to the poem "The Twilight of Freedom" (*Sumerki svobody*, May 1918), Smola remarks that this poem allowed Mandelstam to be attacked both from the right and the left, and argues that Mandelstam here departed from his typical individualism in favor of a broader, "collective" voice that can be traced directly to the powerful force of the Revolution on the poet.[14]

The next few years saw Mandelstam traveling frequently and broadly, but one stop was particularly important for his understanding of the changing literary climate. During the winter of 1920–1921 he became good friends with Vasilisa Shklovskaya-Kordi and Viktor Shklovsky, and also met regularly with several of the writers who joined Shklovsky in forming the Society for the Study of Poetic Language (*Opoyaz*) and in advocating what came to be called the "Formal Method" of literary study. Mandelstam was a regular visitor to the bustling Shklovsky apartment, remembers Vasilisa Shklovskaya-Kordi, and frequently participated in literary evenings where he read his poetry and listened to the other guests, whose number included Formalists Boris Eikhenbaum and Yury Tynyanov.

Those meetings surely produced lively and intense discussions about poetry, linguistics and the study of literature, and Mandelstam would have agreed with some of the Formalist principles: Their respect for the word and for the sound of poetry echoed his own sentiments. Even the call for a fundamentally "scientific" approach to literature was something that Mandelstam would not reject out of hand. But other parts of the "formal method" must have sounded less congenial to a poet like Mandelstam. Indeed, the Formalists' emphasis on the artist as a craftsman, a technician who assembles particular literary devices to produce a poem, could have seemed like a personal challenge to Mandelstam at some of these literary evenings, since he occasionally spent large portions of time huddled under a blanket on the couch, trying to shut out the conversation around him as he mumbled aloud the sounds of the poem that was starting to sound in his consciousness. Once the poem had taken shape in his ears and mind, he would emerge to jot it down—hardly the picture of a technician asserting mastery over a broad array of literary devices.[15]

The literary environment grew increasingly complex and treacherous in the ensuing years, especially for poets. On one hand, the acknowledged shortage of gifted proletarian writers produced a national campaign to raise up a new group of writers, and poetry workshops were an especially popular part of the campaign. On the other hand, established poets started to come under attack if their poetry was considered elitist or not suitable for advancing the goals of the Revolution.

Perhaps two poetry events in May, 1921 best illustrate the turbulence of the times. Symbolist poet Alexander Blok was visiting Moscow and had agreed to recite at several literary events. According to an account of the events by Boris Pasternak, he and Vladimir Mayakovsky went together to hear Blok recite at the Polytechnical Museum in downtown Moscow, where all the biggest literary events were held. The friendly audience received Blok with hearty applause. Mayakovsky had heard that Blok's second reading at the Moscow Press House might yield a very different reception so he and Pasternak hurried off for the reading as quickly as they could. But they had no transportation and by the time they arrived on foot, the chaos Mayakovsky feared had erupted. Eyewitnesses agree on the gist of the remarks addressed directly to Blok by a minor poet named Alexander Struve: Your poetry is dead, you have nothing left to write, and you yourself are dead.[16] The audience, younger and more radical than at the Polytechnical Museum, approved.[17]

Mayakovsky, the leading Soviet poet at the time, was himself walking a fine line, trying to simultaneously recognize the genius of poets like Blok while also leading the Futurist call for a new approach to art. In his 1921 poem "Order No. 2 to the Army of Art" (*Prikaz no. 2 armii isuksstva*), Mayakovsky addresses all the leading poetic groups by name (Acmeists, Futurists, Imagists) and orders them to stop worrying about rhyme, about arias and all the other niceties from the arsenal of art. Instead, he holds up workers as a suitable inspiration for artists, and argues that "Master craftsmen, / Not long-haired preachers / Are what we need now."[18]

Mandelstam did not witness the attack on Blok personally, but he recognized the changing times. In his 1921 essay "Word and Culture"

(*Slovo i kul'tura*) Mandelstam may be expressing his hope rather than his conviction about the status quo when he says that "The separation of Culture and the State is the most significant event of our revolution." Certainly this would have been perceived as a direct challenge to the aspirations of both the Futurists and the proletarian writers' groups, since each hoped to see the state intervene in the cultural chaos by giving them a broad mandate for cultural reform. Mandelstam already sees an emerging threat to literature, and with characteristic bluntness he establishes an absolute dichotomy: "Social differences and class antagonisms pale before the new division of people into friends and enemies of the word: literally, sheep and goats." Finally, he moves directly to some comments that surely reflect the growing clamor for "useful" poetry that serves the state: "There is nothing hungrier than the contemporary State, and a hungry State is more terrifying than a hungry man. . . . Do not demand from poetry any special substantiality, materiality, or concreteness. It is that very same revolutionary hunger."[19]

By 1922 Mandelstam started to feel that "revolutionary hunger" personally. Nadezhda Mandelstam repeatedly marks the period from 1922 to 1923 as a personal fulcrum in Mandelstam's life, the time when his orientation changed dramatically. "It was only after 1922 that Mandelstam's articles took on a highly polemical character and conversation with him tended to end in violent argument," she writes. "Willy-nilly he found himself at cross purposes with his times and his contemporaries—whom, in common with everybody else throughout the world, he had at first taken to be men of a new era."[20]

One factor in Mandelstam's shifting perspective is as mundane as it is central to daily life: lodging. In early 1922 the Mandelstams moved into Moscow's Herzen House, which at that time was already the very center of the nation's literary life. Here they were surrounded not only by the country's leading writers, but also by editors from the competing literary journals and by officials who headed up the rival literary associations. The All-Union Writers' Union, the All-Union Poets' Union and others were housed within Herzen House itself, while several radical proletarian groups had offices next door. By 1922 Mandelstam was being attacked by a number of the journals whose contributors were housed near him in Herzen House, and he was starting to bend under the pressure.

It was also in 1922 that two other traumatic events unfolded in Mandelstam's life. First, Mandelstam was unsuccessful in his efforts to secure a room at Herzen House for Futurist poet Velimir Khlebnikov, whose work Mandelstam repeatedly cited as an example of poetic genius. When the room in question was given to literary scholar D. D. Blagoy instead of Khlebnikov, Mandelstam was despondent. His mood only worsened when he learned that Khlebnikov had died in poverty a few months later.

Even more personal was the arrest of Mandelstam's brother for reasons that are still not clear. Mandelstam's efforts to secure his brother's release brought him into close contact with the state's security forces. Mandelstam started with an appeal to Nikolai Bukharin, the influential *Pravda* editor who interceded for Mandelstam at several crucial points. Bukharin arranged for Mandelstam to be received by the head of the secret police himself, Felix Dzerzhinsky. Mandelstam had seen Dzerzhinsky once before in 1918, and Dzerzhinsky remembered him. Dzerzhinsky ordered the release, but the investigator in charge of the case refused to acknowledge the order. When Mandelstam confronted the investigator in person, he was told that it was "not in his interests" to press for his brother's release. Mandelstam had to make another stress-filled appeal to Bukharin, and eventually his brother was set free.[21]

As Nadezhda Mandelstam remembers 1922, it was also a time when Mandelstam's sense of artistic purpose faded and he started giving ground to the new forces at work in literature. She recalls his "attempted disavowal" of Anna Akhmatova and Nikolai Gumilyov, two of Mandelstam's Acmeist colleagues, in articles written for 1922 issues of the Kiev journal *Russian Art* (*Russkoe iskusstvo*), and considers them a concession to the uproar about Acmeism. "He really was in a state of confusion," writes Nadezhda Mandelstam. "To some degree, as we stood at the crossroads, we all had the temptation to rush after everyone else, to join the crowd that knew where it was going. The power of the 'general will' is enormous—to resist it is much harder than people think—and we are all marked by the times we live in."[22]

One group that knew where it was going more than most was the group of writers and literary bureaucrats that split off from mainstream proletarian writers to form "October" (*Oktiabr'*), the most radical of the proletarian writers' groups. The group officially organized itself in December 1922 and the leaders of October quickly started to maneuver for dominant positions in the growing proletarian writers' organizations. As leading Octobrist G. Lelevich remembers, 1922 marked a significant change in the strategy of the more radical proletarian writers. They were dismayed by the speed with which "bourgeois" literary interests were re-emerging after the end of the civil war, and determined to fight back so that the fragile gains of proletarian writers would not be lost. These radicals had lost patience with the slower-paced approach of the "senior" proletarian writers and started to raise their voices more insistently, writes Lelevich. Finally, at the end of 1922 they set up October and in 1923 organized themselves for more effective opposition.[23]

The Octobrists soon dominated the proletarian writers but they encountered serious competition from other groups in the struggle for literary and cultural dominance. On one side they faced LEF (Left Front of the Arts), a grouping that included Constructivists, Futurists and Formalists. On the other side was the already weakening group of those who advocated a tolerant policy toward the fellow travelers, those artists who resisted complete surrender to the new state. Mandelstam's approach to poetry and culture left him closest to the fellow travelers and certainly set him apart from both LEF and the proletarian groups.

Mandelstam's sense of isolation on the literary fringes may explain some of the harsher judgments he passed on fellow poets in 1922,[24] but not all of his writing that year shows a desire to reconcile himself with the newest cultural forces of the age. In "On the Nature of the Word" (*O prirode slova*) Mandelstam responds to Formalists Yury Tynyanov and Viktor Shklovsky with a rebuttal of the notion of literary evolution, saying that any application of "evolutionary theory" to literature—let alone a theory of literary "progress"—is a harmful manifestation of the scientific approach.[25] For Mandelstam the very notion of "progress" in literature was meaningless, because unlike the proletarians and the Futurists, he didn't see any particular finish line toward which literature was aiming. He especially didn't share their vision of literature's progress toward a social finish line, and even addresses this obliquely in his essay when he argues for a broad humanistic vision for poetry (focused on "Man") rather than a narrower political vision (focused on "citizen"). Some of his pronouncements are extremely blunt: "Futurism, a concept devised by illiterate critics, is devoid of all content or scope; it is not merely a curiosity of vulgar literary psychology. It assumes an exact meaning if one views it precisely as this forced, mechanical adaptation, this distrust of language."[26] The conclusion to the essay comes as something of a surprise after such bold statements, for in the end Mandelstam appears to retreat into the rhetoric of the dominant literary forces, saying that it isn't the idealist Mozart, but "Salieri, the stern and strict craftsman, [who extends] a hand to the master craftsman of things and material values, to the builder and creator of the material world."[27] It cannot be an accident that in the essay's concluding lines Mandelstam includes four of the key terms in the contemporary debate over literature's social function: craft, things, building, and creation. The purpose of this conclusion is harder to identify, but at the very least it shows Mandelstam's effort to remain engaged in the terms of the literary debate, and may show a desire not to alienate himself completely from the dominant forces.

One other article from early 1922 needs to be mentioned here. In "The Birth of Plot" (*Rozhdenie fabuly*) Mandelstam recognizes the increasing influence of prose, and especially the increasing incursion of the "non-literary" into prose. Newspaper fragments, Soviet circulars, and more were finding their way into prose, and the result, says Mandelstam, is that "Prose belongs to nobody. It is essentially anonymous. It is the organized movement of the verbal mass cemented together by anything you please." The increasing dominance of prose is directly attributable to the Revolution, Mandelstam asserts, "because it [the Revolution] promoted the anonymous prose writer, the eclectic, the collector. . . ." The Futurists could well have been thrilled to hear this assessment, because by the end of the 1920s the remaining Futurists (gathered in LEF) identified "anonymous prose" as the apex of their cultural program. The members of LEF would also have been delighted to hear Mandelstam's conclusion that the new prose was dominated by "daily life," although where they saw daily life as the ultimate way to connect literature with a human audience, Mandelstam saw the focus on daily life as an inevitable forerunner to the death of plot.[28]

Already by the end of 1922, then, Mandelstam had serious misgivings about the future of Russian literature, and especially about poetry's place in that future. The new year brought no respite. Nadezhda Mandelstam asserts several times that 1923, the year in which Mandelstam composed most of *The Noise of Time*, was the start of an organized blacklisting of Mandelstam, saying that he "was simply put under a ban."[29] As Lelevich observed, 1923 was the year when the dominant ideology gathered strength and started to flex its muscles more in the literary world. Mandelstam soon felt the squeeze, especially from two new journals that debuted in the middle of the year.

The two journals represented another step in the intensifying struggle between the most aggressive of the proletarian writers and the group known as LEF. It was not accidental that the proletarians' journal carried the martial name *On Guard* (*Na postu*), since one of the new journal's explicit objectives was to guard—and advance—the interests of proletarian artists. Of course, LEF's journal (the self-titled *LEF*) sounded its own military note with its emphasis on being at the "Left Front" of the cultural struggle. Mandelstam, who abhorred violence and had a hypersensitivity to the sounds and words around him, certainly noticed the increasing jingle of military and command rhetoric coming from these two new leaders of the cultural debate.

Much of Mandelstam's own published work in 1923 appeared before the new journals debuted (*LEF* in March and *On Guard* in June), and consists of variously themed articles about twentieth-century Russian poetry. Again he praises Pasternak, Khlebnikov, and Mayakovsky, while giving other poets more ambiguous reviews.[30] Overall, though, there is little in these articles and reviews that would have elicited more than irritation. His article "Humanism and the Present," on the other hand, cuts much closer to the bone of the new age. The article appeared in January, 1923 in the Berlin newspaper *On the Eve* (*Nakanune*) and starts with an ominous introduction to his discussion of "social architecture" when he suggests that some ages treat people the way ancient Egyptians treated their Assyrian prisoners, using people as "building materials" rather than building things for the sake of people. The sense of foreboding only increases when he speaks about the approaching "monumentality" that characterizes the new forms of social architecture, and describes the fear and bewilderment that this awareness already provokes: "[We are] uncertain whether this is the wing of approaching night or the shadow of our native city which we must enter." What will happen to the individual human being, the "little person," in this new age of the grand scale? Already the sense of protection has been stripped away, he writes, because in the new social era "no laws concerning the rights of man, no principles of property and inviolability any longer protect the human dwelling, no laws preserve the house from catastrophe, provide it with any assurance or security." The article gets even darker as Mandelstam nears his conclusion and issues a grim warning: "If the social architecture of the future does not have as its foundation a genuinely humanistic justification, it will crush man."[31]

Nowhere does Mandelstam explicitly accuse the new state of devouring its people, but the implications are not particularly subtle and may have been a significant factor in the increasingly chilly reception that his submissions found in editorial offices, and in the way others reviewed his poetry. The "ban" that Nadezhda Mandelstam remembers may refer largely to Mandelstam's poetry, for we still find a number of Mandelstam's reviews and essays appearing in journals later in the year, but the atmosphere grew increasingly strained. A new edition of Mandelstam's second poetry anthology appeared, but its reception was not particularly reassuring. Nadezhda Mandelstam recalls that the reviews, good or bad, were not substantive—people "no longer had any ear" for poetry, she writes, and people didn't want to make a mental effort to read poetry.[32]

The journal *Press and Revolution* (*Pechat' i revoliutsiia*) took the unusual step of reviewing the anthology twice, though. In its June–July issue for 1923, poet Sergei Bobrov reviewed the first (1922) edition rather sympathetically. Mandelstam started his poetic career writing poetry "about nothing," writes Bobrov, using "some kind of snobbish chatter, lazy and without any meaning." But Mandelstam's post-Revolutionary poems are better, Bobrov continues, and he concludes with the hope that Mandelstam will continue to move away from his Acmeist roots.[33] Valery Bryusov's review of the second edition appeared only a few months later, in the October–November issue, but the tone was very different. In a lengthy footnote he criticizes the soft "impressionism" of Bobrov's review, then takes Mandelstam severely to task for wallowing two thousand years in the past to hide the fact that he "has nothing to say." Poetry like this, "cut off from contemporary life, from social and political interests, cut off from the problems of contemporary science, from the search for a contemporary world view," has nothing to offer, Bryusov concludes.[34]

This is strong stuff, but still completely in keeping with the "plain-speaking" ethos that characterized many of the reviews appearing in all the major journals. Mandelstam dispatched some rather snappy reviews of his own in 1923, including one that appeared in the same issue as Bryusov's article. Certainly he wouldn't like seeing his work disparaged in print, but Mandelstam's horizons were broad enough for him to recognize that the inexorable tightening of cultural theory presented a far more serious threat to his artistic future.

The first issue of *LEF* signaled a harsh up-tick in the cultural rhetoric. A series of flamboyantly aggressive headlines announce the new journal's tone: "What is LEF Fighting For?", "Into Whom is LEF Sinking its Teeth?" and "Whom is LEF Warning?" The articles berate LEF's opponents at length and by name, and announce the principles of the group's own plans. At the heart of the bombast, some recurring principles emerge. Of course, anything related to the old, bourgeois literary patterns has no place in LEF's literary universe. But LEF's leaders also have a lot to say to those who think they are serving the Revolutionary cause in their art. LEF denounces any attempt to "aestheticize" the Revolution and offers a consciously witty reformulation of the old aesthetic question in condemning those who favor only "revolt for revolt's sake." Instead, they want an art that has concrete objectives in the new era: "Our weaponry: example, agitation, propaganda."[35]

In the campaign for a "poetry of concrete results," LEF started to move further and further away from a conception of the poet as an individual artist. Boris Kushner wrote enthusiastically about a new figure who would bring the production values and technical skills of engineering into the cultural realm, a kind of engineer-artist. Osip Brik was much more specific when he explained how the "formal method" should apply to poetry: "There are no poets or litterateurs, there are only poetry and literature," he argues. Someone who writes poetry is nothing out of the ordinary, just "a maker of speech who serves his class, his social group. The subject of his writing is suggested by the consumer. Poets don't make up themes, but take them from their surroundings." One of the advantages of the formal method is that it offers specific ways to study "poetic production" (*proizvodstvo*); the language of "production," so vital to the technological aims of the new state, occupies the central place in Brik's argument and brings the Formalists out of abstraction and into the realm of applied science. Poetry becomes just another production commodity, and its devices can be catalogued and analyzed to see how effectively they produce the necessary finished product. Science and technology merge and virtually eliminate the human poet in the poetic process. The poet becomes an assembler, rather than a true creator, and a "great poet does not express himself, but only fulfills a social order."[36]

This alarming attack on the status of the poet, with its assertion that poets should be considered mere technicians, represented only one side of the increasing pressure on Mandelstam. On the other side were the repeated cries for a "declaration of ideological intent," formulated with characteristic bluntness by the editors of *On Guard*. Already in the journal's first issue its editors had appealed to Communist Party leaders to take a more directive role in eliminating the chaos that characterized literary politics (and offered their own platform as an appropriate model for the Party to adopt). In the next issue, which appeared in the autumn of 1923, the editors decided to issue a cultural ultimatum to all literary figures, challenging them to take a clear ideological stand. The worldview of the Octobrists allowed no room for ambiguity, and they offered only two choices. Maintaining their affinity for military metaphors, they announced that "there are two lines of trenches facing each other": One contains those literary forces with roots in the past; the other contains the forces of revolutionary proletarian literature. "Every writer, every poet, everyone active in literature must openly indicate with whom and for what he stands," they continue. "The moment has arrived when no one can remain on the sidelines in the literary wars that lie ahead."[37]

Mandelstam did not remain on the sidelines, but neither did he respond to this crude challenge. Instead, he launched an attack that sidestepped questions of political ideology while delivering a sharp rebuke to those who were trying to cheapen poetry by turning it into just another occupation for the proletarian laborer. His article, with the appropriately militaristic title "An Army of Poets" (*Armiia poetov*), appeared in two parts in November, 1923 and demonstrates an essential and lasting truth about Mandelstam's literary convictions: When it came to poetry, Mandelstam gave no quarter and expected none. The accounts of Mandelstam's responses to would-be poets who came to him for an evaluation of their work might be humorous to us as readers, but they consistently indicate that Mandelstam did not think poetry—even bad poetry—could ever be a laughing matter. Veniamin Kaverin recalls that when he first visited Mandelstam to receive an evaluation of his poetry, the intensity of Mandelstam's response caught him completely unprepared. "We must protect Russian poetry from people like you," Mandelstam told Kaverin, who felt as though he had dared to walk into a cathedral without first removing his cap. Reflecting on this encounter years later, Kaverin remembers: "It was important to him that I cease writing poetry, and what he was saying was a defense of poetry against me and those tens and hundreds of youths and maidens who were occupying themselves with word games."[38]

This was not an isolated event. Semyon Lipkin remembers that Mandelstam was constantly besieged by "versifiers" who wanted him to read their poems. On one occasion, Lipkin remembers, Mandelstam told a young man whose poetry he despised: "Let's divide the earth into two parts. I will live in one, and you can live in the other." Another time Lipkin was arriving at Mandelstam's building when a young man fled past him down the stairs. He had been complaining that editors kept rejecting his poems when Mandelstam lost his temper completely and chased him from the room. Standing at the top of the stairs, Mandelstam shouted after him: "And did Buddha publish? And did Jesus Christ publish?"[39]

The defense of poetry was also in Mandelstam's thoughts when he argued (in "The Word and Culture" and "On the Nature of the Word") that poetry's extraordinary linguistic density makes it a preserver of history and cultural identity. Gregory Freidin's suggestion that Mandelstam was attempting to define a role for the poet as a mediator "between the most sacred core of the culture and the profane masses" aptly captures Mandelstam's dilemma, because what Mandelstam considered valuable in culture was being rejected on all sides by those who only wanted to look forward, not back.[40] It was maddening for Mandelstam to see what he considered a blasphemous erosion of poetry's authority by a growing notion that poetry was simply another workspace for the proletariat or, even worse, for an idler. "An Army of Poets" becomes an attack on poetry's "enemy without," and Mandelstam tries to describe poetry in terms that a worker will understand. A poet, Mandelstam explains, "is not a person without a profession who is unfit for anything else, but rather a person who transcends his profession and subordinates it to poetry." The most deadly sin of these "poets" is their flippant attitude:

> A person suffering from "poetry disease" is not even interested in poetry itself. He usually reads only two or three contemporary authors whom he tries to imitate. . . . In the majority of cases, writers of poetry are very poor and inattentive readers of poetry. . . . [T]hey are invariably offended by advice to learn to read before they begin to write. It never occurs to them that to read poetry is a most sublime and difficult art, and that the vocation of reader is no less respectable than the vocation of poet. They are dissatisfied with the humble vocation of reader and, I repeat, are born non-readers.[41]

Mandelstam records one final anecdote that reveals the essential hollowness of this "army of poets." He describes a young man who wanted to publish some French translations of Nikolai Yazykov's poetry in a Russian magazine. When the editorial staff politely declined this unusual proposal,

> he went away cheerfully and unperturbed. The insane image of this youth remained in my memory for a long time. It set a record for uselessness. Everything was useless: Yazykov to him, and he to the magazine, and

French translations of Yazykov to Russia. I do not know if it is easy for him to approach people with such a product, but he is an outcast, he is a fop and proud of it.42

To get an understanding of how Mandelstam conceives the bearing of a "genuine" poet, all we really need to do is construct an antithesis to this young "fop": A true poet cares profoundly for all genuine poetry, reads it avidly, and believes that poetry has a genuine usefulness—not the narrowly defined usefulness of nineteenth-century civic poetry, or the "produce on demand" usefulness demanded by the new ideological zealots, but a broader role that shapes the consciousness of the people and the culture. This conviction certainly put Mandelstam at odds with his age, since it left him rooted in the Russian tradition where poets sometimes gained a respect that Freidin suggests was "not unrelated to the traditional veneration of saints." Freidin has adopted the term "charismatic institution" to describe the symbolic power held by Russian poets; he notes the widely held perception that literature is "a potential locus of the sacred" and should thus be treated "*seriously*, even with reverence, by the Russians, and indeed it has been. . . . It is a truth universally acknowledged that the famous poets of modern Russia, Mandelstam among them, have a personal following that borders on a cult."43

This situation may lend a unique gravity to lyric poetry, but it also tends to limit the true poet's options. Faced with such high expectations of poetry—and sharing these expectations personally—a real poet cannot imagine surrendering the high ground of principled poetry, of lowering the standards of poetic Truth, no matter what the cost. As Freidin notes, in a less "ideologically charged" era it may have been possible for a poet like Mandelstam to don a poetic mask, but in the era in which Mandelstam stepped onto the literary stage, with its "emphatically charismatic view of poetry," a true poet could never contemplate such a step.

By the fall of 1923, then, the atmosphere for poets had rapidly become more ominous than even a year earlier. LEF was trumpeting its demands for a technician-poet, the Octobrists were raising the stakes with ultimatums about "ideological commitment," and Mandelstam was outraged over the "army of poets" when he settled down to compose *The Noise of Time* in the Crimean resort town of Gaspra. The growing crisis in culture was certainly in Mandelstam's mind as he wrote, but he addressed this question rather obliquely in the text, folding these specific and pressing dilemmas into the story of his own efforts to find a place in Russian culture.

Much has been written about the compelling sense of history in *The Noise of Time*, and the way Mandelstam divides his life into three historical periods that define the author's psyche while offering a captivating historical analysis of recent decades. This historical approach offers numerous insights that I will not repeat here; instead, I want to focus on the text's powerful cultural orientation, where Mandelstam describes his personal attempt to find a place in the Russian cultural ethos both as a Russian speaker and as a Russian writer.[44] This cultural side of the text introduces a new, more personal tone to the dialogue that Mandelstam had already been carrying on with the new cultural forces in his critical prose. Mandelstam's autobiography is not an isolated and self-absorbed text, but rather a personal story that deliberately engages the cultural crises stirred up by LEF, the Octobrists and others. Mandelstam recognizes the looming threats faced by Russian poets, and *The Noise of Time* becomes a personally framed rejoinder.

Among the numerous insights offered by the historical approach to Mandelstam's autobiography, one in particular offers a particularly useful point of entry into the cultural side of the text. The resemblance between the approach to history in *The Noise of Time* and in Alexander Herzen's *Past and Thoughts* (*Byloe i dumy*) has been noted repeatedly and in the context of the 1920s this linkage was "more than a compliment," says Victor Krivulin. "The figure of Herzen was dually important: officially he was considered the 'grandfather' of Bolshevism, while at the same time the old liberal intelligentsia considered him a 'Russian European.'"[45] Mandelstam knew Herzen's life and work well, and part of the similarity between the two works can be attributed to Mandelstam's inclination to look for models from the past that could be appropriated for the present. But there is another side to this relationship that has been left unexplored. The two men share something even more fundamental than their approach to history, for both Mandelstam and Herzen were by birth interlopers in Russian culture, betrayed immediately by their Germanic names. Herzen was further stigmatized by his illegitimate birth to a Russian aristocrat, and although Mandelstam was not illegitimate by birth, his increasingly precarious status in Russia's literary world brought with it the stark realization that in the eyes of many contemporaries, he was indeed an illegitimate son of his age.

Both Mandelstam and Herzen use their autobiographies to describe their move to legitimacy, but their respective objectives are quite different. Herzen, the illegitimate foreigner, finds a place for himself and becomes a defender of Russia's interests as the country's first real socialist. As late as 1919 or 1920, it might have been possible to argue that Mandelstam could share a similar vision. By 1923, though, Mandelstam's growing awareness of the dangerous forces set loose by the Revolution makes a political or social sense of identity impossible. Instead, Mandelstam's personal mission is to find a place for himself where he can defend Russia's *cultural*, not social, interests. He still wants to find a place, and in this sense the spiritual connection between the two men becomes one of the most significant factors making Herzen's *Past and Thoughts* an ideal model for Mandelstam.

One metaphor used by Mandelstam to inscribe himself in Russian culture is communication and its language-related image cluster. Mandelstam's passion for language and the word, along with his attention to reading, listening and the speech process itself, is readily apparent in many of his essays from 1920 to 1923. All of these combine in the communication process and take on central significance for Mandelstam in the personal cultural pilgrimage that he describes in *The Noise of Time*. On one level, his depiction is very personal. He describes his own family's speech patterns, and especially the way he *heard* them as he was growing up. Hebrew and Yiddish become for Mandelstam the languages of his religious and historical heritage, the languages of his grandparents. Mandelstam describes his family's unsuccessful efforts to help him enter into this heritage, and the memories share a common thread: for each unsuccessful attempt, Mandelstam attributes the failure to linguistic incompatibility. A Russian history of the Jews comes across as written in "the clumsy, shy language of a Russian-speaking Talmudist." A Hebrew tutor's Russian speech is technically correct, but Mandelstam's quick ear recognizes an essential hollowness, something that makes it *sound* false: Mandelstam has a kind of aural truth sense that allows him to spot linguistic impostors. On one of his rare visits to a synagogue, Mandelstam is both entranced and appalled by what he hears. The music captivates him as he listens to the alto and children's choirs; the chants during the service show "an awesome equilibrium of vowels and consonants." But when there is a shift from musicality to ordinary speech, the difference is striking: Suddenly the atmosphere turns vulgar as Mandelstam remembers "how offensive was the crude speech of the rabbi—though it was not ungrammatical; how vulgar when he uttered the words 'His Imperial Highness,' how utterly vulgar [*kakaia poshlost'*] all that he said." Even the very names of the Jewish holidays are alien to him, with their "harsh names" that "grate" on his ears.[46]

When his grandparents (the locus of his Jewish heritage in the text) become more personally involved, the results are no better because Mandelstam cannot communicate with them: His grandmother knows only one Russian word [*Pokushali?* Have you eaten?] and he has no way to respond. Feeling constricted by this mutual incomprehension, Mandelstam wants to leave, but cannot even find a way to say this. He resorts to sign language, but his attempt to escape is met with an even more forceful attempt to assimilate him. Mandelstam's grandfather suddenly throws a cloth over his shoulders and makes him repeat "words composed of unknown sounds; but, dissatisfied with my babble, [my grandfather] grew angry and shook his head in disapproval. I felt stifled and afraid. How my mother arrived just in time to save me I don't remember."[47] This is a fascinating passage: Language is reduced to the phoneme level ("unknown sounds") as Mandelstam shows the completeness of his alienation from Jewish speech in particular, and his entire heritage in general. In the midst of an act of worship—and therefore a literally sacred Jewish moment—Mandelstam feels no affinity. He comprehends the speech as nothing more than babble.

It is his parents that have the most direct influence on Mandelstam's attempt to find himself in Russian culture. Both his father and his mother have left behind the exclusively Jewish orientation of his grandparents, but they now find themselves in a linguistic space mediated by both the Jewish past and the Russian present. Mandelstam recognizes the importance of his parents in creating his own verbal world: "The speech of the father and the speech of the mother—does not our language feed throughout all its long life on the confluence of these two, do they not compose its character?" he reflects.[48] Looking at his father, Mandelstam paints a rather grim picture of someone caught in a linguistic no-man's-land between past and future, someone who has *no language at all*:

> his speech was tongue-tie and languagelessness. The Russian speech of a Polish Jew? No. The speech of a German Jew? No again. Perhaps a special Courland accent? I never heard such. A completely abstract, counterfeit language, the ornate and twisted speech of an autodidact, ... the capricious syntax of a Talmudist, the artificial, not always finished sentence: it was anything in the world, but not a language, neither Russian nor German.[49]

This must have been a terrifying heritage for Mandelstam to contemplate. Attempting to move into Russian culture and language, Mandelstam would find an absence of language tantamount to non-being.[50] Still, there is a sense of progression here. Mandelstam's father attempts to break into new linguistic territory and succeeds in wrenching himself free from the mother tongue—but he is unable to achieve something new. His past and future cancel each other out to leave only non-language.

It is left to Mandelstam's mother to become the family's first "settler" in the Russian language, and he commemorates her success in eliminating virtually all foreignness from her Russian. Her speech has "roots and confidence," even though it is hampered by the inevitable limited vocabulary and trite locution of the linguistic pioneer. Perhaps most important, she has succeeded in entering Russia's linguistic and literary culture to the point where external signs of foreignness have fallen away. This degree of success will not be enough for Mandelstam, of course. He must move beyond the success of the pioneer and become a fully naturalized master of the language. The break with his linguistic past must be complete if he is to become a Russian *poet*, someone who will not just master the language but create with it.

Why is it crucial that *The Noise of Time* depicts Mandelstam's mother, rather than his father, as the one from whom he inherited Russian speech? The answer lies in the Jewish tradition of matrilineal succession, where the children inherit their identity as Jews from their mother. In Mandelstam's account, his Jewish blood heritage confronts his longing for a place in Russian culture—but a fundamental shift takes place as his identity is conferred on him by his mother. The entire text of the autobiography shows that it is the Russianness of his mother, her love of speaking Russian and her appreciation for Pushkin, that Mandelstam inherits instead of her Jewishness. The matrilineal Jewish succession is broken, and paradoxically his mother becomes the source of his entry into Russian, not Jewish, culture. That helps to explain why it is Mandelstam's mother who "rescues" him from his Jewish linguistic plight at his grandparents' house: In the traditional Jewish narrative the mother should provide the link to the child's Jewish past, but here she actually separates him from it—"saves" or "rescues" him, to use Mandelstam's own word. In Mandelstam's world, speech and linguistic linkages are more compelling than blood ties, and his mother guides him away from Jewish and into Russian culture.

These passages, where biographical details from his family tree are presented to the reader but then left behind as Mandelstam shifts the emphasis from biological to cultural pedigree, capture the ambivalence of Mandelstam's attitude toward his past. Some readers see the entire text as a denial of biography, and point to one of the best-known passages in *The Noise of Time* as evidence of Mandelstam's anti-biographical orientation. The text in question appears near the end of the work, at the beginning of the penultimate section where Mandelstam writes:

> My desire is not to speak about myself but to track down the age, the noise and the germination of time. My memory is inimical to all that is personal. If it depended on me, I should only make a wry face in remembering the past. . . . I repeat, my memory is not loving but inimical, and it labors not to reproduce but to distance the past. A *raznochinets* needs no memory—it is enough for him to tell of the books he has read, and his biography is done. Where for happy generations the epic speaks in hexameters and chronicles I have merely the sign of the hiatus, and between me and the age there lies a pit, a moat, filled with clamorous time, the place where a family and reminiscences of a family ought to have been. What was it my family wished to say? I do not know. It was tongue-tied from birth—but it had, nevertheless, something that it might have said. Over my head and over the head of many of my contemporaries there hangs congenital tongue-tie. We were taught not to speak but to babble—and only by listening to the

swelling noise of the age and bleached by the foam on the crest of its wave did we acquire a language.[51]

There is no question that this passage must be considered carefully if we want to understand the work, and most discussions of *The Noise of Time* include some discussion of Mandelstam's remarks here, sometimes referring to them as his "programmatic statement." Most tend to accept Mandelstam's assertion that he has no desire to "speak about himself" because he has no sense of a personal history, no sense of family rootedness.[52] Charles Isenberg, however, responds more skeptically with the observation that the text does not actually support Mandelstam's assertion. Just as books are not—contrary to Mandelstam's claim here—the only things used to show the narrator's history, so there are many more personal and family notes struck than this passage would condition the reader to expect.[53] In the same way, the notion and function of memory is much more complex in Mandelstam's autobiography than he suggests here. The first three words of the Russian text are "I remember well," bringing together both the absolutely personal "I" and the notion of a properly functioning memory—hardly what a reader would expect to find if one were to read this "programmatic" statement first, and then proceed to read through the work from the beginning.

Indeed, one of the most puzzling aspects of Mandelstam's elaborate disclaimer about biography is its location in the text. Appearing as it does in the second last section of the work, it seems vaguely out of place. One might argue that Mandelstam placed it here so that his assertion would not distract the reader by laying bare his method from the outset. However, the sharp polemic thrust of this passage shows that Mandelstam is not trying to be subtle. It would make more sense to declare one's credo at the outset; here, Mandelstam declares himself at the end, and in doing so he invites—and expects—the reader's assessment of how his practice measures up to his stated intentions. Certainly there has been considerable personal material: his attendance at concerts, descriptions of his school days and friends, memories of family vacations on the Baltic shore, memories of the family linguistic and literary pedigree. His past is shaped by much more than just the books he has read.

Why such a strong assertion to the contrary, then? The passage actually responds to contemporary political and cultural trends, and shows Mandelstam's very personal—and somewhat anxious—interaction with these trends. Both the language and the location of the passage tend to support this conclusion. First, Mandelstam's denial of a "personal" biography and his statement that books supercede memory are in no way original statements. In fact, by 1923 they might even be considered cultural clichés. Already in 1918 Alexander Bogdanov called for poets to abandon the too-personal lyric "I" and concentrate on a more collective identity; the need to abandon an individual consciousness became a familiar refrain in the writings of almost all the pro-Revolutionary literary groups and became one point on which even bitter opponents like the Octobrists in *On Guard* and the LEFists in *LEF* could agree. Of course, it was easier to demand an abandonment of personality than to enforce this new mind set. Pavel Lebedev-Polyansky, who became the country's chief censor from 1921 to 1930, grew exasperated with the lyric poem's stubbornly lingering personal voice and condemned it as a holdover from the bourgeois literary past. The emblem of the new age, he argued, was the collective. Mark Steinberg notes a continuing ambivalence in the literary world of the early 1920s, with critics and Party figures demanding a focus on collective identity but many writers still trying to figure out where they fit as individuals.[54]

Eventually the constant drumming of the collective theme produced the desired result. In 1923 P. Ya. Zavolokin set out to collect short autobiographies from the country's worker and peasant poets and he saw a marked tendency to deflect attention from the individual to a broader collective. "Most authors willingly responded, indeed relished telling their personal life stories, although they did not consider the genre of autobiographical sketch the place to write about personal life," comments Steinberg. "A few went further and suggested that it was wrong to write about themselves." Some of the entries seem to be following a narrative track very similar to Mandelstam's. "I am little interested in my own personality," writes Aleksandr Pomorsky, emphasizing his sense of discomfort at the notion of separating his individual account from the broader story of the revolutionary age and unknowingly choosing words that overlap closely with Mandelstam's own denial of individuality.[55] In this sense Mandelstam's apparent move away from family history, or biography, makes perfect sense as an example of what Jerome Bruner describes as autobiography's move towards "culturally canonical" accounts that frequently take the place of a person's individual experiences.[56]

In the same way, the notion of books as a crucial influence in forming personality was also a cultural commonplace when Mandelstam wrote *The Noise of Time*. Describing the many autobiographical tales finding their way into print in the early 1920s, Steinberg notes:

> Culture, especially books, was often central to these portrayals of self-realization. Fedor Kalinin quoted Nietzsche on the power of books to "burn thought into oneself" and to teach the proletariat to "think for themselves." ... In this spirit, almost every memoir written in these years identified books (and occasionally the periodical press) as catalysts that awakened them to their own dignity, their capacity for self-improvement, their inner genius, and the need to fight against insult.[57]

When we recognize that Mandelstam's statements about the importance of books and the irrelevance of individuality are direct echoes of claims being made all around him, we may be less ready to accept them as univocal "good-faith" assertions of authorial intent.

I would argue that they are much more ambivalent. On one hand, Mandelstam's early readers would readily recognize the prevailing rhetoric, and might indeed conclude that Mandelstam was adopting the dogma of the day to signal his willingness to fit into the prevailing cultural and political ethos. On the other hand, Mandelstam may be paying only surface tribute to the abandonment of personality, while underneath a competing and very different message emerges.

That is the possibility that I would like to explore by examining Mandelstam's statement within the larger framework of the text. When we look at the structural context, this passage becomes a synecdoche for the Revolution as a whole, and the individual personality becomes a casualty of the "clamorous time" that tears a hole in history. It acts as a textual separator to mark the change of epochs and to spell out clearly what these changes mean for the individual.

What, then, is it separating? Immediately prior to this passage Mandelstam describes the last desperate days before the October Revolution, with their conspiratorial meetings and debates over minute points of dogma. The language becomes steadily more ominous as he describes conflicts between various competing Revolutionary factions. Events start to affect language itself when "the grim hairy hands of the traffickers in life and death were rendering the very words life and death repugnant." From this pre-Revolutionary setting Mandelstam shifts to the "programmatic statement," then moves on to a reprise of the life-and-death theme, but this time in a post-Revolutionary context: "A revolution is itself life and death," he writes, "and cannot endure idle chatter about life and death in its presence. Its throat is parched with thirst, but it would not accept a single drop of moisture from alien hands." This helps to interpret his earlier comments: In the context of revolution, personal memory is irrelevant and even dangerous, since one can infer that the "thirst" of the revolution is closely associated with life and death. The individual is no longer a safe or suitable topic, since time has "germinated" and produced the upheaval of revolution: One must speak now of the age (or the collective) rather than of the individual. The "pit filled with clamorous time" becomes a metaphor for the historical chaos of the October Revolution, which has left itself like a hiatus between Mandelstam and his age.

From a post-Revolutionary context, a person in Mandelstam's position would have no choice but to deny knowing what his family wanted to say. Even if Mandelstam had wanted to produce a family chronicle in the tradition of Sergei Aksakov, the very fact of the revolution would make such a detailed family reminiscence risky, if not impossible. The revolution stands implacably between the present and the past, and changes everything—including the past. Its noise (the Russian root from the word "noise" is repeated three times in the passage) forces one to "hear" the past differently, and to speak differently. Indeed, Mandelstam takes a deliberate and risky step toward an assessment of the new age by explicitly noting that he, and by extension his contemporaries, do not belong to a "happy generation." In this reading Mandelstam's statements are not a programmatic manifesto that defines the composition of the work, but rather an uneasy description of the way the revolution has forced a shift in personal consciousness.

If we return to our original point of departure, the study of communication-related metaphors in *The Noise of Time*, we find that this sense of uneasy interaction with the age pervades the text and is transformed into a more compelling anxiety in the work's concluding section. It is worth noting that the themes of language, speech and listening are not new for Mandelstam in the autobiography, but had already been key elements in both his poetry and prose for more than a decade. Already in 1910 Mandelstam describes the difficulties of poetic speech and even of drawing breath in the poems "Stifling gloom covers the river bed" (*Dushnyi sumrak kroet lozhe*) and "Out of the evil and miry pool" (*Iz omuta zlogo i viazkogo*), while "Silentium," also from 1910, describes the breathing of the sea and the poet's struggle with muteness. Other poems from this era extend the range of Mandelstam's quest for poetic voice and breath, and in the 1912 poem "I wince from the cold" (*Ia vzdragivaiu ot kholoda*) he describes an inclination toward muteness that is overridden by a celestial command to sing out. The poet's efforts to speak and breathe can be traced through poem after poem of the 1910s and into the 1920s as well.[58]

When he begins to compose *The Noise of Time*, Mandelstam writes with the assumption that a careful reader (like the one described in his 1913 essay "On the Addressee" [*O sobesednike*]) will understand the importance of speech and breath as metonymical associations for poetry, and the significance of the associated notions of listening, deafness, and muteness. The author will be recognized as a poet even though Mandelstam never *claims* the title "poet" directly. These ideas leap out at the reader from the very first sentence, which begins: "I remember well the deaf years of Russia. . . ." The phrase summons the shade of Symbolist poet Alexander Blok, alluding to one of Blok's poems ("Those born in the deaf years / Do not remember their own path") but contradicting it. The reference to "deafness" soon finds its counterpart in descriptions of muteness and decay: The newsboys are "silent" and "motionless," the parks are decaying—it is a dying and impotent age, Mandelstam says. Even the great cultural icons are affected. Figner, the tenor at the

Mariinsky Opera, was losing his voice (the "tool" that he depended on to produce his art) in the 1890s, and society responds not with sympathy, but ridicule: A caricature of Figner makes the rounds, with one part showing him singing and the other side showing him plugging his ears. This attention to the voice of culture carries over into the new era, where Mandelstam emphasizes that it was the actress Komissarzhevskaya's voice, with its musicality and mobility, that lent her greatness: "she raised and lowered her voice just as the breathing of the verbal sequences required. Her acting was three-quarters verbal. . . . The theater has lived and will live by the human voice." The voices of Figner and Komissarzhevskaya combine with the music of Tchaikovsky, Hofman, and Kubelik to show the importance of sound in the artistic realm. The power of musical sound and of the human voice on stage are presented as close relations to the use of the voice in poetry.[59]

Poetry initially appears in *The Noise of Time* in a rather unexpected form when Mandelstam describes someone who might be best termed an "antipoet" in his poetic hierarchy. The poet who becomes the poetic key to the "dark coffin of the 1890's" turns out to be Semyon Nadson, whose most striking features are his "inspired arrangement of the hair" and a fiery but woodenly simplistic expression. Yet Mandelstam claims that Nadson became the emblem of the age and confesses his own inexplicable fascination with Nadson, as if he and everyone else were stumbling in a murky dream world: "How many times, knowing already that Nadson was bad, have I still reread his book?" Mandelstam muses.[60] He genuinely tries to hear Nadson's poetry, but it remains an enigma of "uncomprehended sound" that somehow hypnotized an entire era, drawing listeners, like moths, to the destructive fire of its vapidity. The description shows how Nadson was a good fit with the age, since the deafness of the book's first sentence is revealed more specifically as tone-deafness. Hearing is not eliminated, but it knows no discrimination. People are unable to discern good from bad: Nadson's "bad" poetry is idolized, and the sensational miscellanies of the day are read in place of genuine literature. This "tone deafness" to real literature is a sure sign of the broader deafness to history, as people continue with their lives completely unaware of the historical turmoil just over the horizon.

Mandelstam's description of his later years shows a growing awareness of genuine poetry. He does not identify himself as a poet, but mentions trying to work out his own understanding of poetry: "Modernism and Symbolism somehow managed to live together in my head with the most desperate Nadsonism and the poesy from the journal *Russian Wealth*. I had read all of Blok. . . . The 'thick reviews' bred a kind of poetry to wilt the ears, but it was there that the most attractive little loopholes were kept for the eccentric failures."[61]

The concluding section of *The Noise of Time*, where literature finally comes to the fore and the voice again plays an important role, was not part of the original manuscript that Mandelstam submitted in 1923. Instead, it was attached later, Nadezhda Mandelstam recalls.[62] A careful reading shows a new, more anxious and even belligerent tone in this chapter; the shift can be linked to Mandelstam's changing assessment of Russia's literary climate in 1924. One of the only essays that Mandelstam managed to publish in 1924 was descriptively titled "The Slump" (*Vypad*), a rather pointed effort to assess a precipitous decline not only in the writing of genuine poetry, but also in the capacity of contemporary readers to understand poetry. Describing the many conflicting voices clamoring for poetry to do their bidding, Mandelstam writes that "poetry shies away from the countless revolver muzzles of unconditional demands aimed at it. What should poetry be? Perhaps it is not obliged to be anything, perhaps it is not obliged to anyone, perhaps its creditors are all fraudulent!" Taken as written, this statement is certainly defiant, but not explicitly rebellious. The repeated use of the word "perhaps" keeps it in the realm of the hypothetical, a framing of the question rather than a summary of conclusions. But to the writers and theorists from October, LEF and the proletarian writers' groups, this argument for poetic nonalignment had to sound thoroughly treasonous. Mandelstam's next paragraph would be sure to anger them even more, for his list of contemporary Russian poets includes politically acceptable poets like Vladimir Mayakovsky alongside thoroughly unacceptable poets like Nikolai Gumilyov, who was executed on treason charges in 1921. "A nation does not choose its poets, just as a child does not choose its parents," Mandelstam writes. "A nation that cannot honor its poets deserves . . . No, it does not deserve anything."[63]

Mandelstam's defense of the poet in "The Slump" came at about the same time as a special conference at the Party's Central Committee Press department in May 1924. The conference was organized after a group of writers (including Mandelstam, Boris Pilnyak, Mikhail Zoshchenko, Sergei Esenin, and Vera Inber) wrote a letter complaining about the conduct of the *On Guard* staff. At the conference, the proletarian activists from *On Guard* defended their conduct. I. Vardin argued that the "fellow traveler" writers who signed the letter were not contributing to the Revolution and weren't ideologically "reliable." S. Rodov went further, contending that a work's literary merit was less important than its political and class awareness. Vardin, Rodov and their colleagues pressed hard for the Party to endorse their position, hoping that the encounter would give them more leverage in their struggle for ultimate cultural authority. But Party leaders Nikolai Bukharin and Anatoly Lunacharsky were skeptical and remained unwilling to sacrifice entirely the notion of aesthetic value.[64] Neither side was satisfied, but Mandelstam and his allies must have realized that they had succeeded only in slowing, not stopping, the ascendancy of the aggressive proletarian literary forces.

These disturbing literary encounters accompanied the revisions to *The Noise of Time*'s concluding chapter, where we meet the magisterial V. V. Gippius. This charismatic figure is described by Mandelstam as the person who made literature come alive for him, and Gippius becomes an embodiment of genuine literary values in the text. He stands as an unconventional figure with an idiosyncratic approach to literature, and his *voice* is his most important attribute. He doesn't just summon, but bellows in a voice that demands immediate respect. He is a kind of high priest, demanding and meticulous. Mandelstam describes Gippius's peculiar attitude toward his beloved literature as "literary rage," and it is this extremism that Mandelstam finds so attractive. Genuine passion characterizes Gippius's relationship with literature, and this coexistence was so organic, so all-consuming that literature became his family: "V. V. had established personal relations with Russian writers, . . . filled with noble enviousness, jealousy, even jocular disrespect, grievous unfairness—as is customary between the members of one family." This living interaction, where passion, rage and adoration simmer and erupt regularly, is a stark contrast to the "professional" literary scholars dismissed by Mandelstam as indifferent and insipid. Again, Mandelstam underlines that interaction with literature is verbal above all else, for this supreme commander of the literary barracks is nothing without his voice: It was "in the energy and articulation of his speech that one found all the strength of his personality," Mandelstam says. The disease Gippius feared more than any other was losing his voice.

The steadily building impression in this concluding section of *The Noise of Time* is that Mandelstam has finally found a home and a linguistic base, for in this den of literature Mandelstam at last enters into the wildness of the Russian language. "For the first time I felt the joy of the outward disharmony of Russian speech when V. V. took it into his head to read to us children the *Firebird* of Fet," Mandelstam recalls. Mandelstam even wants to add an ancestral gallery to his literary home, with honor paid to the heroes of previous days. The difference between this gallery and the conventional family portrait gallery, though, is striking. Instead of mere faces, pictorial representations of the writer's physique, a house of *literature* needs to remember the writer's *voice*: "It is only with the masks of other men's voices that the bare walls of my house are decorated," Mandelstam reports, and he hopes that through these voices he can escape the sterility of the present, the "dried-up river" that connects the present and the past, and remember the literature of years gone by. Only the writer's voice can help him.

The master plot of the autobiography becomes clear only in this final chapter, where Mandelstam achieves at least a tentative resolution. The family history that has been interrupted and displaced by the Revolution is now replaced by a filial devotion to Russian culture and genuine literature. Finally, he has found a home and family. In the last sentences of *The Noise of Time* he at last seems to acknowledge his own destiny as a poet when he removes the covering from the winter cap of the writer, and appears ready to put on the "beast of literature" that can keep one warm in the increasing cold of the surrounding winter.

The winter depicted in this concluding chapter is not benign, nor is the depiction of literature unequivocally positive. Instead, winter becomes an active force against which the "shivering and raging" writer must define himself. Winter's chill becomes a proving ground for literature: when bitten by frost, will it crunch and brighten up? "If it is genuine, the answer is yes," Mandelstam answers. But winter's threat can turn deadly as well. The story of one writer whose voice was silenced when his throat was frozen offers a warning against taking winter too lightly. When Mandelstam looks back at the "unrepeatable" nineteenth century, he sees that all the previous decades have been welded together into a single day, a single night, a deep winter. Within this winter "the terrible State glowed, like a stove, with ice," he writes. And literature is also somewhat disturbing. Mandelstam describes the trembling that comes over him when he approaches the writer's fur hat: In the post-Revolutionary age, literature offers a more treacherous family than he had ever imagined. The passion of Gippius, the freedom of genuine literature, thrills and inspires him. But the external threat from the State—a threat still largely mediated by the literary groups vying for supremacy, but destined soon enough to be wielded directly—has already suborned a substantial part of the literary community.

Mandelstam's own conviction that the confrontation between literature and the terrible State is inevitable comes through clearly in the autobiography's final passage: "A beast must not be ashamed of its furry hide. Night trimmed him. Winter clothed him. Literature is a beast. The furriers—night and winter." When finishing *The Noise of Time*, Mandelstam still believed that the collective forces of literature (wild, untamed literature, that is) can find strength in resisting the State's pressure. Just as a beast's fur grows thicker and fuller to fend off winter's cold, a poet's work can gain strength by refusing to bend to the will of the State or its proxies.

But the final confrontation is inevitable, and only one side can ultimately claim victory in the analogy Mandelstam creates. Genuine literature may be a beast, and its fur may grow thick. But the furrier—revealed as winter, or the State—awaits, and a furrier only has business with furs when the beast within is dead. The image is a grim one, and signals

Mandelstam's premonition that the only poetry this State will accept is dead poetry, poetry where the essential living, breathing, independent essence has been removed and only the surface covering remains. This troubling final image showed an almost uncanny prescience in anticipating developments in cultural politics during the remainder of the decade and beyond, for the next few years brought increasing pressure on writers, and especially poets.

3

The Search for Safe Passage

In the years following the publication of Osip Mandelstam's *The Noise of Time*, conditions for poets and poetry deteriorated dramatically. The ominous signs that provoked Mandelstam's alarm were gradually replaced by attitudes of open hostility and when Boris Pasternak turned to his autobiography in 1929, poetry was under siege. Even more, the cultural institution of the poet was being assailed as an elitist relic of the literary past and the poet's status was openly attacked. For a true poet like Pasternak, the threat behind these campaigns was unmistakable. Pasternak's response to the attacks provides a powerful example of artistic courage, for his autobiography *Safe Conduct* (*Okhrannaia gramota*) accepts the likelihood of serious reprisal and makes poetry the very center of the text. Like Mandelstam, Pasternak demonstrates an extraordinary acuity to the escalating hostility and, as if to confound the anti-poetry forces, he responds by raising the stakes himself with an emphatic assertion of poetic identity.

At the same time, a lurking darkness in the text shows Pasternak's increasing personal anxiety about the poet's prospects in the Soviet Union. If *The Noise of Time* traces Mandelstam's attempt to enter into Russian culture and to adopt the ferocious literary loyalty modeled by his mentor V. V. Gippius, *Safe Conduct* tells the story of someone who already recognizes himself as a Russian poet but can't find a safe place for the poet in the increasingly treacherous cultural battlefields. Pasternak has no trouble chronicling his life as a poet, but along the way there creeps in a wary feeling that the specter of Death lurks nearby. Can a poet actually continue to live and write in Soviet reality? Is there a way to accept contemporary reality while resisting its demand for submission?

These are the compelling and very personal questions that drive Pasternak as he examines his own path to poetry in *Safe Conduct*. Indeed, the title of the work is the first signal of its function and it is unfortunate that the most commonly used English translation (which I, too, use here for continuity's sake) can obscure this message. In English, the notion of "safe conduct" can suggest behavior, while the Russian designation *okhrannaia gramota* is more precisely translated as "writ of protection" or "protection order." The phrase was broadly deployed in post-Revolutionary Russia where these "writs of protection" were frequently used to safeguard the bearer or to prove ownership of an object or location in fending off nationalization efforts by overzealous local revolutionaries. The work's original readers would immediately have recognized that the text was setting itself up as a similar instrument of protection.[1]

What, then, was Pasternak trying to preserve? That is the question that I will address in this chapter. There are some obvious answers that give partial satisfaction: on one level, the text preserves an account of Pasternak's own life to this point; on another, it provides a testament to Austrian poet Rainer Maria Rilke, to whom the work was dedicated. But these are at best minor elements. The most profound function of *Safe Conduct* is to act as a preservation order for poetry itself, and to provide a writ of safe passage for the troubled Russian poet at a time of great crisis. Pasternak's text accomplishes this through an examination of his own path to poetry, but the ultimate object of concern is much larger and makes the work a national cultural talisman.

Safe Conduct, which first appeared serially in two different literary journals, did not start off with this orientation, though. Pasternak first conceived his autobiography as a tribute to the recently deceased Rilke when the first section of the work appeared in the journal *The Star* (*Zvezda*) in 1929. But after the suicide of Futurist poet Vladimir Mayakovsky in 1930, the shape of the work changed dramatically. When the final two sections appeared in *Red Virgin Soil* (*Krasnaia nov'*) in 1931, they contained a sharp critique of contemporary cultural developments that was allegorically blurred but still readily apparent to careful and informed readers. *Safe Conduct* appeared as a separate edition later in the year, but that was to be its last publication in Russia until the 1980s. The criticism generated by the autobiography was so strong that a planned 1933 collection of Pasternak's work was suddenly shortened considerably, and *Safe Conduct* was dropped when he was "encouraged" to withdraw it.

It is hard to imagine that Pasternak wasn't aware of the impact that *Safe Conduct* might have for he had been near the epicenter of the debates about literature in general and poetry in particular for most of the 1920s. In fact, Pasternak was associated with the radical LEF until 1927, and he contributed to the very journal that argued for the abandonment of lyric poetry. We can only imagine how Pasternak balanced the competing claims that resulted from this identification with LEF: how could he reconcile his passion for the lyric with LEF's urge to abandon the notion of a creative personality? What was his response in 1923 when he was gaining even more artistic respect for the exuberant lyric anthology *My Sister, Life* (*Sestra moia—zhizn'*, published in 1922) and then saw fellow LEFist Osip Brik's article urging poets to abandon the notion of creative force and look instead at the laws of production?

We do know that Pasternak struggled to find his way in these confusing times. When the post-Revolutionary enthusiasm for lyric poetry faded, most attention shifted toward prose but a number of poets looked for other poetic forms. There was a shift from the intimacy of the lyric to grander and more public genres like the ode and the epic, genres that satisfied an urge to tell "more," to describe the events of the age, and at the same time avoided the risky individualism associated with a too-personal lyric voice. Pasternak's poetry had always been characterized by a unique ability for description, and his poems were bursting with unusual and highly allusive word combinations. He recognized but regretted the steady encroachment of the epic, calling it a "second-hand genre" in a 1925 questionnaire.

Pasternak eventually took several stabs at the epic himself, although these efforts never produced the same success as his lyrics. Perhaps to counter the growing popular sense that lyric poetry was a blight, a kind of illness in the new social order, already in 1923 Pasternak wrote a narrative poem that he called *Sublime Malady* (*Vysokaia bolezn'*) and used its lyric-inspired style to undercut the new epic mode, prefiguring the adopt-but-subvert technique that he would repeat several years later in *Safe Conduct*.[2] Catherine Ciepiela has argued that by publishing *Sublime Malady* in a 1923 issue of *LEF*, Pasternak initiates an internal polemic with his fellow LEFists. By using the present tense to narrate revolutionary events, Pasternak suggests that the push to shift from lyric to epic contradicts history itself because the revolution is an ongoing process. And by injecting an autobiographical thread suggesting his awareness that he as a poet is being pushed into irrelevance, Pasternak laid the ground for his own virtual silence as a poet for the next two years. Later, Pasternak's other epic poems further develop his sense of the link between epic and history and show him using the genre in a way that fits its new status as verse chronicler of the revolutionary age. *The Year 1905* (*Deviat'sot piatyi god*) commemorates the twentieth anniversary of the 1905 revolution, and *Lieutenant Schmidt* (*Leitenant Shmidt*) memorializes a revolutionary hero.[3]

These efforts found their way into print, even into journals where poetry was already being eliminated. When LEF decided to revive its journal in 1927 under the name *New LEF*, Pasternak was again listed as a member of the editorial collective and an excerpt from *Lieutenant Schmidt* was published in the first issue. But the relationship between LEF and Pasternak was not harmonious, according to Pasternak's son, Evgeny, who notes that Pasternak expressed his "sharp disapproval" to the very first issue of the new journal. The editors convinced him not to create a scandal by abandoning LEF at this crucial juncture, since the LEFists' increasing stridency was prompted at least in part by a recognition that they were being outmaneuvered by the proletarian extremists. So Pasternak remained unwillingly on *New LEF*'s list of collaborators until May, when he officially severed all ties with LEF.[4]

If we trace the evolving literary policy advocated on the pages of *New LEF* from its inception in 1927 to its dissolution in 1928, the reasons for Pasternak's disenchantment with LEF become clear. LEF's theorists were confronted by sweeping social and political changes and they scrambled to keep up. The freewheeling era of the New Economic Policy was coming to an end; the start of Stalin's first Five Year Plan had almost arrived. Cultural institutions were challenged to match the changing social environment and the very notion of "artistic" literature was questioned. The new era demanded production, and it tied itself firmly to a pursuit of scientific and technological progress. Could *belles lettres* serve these demands? LEF and other groups decided that *belles lettres* should be left behind, and heralded the reign of the "fact" in literature.

It was the daily newspaper, that ultimate symbol of written fact that excited LEF's admiration most. "Every epoch has its own literary forms," wrote LEF theorist Sergei Tretyakov. "Our epoch is the newspaper. . . . What the Bible was for the medieval Christian . . ., what the didactic novel was for Russia's liberal intelligentsia, that is what the newspaper is for the Soviet activist." Newspapers synthesize social, political and economic issues to indicate their direct application to daily life. Could there be a more appropriate literary contribution to the social and physical construction of the Soviet state? Even the authorship of a newspaper fits the epoch, for "the essence of the newspaper is its anonymity," Tretyakov continues. "Our basic task is not to wait for red epic poets, but to train the entire Soviet audience to read the newspaper, the bible of our day."[5]

An emphasis on "facts" led inevitably to a corresponding emphasis on science and the way science could be applied to the tasks of the Five Year Plan. Nikolai Chuzhak combined a comprehensive explanation of fact-based literature with practical guidance for writers in his 1929 "Writer's Instruction Book" (*Pisatel'skaia pamiatka*) arguing that fact-based literature must be concrete. No more abstractions or metaphors, Chuzhak advises. Instead, every object should be classified scientifically.[6] In "Life-building Literature" (*Literatura zhiznestroeniia*) Chuzhak offers a stark choice to would-be writers: will they concentrate on "the junction of science and literature through the processing of fact" or its opposite, "the useless fantasy of ignorant imitators of life, not to say class enemies?" This astonishing juxtaposition sums up the intense oppositions in literary politics, where Chuzhak and his colleagues defended the new fact-affirming literature as "a question of life and death."[7] Indeed, Chuzhak makes a special point of the links between literature and life: they are not separate entities, and a writer who tries to create psychological space between text and subject has no place in literature. If "all of life shouts about concrete industrial work," Chuzhak writes, how can anyone keep singing the same tired, vague refrains? Revolutionary developments in science and industry need to become central parts of literature, and only the literature of fact will do. Another LEFist, Vladimir Trenin, went even further. If "worker correspondents" in industrial newspapers are the ideal writers for the Five Year Plan, writes Trenin, then the ideal education will not be literary training, but rather intense scientific and technological training.[8] Science dictates not just the subject, but even the technique for those promoting the newspaper.

Not everyone agreed with LEF on these questions. The radical proletarian literary groups had been rebuffed in 1925 when an official Party resolution directly contravened their policy of intolerance toward the "fellow travelers," those writers who did not express the unqualified support for the Revolution demanded by the more aggressive proletarian groups. But the retreat was only temporary, and the proletarians emerged from reorganization with renewed claims to preeminence in Soviet literary politics. Slowly they fought their way to the top under the leadership of Leopold Averbakh and by 1930 they dominated the literary scene. Their sharp claim that proletarian writers must be the leading force in literature was a direct challenge to LEF and other groups. As the literary polemics again heated up, the scope of the debate grew implacably narrower. LEF writer Sergei Tretyakov noted at the end of 1928 that numerous journals which had formerly opposed the "literature of fact" now embraced it as though it had been their idea, and criticized LEF's adoption of the newspaper as the ideal literary form. Tretyakov, warning against the insidious elitism of these rivals, said that LEF would continue to fight against those who try to privilege "higher, larger" forms of fact-based writing (autobiography, biography) over "smaller" forms (reportage and newspaper writing). The smaller forms, he argued, offer the best and most direct opportunity for writers to meet the day's pressing sociological problems: increasing literacy, doubling the harvest, collectivizing agriculture, and raising the level of production.[9]

Earlier, poetry's perceived simplicity had made it one of the favored "small forms." Now, from 1927 to 1928, poetry's status shifted further from privilege toward pariah. As late as January 1927, LEF acknowledged poetry as the featured component in its cultural program, which would "stand on the boundary between aesthetic activity and utilitarian life practice." Poetry needed to renew the language, it needed to have a pointedly ideological base, and it needed to be fact based, but within those parameters it could actively effect change in society. LEF poet Nikolai Aseev describes how a poem that he published in the April 1927 issue of *New LEF* led to direct physical—and thus social—changes in Moscow's urban landscape. In his poem, Aseev describes the eagles that still decorate the cupola of a Moscow church, and regrets that this lingering symbol of the tsarist era has apparently remained unnoticed for almost ten years of Soviet power. "I took them as the theme of the lived-out past, as a concrete illustration of this theme, an example of absurdity that assaults the eyes," writes Aseev. A week after his poem appeared in *New LEF*, Aseev was walking near the offending cathedral when he looked up to the cupola and saw that the offending eagles had been thoroughly covered over with lime. Aseev concluded that the eagles had been hidden by religious sympathizers who wanted to avoid attention, and he thereby missed the chance to build a much stronger justification of poetry's continuing usefulness.[10] He could have argued that the obliteration of the eagles showed how a conscientious "Poetry of Fact" could contribute directly to transformative change in contemporary material culture: Facts and poetry can combine to support the Revolution's social program. Instead, Aseev lapses into the easier rhetoric of antireligiosity, and misses an opportunity (with a blatant ideological bias, to be sure) to argue for poetry's continuing relevance.

Perhaps Aseev considered it futile to advance a defense of "activist" poetry when he wrote about the eagles in early 1928 because by then the converging paths of "science" and "fact" were rapidly squeezing poetry not just off the pages of *New LEF*, but from the literary scene entirely. Fewer and fewer poems appeared in *New LEF*'s issues until after the March 1928 issue the only poems that appear are those sent in by readers. And these are published not because they have intrinsic value but because they make useful case studies when *New LEF*'s editor Vladimir Mayakovsky tries to correct harmful tendencies in amateur poetry. After June 1928, poems disappear entirely,[11] and many readers probably marveled that poetry had managed to survive until then. After all, six months earlier Sergei Tretyakov had expressed LEF's complete support for a Komsomol member who wrote that "one technician is infinitely more useful than ten bad poets." Then Tretyakov added: "We would even agree to toss out the word 'bad.'"[12]

The shift away from poetry became a recurring theme in *New LEF* throughout 1928, and culminated in complete abandonment. In March, the journal criticized efforts to recruit new poets, since "writing poetry is an act of extreme responsibility. . . . If the verse turns out to be particularly dangerous, it can bring about mass poisoning." Later, Aseev declared that he had separated himself from verse and initiated a new genre that he described as the "lyrical feuilleton," a literary mode that emerged from newspaper writing.[13] The final blow came in the December 1928 issue, which turned out to be the last *New LEF* issue ever. V. Pertsov, who had personally outlined LEF's support for poetry in January 1927, now announced a complete reversal. "LEF's program has descended from poetry to prose," writes Pertsov, and describes the transition to prose as a progressive movement from "aesthetics" toward "utility." And what lies at the root of this shift? Society requires this "aesthetic destruction" because prose is the only form that can serve "the natural-scientific interest of the new human," concludes Pertsov. The extremity of LEF's stance was not shared by everyone, but the notion that literature had to perform a useful social function came to be a broadly accepted mark of the new era. This function overshadowed all else, and any suggestion that an author had an excessively aesthetic orientation generated immediate suspicion from all sides.

Even a cursory look at Pasternak's *Safe Conduct* shows that the book could not fail to arouse at least criticism, if not outright hostility, in this environment. This is a work that seems to flaunt its nonutilitarian orientation. The boundaries between fact and fiction blur in the consciousness of the narrator, and the impressionistic tone becomes an important element in Pasternak's overall creative project. Outwardly, he accepts the new emphasis on prose, even the "fact-based" division of prose that includes autobiography. But hidden by this apparent acceptance of the new norms is a subtler subversion, a revolt from within, for this autobiography mocks the very notion of "fact." Fact and fantasy, documentary and artistic, run together in *Safe Conduct*.

The appearance of *Safe Conduct* led to a broad-based attack on Pasternak that featured rare agreement among the various literary groupings. Aleksei Selivanovsky, one of the most influential leaders of the Russian Proletarian Writers' Association (RAPP), called the book an example of "subjective idealism," a charge that in 1931 was almost the same as accusing someone of counterrevolutionary activity.[14] N. Oruzheynikov accused Pasternak of an attack on Marxism. Even *Red Virgin Soil*'s editor Vladimir Ermilov joined in, calling Pasternak's work a bourgeois counterattack on Russian literature—despite the fact that his own journal had published the autobiography's final installments. The attacks continued into 1932, when a special "literary evening" was called in April to discuss Pasternak's literary activities. Although several speakers defended both Pasternak and his poetry, the prevailing hostility toward the poet was noticeable. When he was asked to respond to the denunciations, Pasternak was not sure how to begin. After collecting his thoughts, he spoke about the genuine artist's sensitivity to the environment that surrounds him or her. Sometimes it becomes necessary for a real artist to abandon art for a time, he continued, when reality removes the conditions that make art possible. "Many here have made metaphorical comparisons—shooting, barricades," Pasternak said. "For me this is not a metaphor."[15]

Why this outrage over the publication of Pasternak's autobiography? It was not just the style of the autobiography that elicited such a powerful response. Certainly the elusive narrative line identified the work immediately as a thoroughly modernist creation that didn't fit the increasingly "functional" literature demanded by all sides in the literary debates. But it was more the sense that Pasternak was deliberately flouting expectations, and that *Safe Conduct* was a calculated challenge to the dominant cultural ideology, that increased the intensity of the opposition. As Lazar Fleishman puts it, the work has a "polemical address" that starts from its core: Pasternak's style presents "facts" and then immediately calls them into question, thus showing how blurred the relationship between "fact" and "fantasy" can be when constructed in a narrative, even a narrative as "fact-oriented" as autobiography was construed to be at the time.[16]

Some of the best examples of this narrative approach can be found in two passages that are probably the most frequently discussed passages in this most frequently discussed autobiography. Early in the text, after an impressionistic but still structurally conventional account of his childhood introduction to Rilke on a train, Pasternak launches into a long series of events that he says he will not describe: events from childhood, deaths and attempted suicides, a house fire near the Pasternaks' summer home, his broken leg, his father's panic-stricken ride for home under the impression that his family was perishing, and many more. Of course, even as he provides this extensive list, Pasternak violates his own promise: by mentioning these events, he *does* bring them into the text. In a manner that is repeated throughout the text, he extends a description, then either contradicts it or withdraws it: "I shall not describe how later on when I broke my leg and escaped two future wars in a single evening. . . ." But even as this "nondescription" begins to turn into a narrative event, Pasternak breaks it off. The reason, he says, is straightforward: "I shall not describe any of this. *The reader can do it for me.*"[17] Pasternak's seemingly dismissive suggestion that the reader can fill in the blanks of his life has been interpreted as condescension, or camouflage, or a denial of self.

There is another way to see this appeal to the reader, however. Rather than condescension or denial of self, it shows his awareness that the reader is an active part of a text's creation, and any attempt by an author to "fix" facts will inevitably be "unfixed" by the wide-ranging perspectives of the various readers who encounter these facts. A fact is only a starting point, because it exists both for the author and for the reader—and in that relationship any fact is liable to be reshaped in the reader's consciousness. The author provides the framework and the reader provides the active response. As Paul John Eakin observes, "[in] the world of autobiography the author as reader is matched by the reader as author."[18]

A second passage that illustrates Pasternak's narrative approach comes shortly after he describes his decision to abandon music as possible career. "I am not writing my biography. I turn to it when someone else's requires me to," writes Pasternak. "Together with its main character I believe that only the hero merits an actual account of his life, whereas the story of a poet is utterly inconceivable in such form. . . . And the more a productive individuality is shut in on itself, the more its story is—in a quite literal sense—collective."[19] Pasternak's insistence here that he is not telling just his personal story, that his story is literally "collective," echoes the nearly identical assertion made by Mandelstam in *The Noise of Time* that he does not want to speak about himself, but about his age. Collectivity, the individual's deference to the group was certainly a frequently used autobiographical convention in the 1920s. But what kind of collective identification is Pasternak hinting at here? If we consider that he has just identified himself as a poet—and explicitly sidestepped the title "hero"—then it becomes clear that Pasternak's "collective" consists of poets, and the story he is telling in *Safe Conduct* is not his alone. Instead, this is a story on behalf of all poets—or better still, on behalf of the poet as a cultural figure—in the Soviet era.

There is a certain paradox in writing on behalf of poets as a group, or even on behalf of the poet as a cultural institution, because one essential feature of the Russian poet's identity since the time of Alexander Pushkin has been a sense of independence. The tension between Pasternak's awareness of belonging to a group (poets) while still needing to acquire an independent voice runs throughout *Safe Conduct*, especially the concluding sections. This tension also helps to explain why one of the most important characters in the autobiography is not an actual person at all, but rather a somewhat blurry vision of the poet, existing less in flesh and blood (although *Safe Conduct* is almost overcrowded with "real" poets as well) than in the concept of "poet" as it existed for Pasternak. Struggling with the notion of poet, both as an abstract concept and as he faced it in his own life, he tried to work out a balance between the two.

Like Mandelstam, Pasternak knew very well the Russian tendency to exalt the poet, to turn the poet into a prophet or larger than life Romantic figure (a poet with a capital "P"). Dmitry Segal writes that idealization of poets as the embodiment of Russia's highest spiritual and national values can be traced back to the time of Russia's greatest poet, Alexander Pushkin. Without a readership willing to acknowledge the poet's unique mission in life, of course, this self-understanding will be hard-pressed to survive: after all, a poet with no audience will struggle to maintain a sense of place. But Russia "seemed to take its poets very seriously indeed," Segal remarks. One factor contributing to the near-veneration of poets was the exalted view of Russian as a literary language. Poetry came to be seen as the essential heart of the language and functioned as a metaphor for Russian linguistic vitality; Mandelstam was certainly not the only Russian who instinctively linked poetry and the Russian language.[20]

Pasternak returned to the themes of the poet and poetry throughout his career, beginning with the 1914 publication of his first poetry anthology, *A Twin in the Clouds* (*Bliznets v tuchakh*). These themes become particularly important with the publication of *Second Birth* (*Vtoroe rozhdenie*) in 1932, where the poem "Death of a Poet" (*Smert' poeta*) responds to Mayakovsky's suicide, and "If I had known" (*O znal by ia*, 1931) reflects the ambivalence already surrounding the notion of "poet" in Soviet life:

> If I had known that such things happen,
> When I set off for my debut,
> That verses lead to bloody murder,
> That they will choke and they will kill.
>
> I would have refused point-blank
> To play any games with this reality.
> But it all started so long ago,
> And my first interest was so shy[21]

When Pasternak grapples with the Romantic conception of "poet as prophet" in the pages of *Safe Conduct*, he does so as someone who has been consciously trying to work through this problem for almost two decades. Pasternak's longtime friend Konstantin Loks remembers that during their university years "we talked about the relationship between the biography of the poet and his poetry. Boris talked about it as though it were in some way his own, something long known to him, but the longer I listened to him speaking in his not altogether clear way, the more I sensed that this theme had his attention in a special way."[22]

It seems fitting, then, that *Safe Conduct* is clearly a poet's story from the outset; the narrative describes Pasternak's detours into music and art as he moves toward poetry, but there is no sense of suspense for the reader. The ultimate point of arrival is known; it is the intermediate passages, the process, that provide the justification for the account. *Safe Conduct* is a quest narrative or Bildungsroman, with Pasternak in pursuit of his destiny. The search is described in graphic and even geographical terms, with his quest taking him from Moscow to Marburg, to Venice, and then back to Moscow again.

The opening scene in *Safe Conduct* describes Pasternak's first encounter with Rilke and fulfills several important functions. Most basically, it introduces—without naming him—the poet to whom the work is dedicated, but in describing Rilke as a "silhouette among solids," Pasternak also introduces the otherworldly *fragility* of the poet. Finding this image in his memory, Pasternak shows how Rilke first gave him a sense that life in some other, slightly transcendent, dimension was possible. And of course the choice of words here is important: the poet is described as a "fantasy" (*vymysel*) surrounded by a dense world of "what is not fantasized" (*nevymyshlennost'*). The contrast between the poet and fantasy on one side, and fact and non-fantasy on the other, is unmistakable.

This first encounter introduces a recurring motif that accompanies Pasternak each step along his path to poetry and also ties Pasternak's autobiography to Mandelstam's *The Noise of Time*. Like Mandelstam, Pasternak pays extremely close attention to language and speech throughout his story. His ability to speak serves as a recurring touchstone for the quest: when words cooperate with him—or even better, when they appear unbidden and show him their intrinsic, unimaginable power—he knows that poetry is present. At each stage, Pasternak's ability to communicate verbally is a powerful indication of whether he has achieved his goal. Just as the voice and the ability to speak are a crucial part of Mandelstam's autobiography, Pasternak's quest for a true voice, for a nexus where he and language are organically linked, becomes vital to *Safe Conduct*.

The opening paragraphs show just how difficult it is to achieve this organic union of poet, word, and interlocutor. It takes more than a confluence of mechanical elements to ensure communication: the meeting with Rilke shows that some essential spark is necessary. Pasternak writes that even though he "already knew [German] perfectly" when he saw Rilke's shadowy figure on the platform, "I had never heard it spoken like that."[23] Here we see the poet's challenge for Pasternak: how can one get past the mechanics (knowing German perfectly) to achieve the essence (understanding German when it is spoken "like that")? Pasternak's inability to really *understand* Rilke underlines the fact that Pasternak is not yet a poet: Pasternak is still part of the "non-fantasized" world that surrounds Rilke, and thus cannot occupy the same realm as the ethereal poet. This is only the first of a series of encounters between Pasternak and his great mentors (the poet Rilke, the composer Alexander Scriabin, the philosopher Hermann Cohen), for Pasternak's story shows that he did not know from childhood that he was destined to be a poet. Instead, Pasternak first explores both music and philosophy very seriously, and with enough success to justify making either of them a lifelong pursuit. Each time, however, language helps to show that there is an essential link missing, that Pasternak's demonstrated ability as a musician or a philosopher cannot overcome an inner incompatibility that keeps him from pursuing either path with all his soul.

In the first stage of Pasternak's journey, when he studies music and adores Scriabin, words play a subtle but crucial role in indicating the unlikelihood of the match. When Scriabin first speaks to Pasternak, the young boy "lost the power of reason," as Pasternak explains it. "I would hear myself answer something quite off the point, and everyone would laugh, although exactly what I answered I never heard." There is no shared language between them, and Pasternak's scrambling for words signals a weakness not only in the relationship between Pasternak and Scriabin, but also between Pasternak and music. Six years later, at the fateful private recital that will decide Pasternak's fate as a musician, he prepares to make a crucial confession to Scriabin: how will the great composer respond to his young disciple's admission that he lacks perfect pitch? In writing this account Pasternak admits that if music had really been his destiny the question would not have vexed him so powerfully. But this is the hindsight of a narrator who already knows his place; for the youthful would-be composer, the problem is excruciating. Pasternak has difficulty even approaching the dreaded question, but just as he finally starts to articulate the problem, Scriabin "interrupts in mid-sentence." The Russian expression is even more direct, literally "interrupted in mid-word" (*perebityi na poluslove*) and conveys the sense even more powerfully. It indicates a carving-up of the word itself, and for a poet who sees words and language as the fundamental actors in creating art, the expression is a sure indication of the fundamental incompatibility between Scriabin and his would-be follower.[24]

The use of language here shows how carefully Pasternak's account is built, but there are also other indicators that demonstrate how conscientiously Pasternak depicts the stages on his path to poetry. Christopher Barnes suggests that Pasternak's uneven treatment of his past, the "overemphasis" of some experiences and complete silence about others, "go[es] beyond what one might normally accept as 'self-interpretation,'" and Barnes is quite right in noting that Pasternak gives the impression of abandoning music after his fateful interview with Scriabin even though other sources show that the following months were filled with a flood of musical creativity.[25] Of course, Pasternak as autobiographer has made no pledge of reliability; what these overemphases and rejections demonstrate is his desire to create a linear account, to turn the text into a more teleological progression. In fact, autobiographical theorist Jens Brockmeier has gone as far as suggesting that "in autobiographical narrative, it is impossible to avoid positing a telos because of the inherent narrative constraints of this genre." Brockmeier describes the process as "retrospective teleology," a process in which a teleological pattern is imposed on a life thanks to the broader vision gained through historical distance, and this description certainly fits Pasternak's text. Here the author moves far beyond "self-interpretation," if we take that to mean an approach that shows relative restraint in manipulating memories and events. Instead, he becomes a more radical editor, shifting material in a process of identity construction that focuses more on *siuzhet* (the arrangement of events in the text) than on *fabula* (the chronological sequence of events).[26] For an autobiographer, the priority given to constructing a particular type of identity can easily come to outweigh considerations like a quest for objectivity. And in Pasternak's case this rearrangement of "facts" allows him to confound the expectations of readers who assume they will see reality in autobiography because it is a "fact-based" genre. To return more specifically to *Safe Conduct*'s narrative objective, if Pasternak wants to follow the structure of a Bildungsroman it is important that he construct a text showing steady movement from stage to stage on the way to his goal. Allowing periods of vacillation or paralysis will obscure the more important pattern of progress.

Pasternak himself prods the reader in this direction with his digression on the Greek understanding of stages in human development, commenting that "she [Greece] was careful not to confuse them. She was able to think of childhood as a separate, independent identity. . . . She believed that a certain element of risk and tragedy must be gathered sufficiently early."[27] The implication is that Pasternak, by breaking with music, has gone through an initiation rite of "risk and tragedy" and moved beyond childhood to the next stage of life.

In Pasternak's case this move is not directly to poetry, although the quest line does move away from strictly linear movement here and poetry enters the text. Pasternak points out that he is "deliberately characterising my life in those years in a random fashion," but I believe that any randomness in the text functions more to undercut the conventions of autobiography than to delay progress in his quest. The pointedly nonchronological sequence (from the break with music the action moves forward to "one evening soon after," then six years earlier, then an undisclosed period of time forward) makes a mockery of "normal" chronology and reinforces his struggle against the literature of fact without obscuring the sense of progress. At best, poetry's early appearance at this point in the narrative can be seen as a gestation period, since Pasternak carefully hides his efforts at poetry from almost everyone; when he records the encouragement of the one person who applauds his efforts, Pasternak immediately counters the encouragement with the remark that "On the other hand I was studying philosophy with wholehearted enthusiasm and imagined that the seeds of some future application lay somewhere in this area."[28]

Indeed, Pasternak's next "stage" is occupied by philosophy and takes him across a new border: entering Marburg, Pasternak senses that he is on stage, an actor in some greater drama as he follows in the footsteps of Mikhail Lomonosov. It is the originality of Marburg's philosophy school that has drawn him, along with its appreciation for the past; Pasternak feels a sudden rush of kinship with Lomonosov when he realizes that Lomonosov, too, arrived in Marburg with nothing but a letter of introduction, with his future still unwritten. The sense of connection plays on a broader theme, for Lomonosov was a success both as an academic and as a poet who cared deeply about the Russian language and became the first theoretician of Russian verse.

Pasternak's projected connection with Lomonosov suggests that philosophy may be able to coexist with poetry for him, too. But later in his account, after he has already abandoned philosophy for poetry, Pasternak reflects on earlier experiences that showed the match was always a bad one. The most telling factor, just as it was with the failed attempt at music, is Pasternak's inability to reach a genuinely interactive level of communication with philosophy (or with Cohen, which is the same thing). The words simply will not come to him. He recalls sitting in class when suddenly Cohen asks him a question. Cohen, who refused to tolerate "not just vagueness . . . but also any approximation to the truth instead of the truth itself," becomes impatient with Pasternak's answer. Pasternak becomes flustered and rephrases his remark, "which dissatisfied [Cohen] because it was too tentative." The two continue to move apart as Pasternak's answers "kept varying and getting increasingly complex. . . . But it was precisely the growing clumsiness of the answers that aggravated him." What makes this description even more significant for Pasternak's account is that after this confusion, and after Pasternak's fellow students contribute a wild cacophony of incorrect answers in their attempt to help him out, Cohen "dryly repeated to me my own first answer." Pasternak had been correct all along, but—in an incident that parallels closely his encounter with Scriabin—he didn't have the innate confidence to rest on this truth. He doesn't have the philosopher's "perfect pitch" any more than he has the musician's. In the context of Pasternak's larger encounter with philosophy, this fragmentary incident replicates the whole. There is an affinity for philosophy and it *could* be a future for Pasternak, but he wants more than affinity: He wants identity at the deeper level of unmediated communion. The artificial nature of his philosophy studies is revealed to him (again, the text presents this as a retrospective revelation included only after his conversion to poetry) when he notices that in his scholarship he appeals to the books and ideas of others "not by a selfless interest in knowledge, but by a search for literary references in support of my idea," so that his paper will acquire "an increasingly thick incrustation of bookish quotations and comparisons."²⁹ This artificiality disconcerts him for its lack of genuine interaction; in contrast to his later comments about writers who "receive the word as a gift," here the words of philosophy have to be forcibly extracted and marshaled in defense of some preconceived notion. Pasternak has the disturbing sense that he is not doing anything original in philosophy.

Just as *Safe Conduct* makes it clear that Pasternak abandoned music in spite of his mentor's blessing and even admiration, he now abandons philosophy just when he appears launched on a sure path to success. In his early description of the Marburg school Pasternak notes that an invitation to Cohen's famous Sunday lunches was a threshold event indicating that the invitee had joined the elect and was now guaranteed a successful career in philosophy. But it turns out that this sign is less sure than one might expect: the new career can only begin if the invitation is accepted, and when Pasternak receives his invitation from Cohen it is already too late. He has just returned from Berlin to a "transformed" Marburg and "something never before experienced had invaded the substance of reality."³⁰ Poetry has entered his life and transformed him. Still exhilarated by this new realization, Pasternak now graphically turns his back on an academic career by disregarding the invitation and dismantling the serpent-like book trail that crawls across the floor in his room. The temptation of philosophy with its promise of a "sure thing" is rejected for the uncertainty that awaits him as a poet. He is not a philosopher at heart.

There remains one final encounter with philosophy. The simple non-acceptance of Cohen's lunch invitation had shielded Pasternak from a face-to-face confrontation with his mentor, but a chance encounter leaves him with no escape.³¹ Pasternak sees Cohen walking alone in a deserted landscape and before Pasternak can slip away, "he had noticed me. My retreat was cut off." The resulting encounter highlights again the inability to achieve genuine interaction. "Talking to him was quite frightening," Pasternak reports. After telling Cohen that he has decided to return to Russia,

> My solecism [*oploshnost'*] only compounded it. He led me to realize as much in quite murderous fashion, without saying a word and adding nothing to the mocking silence of his walking-stick propped on the stone. He asked about my plans, and disapproved of them. In his opinion I should stay on to complete my doctorate. . . . I thanked him fervently for his hospitable offer. . . . In the way I presented [my gratitude] he correctly detected some falsehood and absurdity.³²

There is a finality in this exchange, a closure to Pasternak's study of philosophy. From the "frightening" talk with Cohen to his "murderous" silence, the absence of any common language makes it clear that Pasternak's destiny is not in philosophy. His own verbal falsity, even absurdity, finally gives way to a complete loss for words: "How could I tell him that I was abandoning philosophy once and for all . . . ?"[33] That muteness provides a fitting send-off from philosophy.

The account of Pasternak's stay in Marburg includes more than just his departure from philosophy, for philosophy is actually pushed out of his life when the irresistible force of poetry awakens within him. The catalyst for this awakening is the unrequited love that Pasternak feels for Ida Vysotskaya; after she rejects him, he is endowed with poetic vision and voice. Things come to a head for him when he starts to notice how enjoyable it is to spend time with Ida and her sister, and he compares this to the discomfort of struggling to find a voice in philosophy. Pasternak comes to a decision. "In an awful agitation I told her things could not go on like this and that I wanted her to decide my fate," he writes. After backing away—both emotionally and physically—from Pasternak's insistence, Ida "suddenly realised that there was an immediate way of putting an end to all this . . . and she refused me."[34]

This is the first time that Pasternak has not been the active agent in choosing his path. The refusal leaves him stunned and emotionally helpless; he *loses the ability to speak* and cannot even say farewell when he sees Ida and her sister off at the train station, then struggles to make amends by foolhardily leaping onto the moving train. Once again he cannot say goodbye when the train arrives in Berlin, and "my craving for one final and utterly devastating farewell remained unsatisfied. It was like the need for a great cadenza that shatters an ailing music to its foundation in order suddenly to remove it entirely."[35] In the same way, his complete wordlessness is a necessary preliminary stage, a shattering of all existing speech patterns to clear the way for his ultimate encounter with the word, and for his initiation into the realm of poetic speech.

The crushing rejection leads Pasternak through a dark night of the soul but after passing through this misery he is resurrected the next morning by a powerful new sensation. With eyes exhausted by a night of weeping, Pasternak emerges onto the street and realizes that "I was surrounded by things transformed. Something never before experienced had invaded the substance of reality. The morning recognized my face and appeared precisely in order to be with me and never leave me." It is crucial that this time Pasternak is not the active force that directs his fate. The loss of love is inextricably linked to his new sensations, and just as he did not initiate the collapse of his romantic dreams, he has no part in calling out this new vision of the world that awakes within him. It is essential that poetry itself find him and *recognize him as a poet* by transforming him, that it "invade the substance of reality" by making him "otherly" in the same sense that Rilke was a "silhouette among shadows" in the book's opening paragraphs. Feeling—which Pasternak earlier says must have something to conquer—finally triumphs. He has the new vision of a poet, and with this new perception comes an altered sense of reality: "Life's laconic freshness was revealed to me. It crossed over the street and took me by the hand."[36] In this birth to poetry, the poet is not the prime mover but rather an initiate, recognized and chosen. This is much the same description that Marina Tsvetaeva gives of her poetic origins in her autobiographical writing. As she writes in "The Devil," the young girl is not transformed by the devil and formed into a poet; instead, the poet in her (the "space" for the devil, as she puts it) was already there and simply awaited the moment of its recognition. In the same way poetry has been somewhere within Pasternak, latent, awaiting the instant when life itself would recognize this in him. The difference between them is that Tsvetaeva recognizes her calling as a poet virtually from birth, while Pasternak tries on and sheds several other identities before finally recognizing what has been waiting within all along.

Lazar Fleishman notes the significance of poetry's birth as a synthesizing force, coming at a time when Pasternak is surrounded by Cohen (intellect) on one side and Ida Vysotskaya (passion, love) on the other.[37] As with the descriptions of his departure from music and philosophy, Pasternak's account in *Safe Conduct* is intricately constructed in order to convey the supreme significance of his recognition, even animation, by poetry. His biographers have noted that other sources describe Pasternak's growing attachment to poetry quite differently, depicting it as a gradual process rather than as the epiphany experience described in *Safe Conduct*. Pasternak had been writing poetry for some time already, and even his encounter with Ida Vysotskaya was not his first experience as a frustrated suitor. "Retrospectively," Christopher Barnes writes, "Pasternak perhaps poeticized what were really two separate events, which vividly coincided in Marburg in late June and which he never saw fit to disentangle. The emotional upheaval of Vysotskaia's [Vysotskaya's] refusal merely precipitated a decision which was already overdue.... the urge and ability to write were too assertive to be ignored."[38] In *Safe Conduct* the incidents are conflated, and poetry is not something that Pasternak consciously adopts. Instead he is a chosen one, set apart when life itself recognizes that he *is* a poet.

We can get another perspective on this encounter by juxtaposing the way Pasternak retold the experience in lyric form. The poem "Marburg," written in 1915, describes both Pasternak's rejection and his transformation. Here Pasternak conveys the essence of the episode, including the sense of newness that he felt when emerging after his troubled night:

> I quivered. I flared up, and then was extinguished.
> I shook. I had made a proposal—but late,
> Too late. I was scared, and she had refused me.
> I pity her tears, am more blessed than a saint.
>
> I stepped into the square. I could be counted
> Among the twice-born.[39]

Where *Safe Conduct* provides a telegraphic account of Ida Vysotskaya's refusal and creates a sense of powerful forward movement, of leaving this rejection behind, the poem describes things differently. There is more emotion in the poem as the poet recalls how he "quivered," "flared up," and "shook." And even though at the outset he affirms the sense of being born anew, this conviction proves to be more transitory. His memory takes him back to that final scene, to the disappointment, and the poet finds himself reeling aimlessly through the city, ready to howl at any moment. "What will become of me, ancient tiles?" he asks in near despair. The rejoicing at poetry's arrival, such an essential part of this encounter in *Safe Conduct*, is largely hidden in the poem. The difference between the two accounts highlights the prose version's function in the larger plot of the autobiography, where it functions within the teleological presentation of Pasternak's progress toward and into the realm of poetry.

If *Safe Conduct* were only an account of the quest that describes Pasternak's finally finding himself to be a poet, the narrative could end with the epiphany in Berlin. The significance of the remaining chapters, though, is that in Germany Pasternak has still not found his *own* poetic voice. He is still being transformed, and that is why his story must continue through Venice and back to Moscow, where he faces his final and most dangerous confrontation, the encounter with Mayakovsky where Pasternak refuses to re-create himself for a fourth time and where he instead moves to differentiate himself from Mayakovsky and other poets by gradually building his own identity as a poet. Before that, though, Pasternak must pass through ancient Venice to begin the process of finding his voice in the world, to encounter art and its power in the broadest sense.

The trip to Venice by train is treated as a rite of passage in *Safe Conduct*. Leaving philosophy behind as he has earlier left music, Pasternak bids farewell to this second stage of his life as the train pulls out of Marburg: "Farewell, philosophy! Farewell, my youth! Farewell to Germany!" The time on the train to Italy brings with it a series of biblical allusions, but the most powerful is the recurring reference to Pasternak's inability to stay awake. He identifies the referent to this experience when he writes: "The one night in my life when I should not have slept —it was almost like 'Simon, sleepest thou?' May it be forgiven me. But there were still moments when I did awake and when I stood for a shamefully short time by the window. 'For their eyes were heavy,' and then . . ." The allusion is clearly to the night before Jesus's crucifixion; the two quotations are taken from the Gospel of Mark, and refer to Simon Peter's inability to maintain a faithful vigil while Jesus moves off to pray and wrestle with his approaching crucifixion. With the sense of importance that Pasternak himself gives to the journey ("the *one night* in my life") the context of this passage seems to be particularly oriented toward what lies ahead for Pasternak in Venice. Simon's sleepiness elicits an unambiguous exhortation from Jesus against falling into temptation, and a warning that betrayal awaits.[40]

In Pasternak's case, the exhortation to remain faithful and the announcement that betrayal is at hand are particularly relevant for what he encounters in Venice, since this second difficult night—the first one emptied his emotions to prepare him for poetry—gives birth to a new understanding of the poet's role. Pasternak does not portray himself as a Christ-figure; in *Safe Conduct*, that role with its transforming power can be assumed only by Art itself. Instead, he is one of the disciples. The responsibility he carries as poet-disciple is to hold up the cause of art, and Pasternak proceeds with a vigorous defense against the notion of state control over art. Just as the story of Simon Peter's slumber in Gethsemane ends with Judas's arrival and betrayal, there is a corresponding betrayal here. Judas was a faithful disciple before succumbing to temptation, and the new traitors are also from within: formerly eager in their pursuit of art, they have now sold themselves and become tools in the state effort to control literature.

The multiple layers of this "betrayal" theme correspond to the structural complexity of an autobiographical text. On one level, Pasternak's description is prompted by what he actually experienced while traveling in Italy as a student; on another level, the description refers quite clearly to the literary reality that surrounds him as an older and much wiser narrator in 1931, when he rewrote the final sections of the text. By then, Pasternak's former colleagues in LEF had started to be consumed by their own creation. As Lazar Fleishman puts it, the theories which LEF promoted had seemed "dangerous but absurd" only a few years earlier, but had now become official policy and were turned loose on their creators: the result was Mayakovsky's death and a strangling of art.[41] It was Mayakovsky's death that prompted Pasternak's sweeping revision of the plan for *Safe Conduct*, for it was now painfully obvious to Pasternak that Soviet culture had become a Kronos devouring its own most talented young. In light of this betrayal of art, how could a poet continue to function as a genuine poet *and survive*? To be genuine, a poet must remain true to an internal truth-meter; nowhere is this more explicitly stated than in Pasternak's comment that an artist's creation will "deceive" a patron because there is something uncontrollable about genuine art. It refuses to be constrained and its implications spill out in directions unforeseen even by the artist.

In the Venice chapters Pasternak takes aim directly at the disastrous results of LEF's policies, and of state efforts to control art; earlier, though, he outlines his aesthetic principles more theoretically. In a digression during his account of philosophy studies in Marburg, Pasternak suggests that if he were to articulate a philosophy of creative aesthetics, it would be based on the dual foundations of power and of symbol. The notion of power indicates art's fundamental intransigence, its resistance when a client or patron tries to exert control. You can't point art the way you point a telescope, Pasternak remarks. No matter how closely you study the way art is created, the way the Formalists examined the literary devices used to compose verse, you cannot capture the essential life within the creation. A poem is more than the sum of its devices.

The continuation of this aesthetic outline reveals a dual paradox closely tied to the cultural debates of the late 1920s and early 1930s. "As activity, art is realistic, and as fact it is symbolic," Pasternak writes, effectively defining art in a way that stands the notion of "literature of fact" on its head. First, Pasternak asserts that art's "realism" can be proven by its use of metaphor, since metaphor is not something invented by art but rather something that art takes from nature and then "realistically" reproduces. This assertion alone would surely anger those who in 1931 were already trying to identify the best way for Soviet writers to depict reality, a search that eventually led them to the cultural doctrine known as socialist realism. But Pasternak did not stop with this outrageously provocative assertion. Instead, he continued by saying that a fact is symbolic in and of itself. In other words, it is impossible for art to be anything but an "art of fact"—and therefore all literature is unavoidably a "literature of fact." The fact is symbolic a priori, since its appearance is based on a shift implicit in any statement that displaces reality. This claim would not fail to raise the hackles of those who, maintaining an exalted notion of the fact, saw fact-based literature as a way to avoid aesthetic elitism that they attributed to bourgeois literature. In effect, Pasternak's neat little formula renders meaningless any debate about the merits of symbolism or realism because symbol and reality are both revealed as fundamental elements in art.

The most explicit rebuttal of LEF and its agenda is found in Pasternak's extended discussion of lion-related words and images in his Venice chapters. Fleishman notes that the lion had been a symbol associated with Futurism since its earliest appearance on the literary scene, and Pasternak makes full use of this connection in *Safe Conduct*.[42] To the Russian ear the connection is aural and instant, since "LEF" and "lev" (the Russian word for "lion") are homonyms in spoken Russian. The LEFists themselves punned on this sound similarity in their journal, with articles like "Into

Whom is LEF Sinking its Teeth?" Assuming that readers will make the connection between the "lions" and "LEF," Pasternak takes a huge risk in writing what follows.

He starts off rather innocuously with the puzzling inclusion of an etymology for the word "pantaloon." Noting that it has a close connection to Venice and comes from the Italian *pianta leone* ("hoister of the lion"; a lion was depicted on Venice's official banner), Pasternak notes that the phrase originally carried an association with military victory since it describes how Venice's banner would be hoisted in triumph after vanquishing a foe. Then, a few paragraphs later, he uses the same phrase (*pianta leone*) to show how "triumph" withered and decayed until it choked itself out. In a sure sign of how important this is, Pasternak couches his analysis in terms of a sick and dying *language*: "The language of the palaces turned out to be a language of oblivion, and not at all the *pianta leone* language that was erroneously ascribed to them. The aims of pantaloonery decayed."[43] In effect, Pasternak seems to be saying that the language of LEF and the Futurists cannot stand: it holds within itself the seeds of its own decay.

Even more indicting, though, is the description of the Censors' staircase in the city center. Here the lion becomes unambiguously sinister, no longer devouring only itself but others as well: "the slit for depositing secret denunciations was sculpted in the shape of a lion's maw. It is well known what terror this 'bocca di leone' struck into the hearts of contemporaries, and that gradually it became a sign of ill-breeding to mention any persons mysteriously fallen through that exquisitely carved orifice when the authorities themselves expressed no regrets." The connection to the contemporary Soviet Union is unmistakable, especially since Pasternak has already made eloquent allusion to the Revolution in his comment that "we had had a taste of independence and then had to renounce it and fall, at the powerful suggestion of things, into a new childhood."[44]

The following chapter of *Safe Conduct* is so explicit that portions were deleted by censors and did not appear in the Soviet edition of 1931. Here the lion's odious role in art comes into sharp focus. While genius struggles to function, Pasternak writes, "all around there is the haunting sight of lions' muzzles, nosing into every privacy, sniffing everything, lions' jaws that devour one life after another in the secrecy of their lair. All around there is the leonine roar of an imaginary immortality, conceivable without laughter only because everything immortal rests in its hands and is held on a stout lion's rein."[45] The connection between the "lions' jaws that devour one life after another" and the denunciations slipped through the lion's jaw in Venice is completely transparent and doubtless led to the paragraph's suppression.

Just as noteworthy, though, is Pasternak's characterization of how genius reacts to all this leonine opposition. Confronted by the lions' intimidation and interference, the genius recognizes that oppression has become so customary that it is now *unnoticed* by the crowd. It is this lack of recognition that makes the infuriated genius boil over, and the fury comes out as art. Perhaps most striking of all in this passage is Pasternak's specific characterization of this eruption as "a slap in the face,"[46] a phrase that could not help but recall the radical manifesto unveiled by the Futurists almost two decades earlier as "A Slap in the Face of Public Taste."

Other elements in Pasternak's reminiscences of Italy are not directed so clearly against LEF, but reflect a daring and combative stance toward broader literary authority. One of the most open challenges comes in his mention of Savonarola, the Dominican friar from Florence who wrote poetry, fought for church reform, and used his own brand of revolutionary republicanism to gain a broad popular following that contributed to the expulsion of the Medici family from Florence in the 1490s. Yet Savonarola also instituted an insidious spy system and burned poets' books, according to popular local legend. It is this terrifying combination of programmatic idealism and repressive deeds that destroys literature, and Pasternak explicitly warns of the destructive forces that can be unleashed by an "untamed Savonarola."

The comments at the start of several of the "Italian" chapters draw specific attention to the fact that all of what Pasternak has written must be understood in a contemporary context. They point out the inevitably dual chronology of an autobiography's text, and identify hidden layers of meaning in Pasternak's comments about Venice and its art. But they also have a broader function and suggest, for those who need the hint, that other parts of the text must be read the same way. In this light the opening paragraphs' characterization of Rilke as a "fantasy in the thick of reality" becomes a deliberate statement against the "literature of fact," although the full impact is felt only much later, when Pasternak reveals the identity of that initially nameless figure. The description of Pasternak's abandonment of music also comes to mind: he has attributed it to his lack of perfect pitch, an undeniable fact. But this lack of perfect pitch is also a symbol for a greater and deeper unease, and illustrates how a "literature of fact" can never be *only* about facts in the narrow definition favored by LEF.

As Pasternak leaves Venice and the narrative of *Safe Conduct* carries him back to Moscow, then, the newly discovered poet has passed what can be seen as a crucial rite of initiation: he has remained faithful to Art by standing up to Art's betrayers, the state-dominated literary hacks represented by the radical LEFists. But despite all this, he has still not found his *own* voice. His attempt to speak Italian leads to babbling in a "nonexistent dialect," and he realizes that he will be verbally free only in his native Russia. On his last night in Venice Pasternak notices that on the cathedral portico's roof "was a team of four horses, which swept at a gallop from ancient Greece and seemed to halt there on the brink of an abyss."[47] The Greek notion of the ages in human development is recalled, and signals yet another stage completed. But the future is ominous: will there be a plunge into the abyss?

The return to Russia brings this question to life as Pasternak faces the most dangerous stage of his poetic journey. Not only will he face the "lions" of literature in real life, but he must deal with the fact that he is only one poet among many. His version of a poet's progress continues in a Russia densely populated by other poets. Dominating all others is Mayakovsky, but even a partial listing is impressive: Khodasevich, Blok, Pushkin, Bely, Tsvetaeva, Anisimov, Bolshakov, Bobrov, Baltrushaitis, Khlebnikov, Severyanin, Esenin, Selvinsky. Perhaps the clearest sign that Pasternak is still a fledgling poet is his membership in one of the groups of novice "innovators," as he describes them. Pasternak senses the artificiality of his involvement with the group known as Centrifuge, and wonders why he is willing to sacrifice "both taste and conscience" on behalf of the Centrifugists. Eventually an encounter with Mayakovsky propels Pasternak out of this circle of mediocrity. Centrifuge has been embroiled in an artistic dispute with Mayakovsky's group, but despite Pasternak's expectation that he will have to betray his principles to remain loyal to Centrifuge, when the meeting finally takes place he finds himself incapable of betrayal. Instead, upon finally having the opportunity to see and hear Mayakovsky at close range, Pasternak realizes that he sees before him the quintessential Poet-priest. Far from conquering Mayakovsky, Pasternak finds himself on the path to becoming Mayakovsky's disciple.

The force of his encounter with Mayakovsky jolts Pasternak away from the clutches of Centrifuge, and he starts to measure himself against other poets. The most concentrated example of this poetic pulse-taking is a poetry recital that brings together leading representatives from both generations of Russian poetry. The meeting is set up as a new stage in the perpetual showdown between fathers and sons: the elder statesmen Symbolists are led by Andrei Bely and Konstantin Balmont, the upstart Futurists by Mayakovsky and David Burlyuk. Lesser figures on both sides complete the gathering. Aside from Mayakovsky, who is always a special case for Pasternak, the only figures singled out as rare and genuine poetic talents are Bely and Marina Tsvetaeva. At the time of the recital Pasternak did not know her poetry, but still sensed in her a kindred spirit. She becomes for Pasternak a "living palladium," a sacred preserver of poetry in the midst of a group whose members impress him more for their complacency than for their poetry. The recital begins as poets read their work rather ineffectually according to seniority. But it is their response to Mayakovsky's recitation that carries the most weight in Pasternak's assessment. Tsvetaeva's expression is hidden from him but of the rest, the only one to emerge with honor is Bely. While others remain constrained by a sense of their own self-importance, Bely abandons himself completely to the reading, carried away with joy and gratitude.

This meeting shows Pasternak that the true poet is a rarity, and shows implicitly that he is numbered among this select few. His ability to participate in true communicative interaction with genius grants him entrance, for only Bely and Pasternak are able to grasp the profound essence of Mayakovsky's words. If we compare Pasternak's incomprehension while listening to Rilke in the book's opening paragraphs to the complete union evoked by this encounter with the genius of Mayakovsky, we can see that Pasternak has truly emerged as his "own" poet. Pasternak also recognizes with a sense of finality that he (as one who treasures the gift of Mayakovsky's poetry on its own terms, with no fear that admiring someone else's poetic gift will lessen his own worth) is different from the crowd, even the crowd of poets. In earlier encounters he has set himself apart from individual poets, or poets in pairs. This time the differentiation is more comprehensive, and effectively removes him from the collective of complacent, self-absorbed poets. Only the "great" and genuine poets remain within his orbit.

Of these great poets, though, one stands alone. This giant, the towering figure who has been looming in Pasternak's consciousness since their first meeting, is Mayakovsky. It is the account of his struggle to understand and come to grips with Mayakovsky that brings Pasternak to the final stage in his journey of poetic self-discovery. The struggle begins with their first meeting, when Pasternak recognizes that Mayakovsky is a phenomenon that appears perhaps once in a lifetime. The "largeness" of Mayakovsky is emphasized, and he clearly becomes something superhuman in Pasternak's perception: "Whenever Mayakovsky appeared it seemed miraculous and every head turned in his direction. What was natural in his case appeared to be supernatural. . . . He seemed to exist as on the day after completing some immense spiritual life. . . . [He recited] particularly profound snatches of his own and other people's verse, like extracts from the liturgy."[48] Pasternak appeals directly to the conception of the poet as a larger than life Poet, a prophetic or even divine figure.

The attraction to Mayakovsky is intensified in succeeding chapters. When Mayakovsky recites his *Vladimir Mayakovsky* to Pasternak the next day, Pasternak responds with rapture. Mayakovsky is colossal. He can hold the world in his hands and "either set it in motion or bring it to a standstill." Pasternak begins to lose his own identity as admiration rapidly turns into worship: "whenever I was invited to say something about myself I started on about Mayakovsky. It was no mistake on my part. He had become my god. I saw him as a personification of my spiritual horizon."[49]

Mayakovsky's greatness is so dominating that it threatens to consume Pasternak entirely, and this serves as the motivation for Pasternak's renunciation of Mayakovsky in *Safe Conduct*. It is not Mayakovsky's *poetry* that Pasternak rejects (although he does reject Mayakovsky's later efforts as unworthy of his talent), but the romantic role of Poet that Mayakovsky personifies so intensely. Pasternak says that he could have given up literature entirely, but "after so many transformations I had not the resolve to change course a fourth time.... [Instead,] I renounced the romantic manner."[50] Christopher Barnes warns that Pasternak's "overgrateful" account of his response to Mayakovsky could easily lead to distorted readings of Pasternak's early poetry,[51] once again underlining the danger of assuming that an autobiographer's account is a direct and reliable link to real life, that its "orientation to authenticity" is firm and absolute. Instead, readers should try to understand the function of such excess. In effect, Pasternak's portrait of Mayakovsky builds Mayakovsky up into an enormous figure, a colossal Poet, and establishes a rationale for Pasternak to respond on a similar scale, to act in a way that is correspondingly "huge." The intensity of Pasternak's initial attraction to Mayakovsky makes the eventual break with him that much more important for Pasternak as a poet: the closer the ties, the more significant the conscious decision to separate.

The compelling force of Pasternak's struggle to free himself from Mayakovsky's spell derives from his awareness of the ultimate fate that awaits a poet who takes the role of Poet-hero, who does not resist the temptation to be a Poet in the Romantic or prophetic mode. Pasternak senses how the "drama of Mayakovsky" will end: He recognizes that Mayakovsky has surrendered himself to his own genius, a decision that Pasternak characterizes as a "lack of will" that will eventually lead Mayakovsky to succumb to the "insatiable demands" placed on the Poet-hero.[52] It is with Mayakovsky as the embodiment of "poetic genius," as a *hero* in the world of poetry, that Pasternak struggles. Catherine Ciepiela argues that this was not the first time Pasternak refuted this notion: In the narrative poem *Spektorsky* he counters a similar maximalism that he finds in Tsvetaeva, and as Ciepiela puts it, argues that the temptations and pressures for compromise would be less likely if the poet were a less prominent cultural authority.[53] (And soon after the completion of *Safe Conduct*, Pasternak will attempt to counter an even more determined maximalism in Mandelstam.) While writing *Safe Conduct*, though, Pasternak's focus is largely Mayakovsky; he recognizes that Mayakovsky's surrender to genius carries the certainty of death (either artistic or physical, depending on the path Mayakovsky chooses), and he battles within himself to seek an alternative: Can a poet renounce becoming the Poet? Can a poet still have a life? These are the issues that erupt into literally life-shaping—and life-threatening—choices in his repeated encounters with Mayakovsky, but they have been haunting his path all along.

The ominously recurring images of death are a constant reminder of how important Pasternak's choices become. When we remember that the project started as a tribute to the recently deceased Rilke and concluded as an attempt to understand the implications of Mayakovsky's suicide, we realize that the theme of death "bookends" the work and encloses everything within it. Mayakovsky's powerful presence, followed by sudden and shocking absence, make this an almost inevitable theme for a poet trying to understand his own fate in the aftermath of another poet's suicide. As Richard Sanderson explains, "Because suicide is a communication rather than an arbitrary natural event, the survivor seeks to decipher it: 'To take one's life is to force others to read one's death.'"[54] This helps to show what Pasternak is doing in *Safe Conduct*: he is trying to decipher Mayakovsky's suicide for his own life, and the effort results in a fundamental reconception of his approach to the autobiography.

This revised approach makes the frequency of death references within *Safe Conduct* even more important, especially in passages that describe Pasternak's movement from stage to stage on his path to poetry. Death is present in Pasternak's early recollections of childhood, when he mentions a neighbor child who drowned, and a young woman's repeated suicide attempts. It lurks in his father's fear that the family has perished in a blaze, and in Pasternak's observation that "the image of inevitable death" anchors his view of history. When Pasternak sets out for his fateful encounter with Scriabin, which was written before Mayakovsky's suicide, the allusions to death and mortality are oblique. He describes himself approaching a "terrible goal" and immediately after the meeting he feels that "something was tearing" inside him, accompanied by weeping. Finally and most explicitly, after describing the Greek concept of the ages of man Pasternak adds that growth demands tragedy, and "death itself had to be experienced in some memorable likeness." As a self-instigated "death," the break with music certainly functions as a metaphorical suicide.[55]

The final encounter with Cohen in Marburg is preceded by a similar morbidity. On the way into town, Pasternak views "drowned corpses" and "martyrs" in the windows that line his path. A "murderous silence" results from Pasternak's announcement that he is leaving Marburg, and Cohen considers Pasternak's decision something that "artificially shortens" his life. The implication is clearly suicide, despite the use of "murderous" to describe Cohen's response. There is, however, one episode in Marburg where death is unambiguously the result of an external force. As mentioned above, in contrast to the breaks with music and philosophy where Pasternak makes his own choices as the agent of his fate (thus the suicide allusions), the end of his love affair is determined by Ida Vysotskaya, not by Pasternak. The references to death here are quite open. On the night before his marriage proposal, a waiter jokes that Pasternak is having one last meal before his execution. The joke becomes real only the next day with the rejection that kills his love, but indirectly gives birth to poetry. Vysotskaya's rejection is carefully phrased. As an imploring Pasternak advances toward her, Vysotskaya "puts an end to all this." It only gradually becomes clear that what is ending is not just a love affair, but a whole mode of nonpoetic life. Pasternak's desperate leap at the train station, where he says that the guard "seized me by the shoulder lest I . . . go and sacrifice my life" offers yet another example of the pervasive death and suicide references that surround the collapse of love and the start of poetry.[56]

These early deaths are only metaphorical and actually lead Pasternak into new and better stages of life. The death of Mayakovsky is something else entirely. Here the metaphor is realized in all its grotesque horror, and Pasternak recognizes that this too-real death could destroy him as well. In Mayakovsky, Pasternak recognizes an arch-Romantic figure, someone for whom life is "life on show, 'biography as spectacle,'" as Angela Livingstone puts it.[57] In struggling to reject Mayakovsky and the romantic manner, Pasternak crystallizes the poet's ultimate dilemma: Can an artist's need to "resist the inevitable" (one of Pasternak's definitions of art in *Safe Conduct*) coexist with a second, seemingly incompatible impulse to maintain some form of tolerant relations with contemporary life?

Pasternak's attempt to bring these two together is a crucial effort on behalf of all genuine Russian poets. It is based on his rejection of romanticism, and it leads him to a new and startling conclusion: Not only is it possible for resistance and tolerance to coexist, but it is necessary if the poet is to find a place in life. The problem with Mayakovsky is that *he did not resist the mantle of Poet*. And by not resisting this pull, by not fighting to free himself from the insidious claims put on him by the state that longed for a Poet to call its own, he allowed himself to be drawn along the path that led to his death.[58] Pasternak recognizes the signs of this during one meeting, where he says that Mayakovsky "showed great skill in concealing his agitation. Something was happening to him. He was undergoing some crisis. He had realised his purpose in life. He was openly striking a pose, but he did so with such hidden anxiety and feverishness that beads of cold sweat stood out on his adopted mask."[59] The signs are chilling in their implications for a poet: Mayakovsky has surrendered to a purpose, and his inner turmoil signals his own foreboding about where this will lead. His choices and behavior shape his own destiny.

Still, Mayakovsky does not resist. Recognizing the danger, Pasternak tries to save Mayakovsky from himself. The failed rescue attempt is their last real encounter in *Safe Conduct,* and takes place during the transitional time between the two 1917 revolutions—perhaps there is still hope. Pasternak is already moving away from Mayakovsky's orbit, and when Mayakovsky wants to hear Pasternak's response to his new "War and the World" (*Voina i mir*) Pasternak has nothing to say: "he could read it all in my eyes." The essential communicative link of language, of *words*, no longer exists between them; but even though it is Pasternak who does not speak, the link is broken by Mayakovsky's shift from "us" (the group of genuine poets) to "them" (a bard for the state). There is nothing accidental in Pasternak using this crucial juncture to reveal his attitude toward Futurism for the first time, suggesting how wonderful it would be if Mayakovsky "publicly sent the whole thing to hell." Pasternak adds that Mayakovsky laughed, and almost agreed. It is unlikely that Mayakovsky really did come so close to agreement with Pasternak, but the specifics of the narration are important for Pasternak's *story*: He tried to draw Mayakovsky from his path to destruction before the final Revolution, but was unsuccessful. From that point on their mutual incomprehension, their inability to speak to each other, is complete. It is broken only when death finally frees Mayakovsky's voice from the bondage of the role he has chosen: "he again reminded me of himself *at the top of his voice* as once he used to do, but this time from beyond the grave."[60]

Pasternak's reference here is to Mayakovsky's last great poem *At the Top of My Voice* (*Vo ves' golos*, 1930), written shortly before his death and seemingly an attempt to wrench himself off the poetic path he had been traveling. Mayakovsky already appears to sense that his end is near, and addresses his reader as a future reader, a reader who will read these lines only after the author is gone—a situation that was indeed realized by Pasternak. "Respected / comrade descendants," Mayakovsky begins, "Digging around / in today's / petrified crap, / Exploring the darkness of our days, / you / may perhaps / ask about me as well." He then deliberately informs the reader of his intent to interpret his times and himself, fashioning a lyric monument to himself in the tradition carried forward from the time of Gavrila Derzhavin. Pasternak would surely have been shaken by the lines that came to be known as the essential formula of Mayakovsky's terrible choice:

> But I
> > abased
> > > myself,
> > > > standing
> > on the throat
> > > of my own song.

> Listen,
> > comrade descendants,
> to the agitator,
> > to the ringleader of the brawlers.
> Suppressing
> > torrents of poetry,
> I will step over
> > the lyric anthologies,
> As someone alive
> > speaking with the living.
> ....
>
> My verse will reach
> across the crests of ages
> and over the heads
> of poets and governments.[61]

Mayakovsky's self-suppression, his willingness to silence the inner voice of real poetry, haunts him and finally exorcizes itself in this last great lyric flow. But the lesson for Pasternak is chilling: a poet can avoid Mayakovsky's grim fate and survive only by generating resistance both externally and internally. External pressure will try to prescribe the poet's role and work, while inner pressure will try to lure the poet into becoming a Poet-hero. If a gifted poet succumbs to both temptations, the state will have found the longed-for successor to Mayakovsky. If a poet succumbs to just the external temptation, he or she will lose artistic integrity and become a mouthpiece for the regime. And succumbing to just the inner temptation will lead inevitably to romantic tragedy, for an independent Poet-hero cannot be tolerated by a state jealously guarding its cultural flanks.

While writing *Safe Conduct*, Pasternak grappled with this theme in lyric form as well. In 1931 he wrote a poem that he called "To Boris Pilnyak" (*Borisu Pil'niaku*), knowing that the censors could hardly allow a title that honored a writer who had been the subject of a vicious smear campaign less than two years earlier. Pasternak had to find an alternate, and the result was a less concrete but perhaps more fittingly general title, "To a Friend" (*Drugu*):

> Do I not know that, fussing about in the dark,
> Darkness would never make its way out into light,
> And am I a monster, and is the happiness of hundreds of thousands
> Not closer to me than the empty happiness of a hundred?
>
> And do I not measure myself with the Five Year Plan,
> Do I not fall, not rise along with it?

> But how can I carry on, with my ribcage,
> and being more sluggish than any sluggishness?
>
> In the days of the great council,
> Where seats go to those with the most passion,
> The poet's place is left vacant in vain;
> It is a dangerous spot if not left empty.⁶²

The concerns about the poet's dilemma from *Safe Conduct* are compressed almost unbearably and emerge telegraphically, line by line: anxiety about being considered a monster/elitist, recognition that the artist must be in tune with the country's plans, equivocation about compatibility with the new system, and finally the ultimate refusal, the poet's unwillingness to become the state's new poet-priest. Even more, the poet issues a grim warning that the place of the state poet, so recently and absolutely vacated by Mayakovsky, is a treacherous one. That place must remain empty, for it will swallow its occupant if it is ever filled again.

What may be most puzzling in Pasternak's autobiography is the complete absence of one poet who should logically have found a place there. Pasternak and Mandelstam were never close friends, but they certainly knew each other better and had more in common than many of the other poets mentioned in *Safe Conduct*. One very real possibility is that it would have been dangerous, or perhaps even impossible, to include Mandelstam at this point, for in Mandelstam Pasternak sees a fortiori a poet who will not reject the role of Poet-hero. By 1931 Mandelstam's resistance to the state was starting to express itself in covert but still potentially lethal acts of defiance; where Mandelstam preferred a direct approach, Pasternak was more oblique, Barnes suggests.⁶³ Mandelstam was sometimes openly critical of Pasternak's attempt to find a less confrontational (or non-heroic) path, and on at least one occasion Pasternak cautioned Mandelstam against misunderstanding his behavior with the comment that his feelings were no weaker than Mandelstam's, even if they were expressed differently.

The extent of their differences was revealed most fully a few years after the appearance of *Safe Conduct*. It was 1934, Pasternak recalled, when he and Mandelstam took a walk through Moscow together and Mandelstam recited his fateful poem about Stalin. Pasternak was horrified, and told Mandelstam: "What you have read to me has no relation to literature, to poetry. It is not a literary fact, but an act of suicide that I don't approve of and in which I do not want to take part. You didn't read anything to me, I didn't hear anything, and I ask you not to recite this to anyone else."⁶⁴ Obviously this encounter could have had no bearing on Pasternak's thinking as he wrote *Safe Conduct*, but it must have been a chilling confirmation of his sense that a poet who embraces the role of Poet-hero in the Soviet era simultaneously embraces the likelihood of an untimely death. In Mandelstam's poem he saw not passive acceptance of possible death, but an active movement in that direction. It could only have been a confirmation to Pasternak that his best—even only—way forward as a poet was to keep resisting on two fronts, against the state on one hand and against the call of the hero on the other. To Mandelstam this might look like compromise, but it was the only way Pasternak could see for the survival of poets, and more importantly, for poetry itself.

Perhaps one reason for Pasternak's horror at Mayakovsky's self-destruction was his recognition that the seeds of self-destruction lay within himself as well. Pasternak's letters show a strong sense of his own mortality in these years, and when the rush of abuse generated by *Safe Conduct* coincided with more personal family crises, Pasternak himself succumbed to suicidal thoughts. Details remain shrouded in the haze of allusion, and it isn't clear how sincerely he wished his suicide attempt to succeed, since it was carried out within hearing of people in the next room. But this wasn't the first time Pasternak had considered suicide. In a 1917 letter to his old friend Konstantin Loks, Pasternak wrote: "In everyone there is a whole host of suicidal inclinations. I have known times like that, when I have had to devote all my energies to rebelling against my own instincts. . . . It was while I was subject to a whole series of moods of that kind that I abandoned my music."[65] Suicide was an impulse well known to Pasternak.

But he survived. He survived his own impulse toward self-destruction, he fended off attempts to install him on the poetic throne left empty by Mayakovsky, and he largely resisted the pressure to write something that would please the literary authorities. It was not an easy survival. The captains of literature resented his independent streak, and suspected rebellion. Overt dissidents wondered whether he wasn't collaborating too closely with the state. And Pasternak himself recognized the tenuousness of his position, constantly having to triangulate between his conscience, the demands of the state, and the realm of the possible. What he accomplished, however, was significant: In *Safe Conduct* Pasternak was able to carve out a path that would carry the poet into the heart of the new era. In 1931, no one could know where the path would end, whether in a poetic sanctuary or an eventual dead end. Still, it was a courageous stroke, an attempt to stand up for the integrity of poetry and the survival of the poet. In 1931, voices willing to speak out with such force were hard to find, and this literary "fact" guarantees its author's place as a reluctant hero in the battle for poetry.

4

Fighting for Breath

At the end of the 1920s, Osip Mandelstam abandoned prudence. While Boris Pasternak was exploring a way for poets to pick their way through the cultural minefield and emerge safely on the other side, Mandelstam was preparing a much more radical response to the increasing political and literary pressure faced by poets. The result was a personal manifesto that not only rejected the authority of the literary establishment, but also announced his intention to fight back. Even if Mandelstam had to act as an army of one, he would challenge the cultural ideologues with a determined poetic insurgency. The work in which Mandelstam's defiance emerged with such blistering force is the short autobiographical statement called "Fourth Prose" (*Chetvertaia proza*). It was never officially published in the Soviet era, of course, and its very survival was under constant threat. Mandelstam dictated it to his wife, Nadezhda, and she gave copies to several trusted friends for safekeeping after memorizing the entire work. Few people even knew that "Fourth Prose" existed.

The arrival of *samizdat* (self publishing) changed everything. Armed with typewriters and carbon paper, a new generation picked up where Mandelstam and other rebel voices had stopped. The result was "Fourth Prose's" emergence as a literary legend and *samizdat* bestseller, according to Viktor Krivulin. He notes that "['Fourth Prose'] was constantly confiscated during searches; possession of it incriminated the owner with 'antisoviet propaganda,' and the archives of the KGB grew to contain tens of thousands of copies."[1] Anna Akhmatova read "Fourth Prose" not long after it was composed, and years later she saw it gaining a huge underground following. "I am constantly hearing, mainly from young people who go crazy over it, that in the entire twentieth century there has never been such prose," she wrote.²

"Fourth Prose" has often been seen as a crucial turning point in Mandelstam's creative life. It came at the end of a five-year period in which Mandelstam seems to have been completely abandoned by his muse. Provoked by a translation scandal, "Fourth Prose" exorcized the personal demons that had been keeping his voice still. The poet who takes shape in "Fourth Prose" is fundamentally different from the hero of *The Noise of Time* or Mandelstam's early lyrics: Here we find a survivor who has lost his illusions about the hypocrisy of "official" literature; a poet whose voice is his only tool; and a patriot who recognizes that he is part of a painfully small remnant of literary loyalists.

The writing of the essay was provoked by a series of incidents that convinced Mandelstam that his own existence in the Soviet literary world might soon be snuffed out. Briefly put, the problems began when Mandelstam was commissioned to revise two existing Russian translations of Charles de Coster's *La légende de Thyl Ulenspiegel*. When the revised editions were published in 1928, Mandelstam was shocked to find that he had been listed as the sole translator. He tried unsuccessfully to have corrections pasted into the printed copies, and contacted original translator A. G. Gornfeld to explain the situation and offer his royalties as compensation for the unintended slight. Gornfeld responded with a published charge of plagiarism and events escalated quickly. Mandelstam wrote a public letter answering the charge, the writers' organizations got involved, and eventually a Conflict Commission was established to investigate. After numerous exhausting interrogations, Mandelstam learned that the affair had been "resolved" by the Federation of Soviet Writers' Organizations (FOSP). FOSP decided that Mandelstam had been treated unfairly, but that he still bore moral responsibility for the error. At this point Nikolai Bukharin interceded by offering Mandelstam a trip to Armenia; Mandelstam and his wife Nadezhda set out in May 1930, and the scandal faded from public view.

The whole "Ulenspiegel Affair" left Mandelstam with a bitter feeling of betrayal by the literary community of Soviet Russia and "opened M.'s eyes to what was happening around us," says Nadezhda Mandelstam. The result, she continues in a frequently quoted passage, was that "M.'s voice was henceforth the voice of an outsider who knew he was alone and prized his isolation. M. had come of age."³ She exaggerates here, however, and we do well to note this at the outset: Even though "Fourth Prose" did serve as a declaration of literary independence that restored Mandelstam's poetic vigor and led to a flood of new poems, there is more to the story. Mandelstam's stance and his poetry in the 1930s are not as unequivocal as these assertions by his wife would lead one to believe. So while the fatal poem "We live without sensing the land underfoot" (*My zhivem pod soboiu ne chuia strany*, 1933) does show the ultimate reckless outsider described here by Nadezhda, the notorious "Stalin Ode" (1937) and other poems of 1936–1937 show a different, much more conciliatory posture in relation to the state's focal point, Stalin. As I wrote earlier, these contradictory elements need to be acknowledged; at the same time, they should not lessen our appreciation for the courage and conviction that imbue "Fourth Prose." My primary concern here is to examine "Fourth Prose" in relation to the context that led to its formation; within that framework, Mandelstam's subsequent arrest and exile, the immense physical and mental strain that he and Nadezhda suffered together, and the way in which these events figured into his poems to Stalin, are important because they point out that even a statement as powerfully cathartic as "Fourth Prose" cannot present a foolproof blueprint for real life.[4]

The years after the 1925 publication of *The Noise of Time* had been increasingly difficult for Osip and Nadezhda. Mandelstam wrote no poetry and few essays, and the couple survived by borrowing money from friends and earning what they could through translation assignments. The temporary rebuff suffered by the proletarian writers in 1925, when the Party dictated tolerance toward nonaligned writers, did not improve his mood or his prospects. He watched the decline of the lyric and the rise of the epic, but did not try to turn himself into an epic-writer. The bold denunciations of poetry in *New LEF*, and the assertion that only a fact-based literature could satisfy the social and literary needs in the Soviet Union, surely alarmed Mandelstam just as much as they did Pasternak. And even though Mandelstam did not produce any new poetry during these years, he still saw himself as a poet. On January 24, 1927, Mandelstam applied for admission to the Leningrad section of the All-Russian Poets' Union and was accepted four days later.[5]

The year 1928 was especially odd and contradictory. An outsider looking only at a list of Mandelstam's publications might be excused for considering 1928 the high point of his writing career, since three separate books of Mandelstam's work were published in that year: a collection of short prose, an anthology of verse, and a cycle of essays about poetry. However, the three books contained almost no new material, and only appeared because Mandelstam's few remaining influential friends interceded for him. New writing was almost impossible to publish, and good translation assignments were hard to find. Together Osip and Nadezhda shared the strain of constantly looking for new commissions, negotiating payment, and meeting publication schedules. The near-simultaneous publication of three books certainly didn't make Mandelstam's literary circumstances any easier. It may even have had the opposite effect, pointing out that Mandelstam still retained some literary influence and attracting the attention of those who would certainly consider Mandelstam an obstacle if not a threat.

The summer of 1928 was particularly difficult. P. N. Luknitsky remembers that when he came across the Mandelstams in Yalta in mid-August, they were almost completely out of money. When payment for a translation finally arrived, it all went to pay back the arrears on their room; the landlord promptly increased the rent and told them to find a new place to stay. Mandelstam tried to raise money at the bazaar by selling an old fur coat and other clothing articles, but still had to borrow money constantly. Luknitsky even remembers a conversation on August 17 when Mandelstam said that the term "poet" was a "shameful name," and should be replaced by "master" or "thinker." Luknitsky thought that this was Mandelstam's way of saying that he was looking for a new, nonliterary career but it could also have been a reaction against the increasingly compromised position of most poets. Conformity simply may not coexist with the notion of poet. Or it may be that Mandelstam experienced a moment of personal despair and couldn't foresee a time when poets might once again regain their lofty moral stature in Russian culture. After all, Mandelstam certainly followed the literary trends as closely as Pasternak, and he witnessed the increasing attacks on poetry and on the poet's independence. The increasing authority of the proletarian writers' groups, and their dominance in the official literary hierarchy, was only too familiar to Mandelstam.

I think that the most significant aspect of Luknitsky's account, though, is his description of how Mandelstam responded to these troubles. Rather than allow the controversy to die down, Luknitsky writes, Mandelstam seemed determined to keep it alive. When the Mandelstams' landlord tried to force them out, Mandelstam argued vigorously and resisted efforts at mediation. It was as though Mandelstam *wanted* to provoke a heightened response, as though he needed the confrontation to fuel an inner sense of purpose, Luknitsky writes.

I draw attention to Mandelstam's "maximal" response to a rather common domestic dispute only because it acts as a small-scale dress rehearsal for the larger and much more dramatic scandal that was just starting to bubble up around the Ulenspiegel translation. Both Luknitsky and Nadezhda Mandelstam emphasize that the Ulenspiegel affair would have died down much sooner if Mandelstam had not kept it alive, and I think that their insistence on this point deserves more attention than it has received in the past.[6] If they are right—and I think they are—then Mandelstam was deliberately protracting a struggle that gave him an opportunity to overtly resist the new literary hierarchy.

In other words, we need to recognize that Mandelstam did not see himself as just another victim of the new regime. He recognized the injustice done to him, but his fundamental orientation was *active*, even aggressive, rather than passive. Mandelstam turned the accusation against him into a personal rallying point, focusing his energy on a new determination to resist the literary community en masse. He had been pushed too far, and now he was determined to push back. The chain of events shows a steadily escalating rhetoric, and eventually Mandelstam demanded action from his fellow writers through a direct request for their support: Were they willing to take a stand for genuine, unfettered literature? In essence, he used the scandal in a failed effort to incite a counterrevolution from within, unsuccessfully trying to persuade his fellow writers to demand replacement of all those responsible for the "attack on literature" symbolized by the accusation against him personally. When this counterrevolution in the world of flesh and blood failed, Mandelstam shifted the focus of his resistance in a new direction with the composition of "Fourth Prose."

The controversy really started when A. G. Gornfeld accused Mandelstam of plagiarism in a letter to *Red Evening Gazette* (*Krasnaia vecherniaia gazeta*), saying that he could recognize "even in its changed condition, my coat that was yesterday hanging in my foyer."[7] This phrase appears to have been instrumental in provoking Mandelstam's outrage and he responded almost immediately with a letter to *Evening Moscow* (*Vecherniaia Moskva*) in which he rails against Gornfeld's suggestion of petty thievery and moral baseness:

> Now that my apologies are made and I have abandoned all sentimentality, I, a Russian poet and man of letters, having erected over twenty years a mountain of independent labor, ask the literary critic Gornfeld how he could have stooped so low as to permit himself the phrase about the "fur coat" [*shuba*]. My mistake and Gornfeld's transgression are incommensurable. . . . Gornfeld has shown so much indifference to his younger contemporary, a man of letters, so much disdain for this man's work, . . . that both man and writer are horrified.[8]

Gornfeld, a figure made so reprehensible in "Fourth Prose" and in Mandelstam's letter, was a representative of the old-school translators and was himself being swept aside by the "new people" of the literary world. Isolated from this case, Mandelstam probably would have felt sympathy for him. But it is the way that the charge was leveled directly at Mandelstam, rather than including the publisher who bore greater responsibility for the mistake, that made Mandelstam sense hidden hands behind the accusation.

The accusation was even more offensive because of Gornfeld's metaphor about a stolen coat. Coat metaphors had been a recurring motif in Mandelstam's writing since the early 1920s, when he made "Fur Coat" the title of a short autobiographical article that appeared in *Soviet South* (*Sovetskii iug*) in February 1922. There Mandelstam describes how he acquired a fur coat that kept him warm through the dreadful Petersburg winters of unheated apartments and scant food, while living next to Viktor Shklovsky in the House of Arts. It is not difficult to see how this was reworked to form the concluding chapter of *The Noise of Time*, with its description of V. V. Gippius in a cold Petersburg literary winter, and it becomes clear that the coat metaphor was more than a whim to Mandelstam. Even though Gornfeld's letter actually referred to a "coat" [*pal'to*] rather than a "fur coat" [*shuba*]—and Mandelstam reproduces this accurately when he quotes the offending passage from Gornfeld's letter as an epigraph to his response—in Mandelstam's rebuttal the term is consistently "fur coat". This way he maintains a semantic continuity with the original accusation but also points to his own literary work, where he effectively transformed the term *shuba* into a metaphor for Russian literature. In effect, Mandelstam raised the stakes from the outset, deciding immediately that this was no trivial accusation.

It is possible that the scandal would gradually have died down after this exchange, but in April 1929 Mandelstam went on the attack with a sharply critical article in *Izvestiia* about contemporary Soviet translation practices. The article, with the unyielding title "Torrents of Hackwork" (*Potoki khaltury*) minces no words from its very beginning: "Speaking bluntly, the Russian translations of *belles lettres* that are currently flooding the marketplace are no more than torrents of hackwork. . . . The average reader, who knows only his native language, is systematically deluded by the publisher," he writes. Translations are simply a way of publishing books without paying royalties, Mandelstam argues, and then takes his fellow translators to task for putting the most varied of foreign authors into a uniformly clumsy Russian: "From [translators'] hands we receive the riches of foreign nations in a debased and tendentiously degraded form."[9] This is strong language indeed, especially when we remember that here Mandelstam is attacking an entire industry—and that he was relying on this very industry for survival at the time he wrote.

The effect of Mandelstam's bold critique was like pouring gasoline on a smoldering fire. It reignited the entire Ulenspiegel scandal and prompted a turbulent exchange of accusations and rebuttals that flowed through the pages of *The Literary Gazette* (*Literaturnaia gazeta*) for all of May 1929. David Zaslavsky launched his career as a literary hatchet man in the May 7 issue with the publication of "On Modest Plagiarism and Ostentatious Hackwork," a personal attack against Mandelstam. Mandelstam's letter accusing Zaslavsky of slander, accompanied by a statement of support signed by fifteen writers, appeared a week later. Zaslavsky responded the following week and included Gornfeld's original letter of complaint.

By now the Leningrad writers had been drawn into the controversy, and a group that included Anna Akhmatova, Boris Eikhenbaum, Yury Tynyanov, and more published their own defense of Mandelstam in the last May issue.

Meanwhile, the leaders of FOSP had set up a Conflict Commission to review the entire affair. Mandelstam had little faith in the outcome, since he was convinced that FOSP's machinations lay at the root of the original accusation and especially Zaslavsky's involvement.[10] Knowing that the commission was scheduled to meet on June 21, Mandelstam fired off an urgent telegram to his fellow writers in Leningrad, begging them to take some decisive action. "Words are powerless here. It is necessary to act," he wrote, so that those carrying out this "executioner's work" would be held to account. Mandelstam makes it clear that there is a lot more at stake here than just his own predicament. It is time for writers to stand up for "their own honor, the honor of literature," he urges.[11]

But Mandelstam was still not ready to let the affair die. In July he published the article "On Translations" and renewed his attack on the publishers of translations. Publishers view translators merely as "cheap brainpower," he accuses, and readers are typically philistines who want to appear cultured but can't read the works in the original languages. Of course, this can have the beneficial effect of stimulating an interest in language study, but in the present social structure even language study becomes a tool for social control: "Knowledge of languages is a mighty weapon in the hands of the ruling class. With the aid of this weapon the composition of the entire cultural present is counterfeited and world literature is falsified until it reaches the condition demanded by people of position."[12] These are hardly conciliatory remarks, and the affair dragged on with a series of lengthy interrogations that started to work backward through Mandelstam's career, looking for suspicious material in works that had been published years earlier. In letters to his wife, Mandelstam describes the interrogations and sounds a note of loneliness, if not despair: "I'm alone. *Ich bin arm.* Everything is irreparable. . . . Just write to tell me what I should do, help me to stand firm, help me to avoid all lies and vile people. . . ."[13]

The moves and countermoves escalated. The Leningrad section of the Poets' Union expelled Mandelstam on September 30, 1929, ostensibly because he had not kept up his dues.[14] The investigation by FOSP's Conflict Commission was supplemented by additional pressure on Mandelstam from even higher layers in the organization's bureaucracy. At the Land and Factory (*Zemlia i fabrika*) publishing house a new administrator took over and promptly launched a criminal case against Mandelstam in a Moscow court, denying that the publishing house bore any responsibility in the affair.

Harassed from all sides and feeling completely isolated, Mandelstam composed (but apparently did not send) an "Open Letter to Soviet Writers." The lengthy letter includes a summary of all the processes initiated against Mandelstam and a denunciation not only of the charges, but of a literary bureaucracy that would stoop to the persecution of its own kind. Mandelstam notes that he has observed the "suspicious flexibility" with which FOSP's judicial process responds to pressure from above. Much more inflammatory, though, is Mandelstam's accusation that "The society of writers, allowing the transformation of their own agencies into torture chambers, . . . becomes in the process a concrete threat for every writer."[15]

Toward the end of this lengthy process, in late 1929 and early 1930, Mandelstam started to compose "Fourth Prose."[16] The work that emerged is an extension of the defiance that Mandelstam showed in publishing articles like "Torrents of Hackwork" and "On Translations" (*O perevodakh*). Now, however, Mandelstam abandons all restraint. There are defiance and resoluteness in this text that go far beyond even the final chapter of *The Noise of Time*, which seems tame in comparison.

Perhaps the most striking difference between "Fourth Prose" and *The Noise of Time* is the identity of the narrator. While the narrator of *The Noise of Time* never directly claims the title "poet," in "Fourth Prose" the narrator assumes this title proudly and resolutely. But this is a poet not often seen in Russian literature. This is not a Symbolist declaiming about otherworldly ephemera, or even a Futurist at his provocative, scandalous best. "Fourth Prose" transcends all of this with the directness and the implacability of its challenge to the literary establishment. It is the conscious nature of this assault that makes "Fourth Prose" difficult to fit into a strict generic category: "Is it autobiography, anecdote, or jeremiad?" asks David Bethea, observing that "Fourth Prose's" "generic outlaw status" is itself a liberating force.[17]

Mandelstam was not completely alone as he created such an intensely personal response to persecution, though. We know that Mandelstam always tried to keep a small number of books with him wherever he went; included were Dante's *Divine Comedy* (in a small edition so that Mandelstam could take it with him if arrested suddenly), the autobiography of the Archpriest Avvakum, and the writings of Alexander Herzen. These became his "companion books," as Nadezhda Mandelstam describes them.[18] Mandelstam's choices may seem an unlikely combination for an essential library, but Gregory Freidin suggests that "Herzen and Avvakum went well together. Herzen was the first to present modern Russian authorship as martyrdom, and Avvakum, seen in this light, was Russia's first martyred author."[19] If we believe Mandelstam's claim in *The Noise of Time* that the books one treasures reveal one's biography, then these three exile-authors offered more than just inspiration and comfort to Mandelstam.

They also offered him model biographies, ways in which he could either structure his own life, or at least structure the *account* of his own life.

Mandelstam approached each of these spiritual ancestors at different times and in different ways, but each became an important interlocutor for Mandelstam at a crucial point in his life. Herzen's personality and style anchored the composition of *The Noise of Time* in the mid-1920s. Dante became Mandelstam's inspiration of the 1930s, when Mandelstam started studying Italian in an effort to get closer to the great Florentine poet and then brought Dante back to life in the extraordinary literary study and self-portrait called "Conversation about Dante" (*Razgovor o Dante*, 1933).

But although both Herzen and Dante are important figures in "Fourth Prose," with Herzen even called by name, I believe that it was Avvakum—who has never before been explicitly linked to the work—who was Mandelstam's most important model when it came to "Fourth Prose." Avvakum's raging defiance provided Mandelstam with the literary model that most suited his mood and objective in the aftermath of the Ulenspiegel scandal. When he opened the pages of *The Life of the Archpriest Avvakum by Himself* (*Zhitie protopopa Avvakuma im samim napisannoe*), Mandelstam found the unvarnished story of another tormented soul, someone willing to suffer and even die for a cause that he believed in completely. As Mandelstam fought off the increasingly direct attacks of FOSP and other representatives of the literary bureaucracy, he surely sensed a profound spiritual connection to Avvakum.

The ties between the two men are not direct, of course, and this may explain why the relationship has never been noticed. Avvakum was a priest whose refusal to conform to the status quo insured that his journey through life would never be smooth. Appointments to various parishes seemed to lead inevitably to violent rejection by his parishioners, for Avvakum invariably demanded submission to his spiritual authority. In one parish he was severely beaten and driven from his home twice; elsewhere, fellow priests joined Avvakum's opponents when he declared their local customs immoral. When the new Patriarch Nikon decided to formalize Orthodox liturgy and rejected many popular parts of church practice, Avvakum's eloquent and charismatic voice of opposition became the focal point for resistance, and his followers came to be known as the Old Believers. Avvakum rejected all efforts to secure his cooperation and was sent into monastic exile; this was followed by exile to Siberia, where two of his sons died of starvation. After Nikon's death, Avvakum was called back to Moscow and Tsar Aleksei offered him a post in the Kremlin in exchange for his support. When Avvakum refused, he was sent back into exile and a church council anathematized him. Eventually he was burned at the stake after almost thirty years of exile, hardship and torture.

The similarities between Avvakum and Mandelstam stand out sharply when we remember Mandelstam's reverent, almost religious fervor for genuine poetry. He resisted those willing to profane poetry by throwing it open to any dilettante who could cook up a few rhymes in the "poetry kitchens" that sprang up when proletarian cultural groups decided to train new poets. These idlers from the "army of poets" inspired only contempt in Mandelstam, who saw it as his mission to resist them in the name of all real poets.[20] Mandelstam's horror at the desecration of Russian culture finds a ready parallel in Avvakum's righteous indignation at the sweeping reforms transforming (or deforming, as he saw it) the church liturgy of his time. Both Avvakum and Mandelstam are willing to suffer for their convictions and describe their tormentors in very similar terms. Mandelstam describes the literary elite that threatens him as a group of priests only too willing to use violence in achieving their literary-political ends; Avvakum's account shows that his most relentless tormentors are priests who formerly served with him and now represent the "reformed" Orthodox church. Just as Avvakum considers himself to be part of a faithful remnant, Mandelstam sees himself as a minority of one, standing alone to defend genuine literature.

The two works also share a similar style. Avvakum's writing is earthy, unpretentious and sometimes surprisingly coarse—but it is renowned in Russian literature as one of the purest and most powerful prose works ever written. In fact, says A. N. Robinson, Avvakum's writings on the Russian language became a sensation when they were published in a small edition in 1916. Among the documents published was a letter by Avvakum to the tsar, in which Avvakum wrote: "You're a Russian, after all, not a Greek. Speak your natural language. Do not demean it either in church, or at home, or anywhere. God loves us no less than he loves the Greeks."[21] Mandelstam shared Avvakum's passion for the Russian language, and "Fourth Prose" shows that passion in its raw, unsophisticated directness. The style here is a far cry from the elegant flair found in *The Noise of Time*. In "Fourth Prose" Mandelstam's language descends right to the gutter: "all around the bitch pack writes. What the hell kind of writer am I?! Get out, you fools!"[22] Other descriptions may not be quite as crude, but are still far from the polished style of *The Noise of Time*; Mandelstam's accusations crash against his persecutors and all those who have betrayed literature, who have sold out to the new regime and now function as the state's mouthpieces in the literary realm. Avvakum's directness shows a similar gift for description, for conveying emotional intensity. He minces no words when describing his tormentors, reserving his harshest words and choicest earthy expressions not for those who attack him physically, but for those who betray the Church. For both Mandelstam and Avvakum the physical trials they face are much less important than the sanctity of the faiths they guard.

While Avvakum becomes a spiritual brother for Mandelstam in "Fourth Prose" and models maximal resistance to an oppressive, heretical regime, Alexander Herzen becomes a disappointment, if not a traitor. After the appreciation that Mandelstam shows for Herzen in *The Noise of Time*, the sharp change in attitude that we see in "Fourth Prose" is striking—but the shift in tone and its significance have gone virtually unremarked. The repeated references to Herzen and Herzen's House, which in Mandelstam's day housed the main writers' organizations and in which Mandelstam actually lived from 1922–1923, indicate that Herzen remained an important figure in Mandelstam's thinking when he wrote "Fourth Prose." As we saw in looking at *The Noise of Time*, Mandelstam believed that there was a real affinity between himself and Herzen. Both suffered for taking principled stands against authority. For both, skill with words served as the most effective response to the forces that tried to silence them. In his own time Herzen was one of only a few voices demanding justice and social change, and after repeated run-ins with authority and a first-hand experience with internal exile, Herzen emigrated to England. From there he used his literary voice to carry on the struggle. This picture of refusal to conform, combined with a commitment to social justice, drew Mandelstam to Herzen, and Nadezhda Mandelstam writes that Herzen "was undoubtedly one of the formative influences in [Mandelstam's] life."[23]

But there is a gap between *The Noise of Time* and "Fourth Prose," and during that gap a fundamental shift has occurred in Mandelstam's orientation. He has new and painfully personal evidence that Herzen's ideals have gone off course: Herzen's intentions may have been admirable, but now Herzen's ideals have all been swept away as the state consumes increasingly large pieces of its subjects' lives. The Revolution has turned out to be even thirstier than Mandelstam suspected when he wrote *The Noise of Time*. But the bitterest pill of all is that literature, Mandelstam's greatest love, appears to be leading the campaign against him. It becomes much more than mere irony, then, that FOSP actually has its physical headquarters in Herzen's former house. Instead, this becomes a concrete representation of how Herzen's "property" (both intellectual and physical) has been misappropriated by the state, and a sign to Mandelstam that Herzen is no longer the hero he once was. Letter drafts from 1930 show just how powerful the link between writers' organizations and Herzen House became for Mandelstam. In one unsent letter to Soviet writers, Mandelstam writes: "You will no longer have to 'defend the virtue of Soviet literature against Mandelstam' (an actual expression from the All-Union Writers' charter, prepared in Herzen House) . . ."[23] In "Fourth Prose," Mandelstam repeatedly uses the metonymic shorthand "Herzen House" when he wishes to refer to FOSP, the Writers' Federation.

Eventually Mandelstam decides to go beyond the current tenants of Herzen House and he appeals directly to Herzen himself:

> Aleksandr Ivanovich Herzen! . . . Allow me to introduce myself. . . . It was, it seems, in your house. . . . As host, you are in some sense responsible. . . .
> You were so good as to go abroad, were you? . . . Meanwhile, something disagreeable has happened here. . . . Aleksandr Ivanovich! Sir! What am I to do? There is absolutely no one to turn to![25]

The phrase "in your house" refers most directly to the building that houses the nefarious Writers' Federation, but it also has a wider application to the entire country. As the "first socialist" Herzen took some of the earliest steps on the path that led to Mandelstam's current predicament, and is thus a kind of shadowy host who must take some responsibility for the events unfolding before Mandelstam's eyes. But Herzen chose to go abroad rather than stay behind, and in his absence "something unpleasant" took place. Herzen's struggle against tyranny has been cruelly successful: The long awaited changes finally came, but a new authoritarianism quickly took the place of the old. The best description of this in "Fourth Prose" is the portrayal of young Vasenka in part 2. Vasenka's goatskin boots and dress coat, along with his entourage of "mamas, grandmothers and nannies" clearly show that he is from the privileged class. In the new Soviet reality, though, Vasenka is part of the Komsomol, not a member of the hereditary aristocracy. The revolutionaries have swiftly metamorphosed into the new Establishment, assuming positions and attitudes of privilege. In a passage that could easily be taken as a direct commentary on this section of "Fourth Prose," Nadezhda Mandelstam writes: "It would have been a hopeless task to justify what was happening in the name of Herzen—indeed, in the name of Herzen it could only be condemned. It is true that Herzen reserved the right to retreat into proud isolation . . . but such a course was not for M."[26]

The confusion at the end of the passage quoted above ("What am I to do? There is absolutely no one to turn to!") reflects the poet's dilemma. There is a sense that he was not entirely opposed to Herzen's ideas, but was shocked by what happened after the anticipated Revolution actually took place. This sense of dismay is made more intolerable by the absence of any court of appeal ("no one to turn to").[27] No new Herzen has arisen to defend the rights of the oppressed.

The final allusion to Herzen is the most subtle and has never previously been mentioned in discussions of "Fourth Prose." In Part 16 Mandelstam offers a summary of his argument, a concise recapitulation of the charges brought against him and his response to the accusations:

No matter how hard I would work, even if I would carry a horse on my back, even if I would turn millstones, all the same I would never become a workman. My work, no matter what form it might assume, is taken as mischief, lawlessness, mere accident. But such is my will, and I give myself to it. I'll sign to it with both hands.[28]

In this paradise of the working proletariat, Mandelstam acknowledges that he will never be considered a worker no matter what Herculean efforts he may make. But instead of remaining passive and taking his identity only from what others think of him, Mandelstam asserts the force of his own character. His path is not one that has been forced on him, but a choice made by his own will, he insists. His defiant conclusion ("I'll sign to it with both hands") is almost a direct quotation from Herzen's memoirs. In *Past and Thoughts* (*Byloe i dumy*) Herzen describes a talk with his French tutor as a key moment in forming his youthful ideas about authoritarian rule and autocracy. Herzen's tutor had been describing the events surrounding the French Revolution when Herzen asked, "Why was Louis XVI executed?" The tutor responded: "Because he was a traitor to his people." This prompted Herzen to ask: "If you had been among the judges, would you have signed the death sentence?" "With both hands," answers Herzen's tutor.[29] The lexical correspondence is no coincidence, and although this phrase is not uncommon in Russian as an intensifying expression, the context of "Fourth Prose" and Herzen's place in it suggest a more deliberate linkage. Just as the passage from Herzen's memoir describes a formative moment, Mandelstam's statement comes at the crucial juncture when he recognizes that he can no longer maintain any illusion of playing by the state's rules. He must embrace his "lawlessness" and "mischief" with all his might and with his full voice.

The second parallel, I would suggest, is between the death sentence that Herzen's tutor would gladly sign and the work that Mandelstam will never see officially recognized. In Mandelstam's eyes, his work is tantamount to the strongest possible condemnation of the state and its culture of violence. It is a figurative equivalent to the literal death sentence referred to by the long-dead French tutor. In a country where a tribe of literary stooges can flaunt its usurpation of Herzen's house, Mandelstam's voice (his "work") utters a continuous denunciation of the new autocracy. He utters this condemnation with all his might ("with both hands") because the new forces of literature are no longer true writers but mere thugs catering to the sinister whims of Soviet ideology. Even though his solitary voice of defiance may hasten the pronouncement of a death sentence on the poet himself, he will not back down.

Mandelstam's emphasis on his voice throughout "Fourth Prose" provides a crucial insight into what he considers the most effective form of resistance to Soviet reality, and reinforces his natural attraction to Avvakum. Avvakum's reputation for passionate, articulate speech and his very literal appointment as a priest of the word (since church liturgy is verbal), make him one of Russia's great voices. Even more, Avvakum tells of leading a healing service that miraculously restored speech to a young woman. Avvakum finds a perfect heir in Mandelstam, for the two share a passionate belief in the awesome responsibility that accompanies the voice's production of the sacred word.

In Mandelstam's own generation there were others who wrote fervently about the power of the word, but none surpassed him. It is no surprise, then, that the semantic network of word, voice and language emerge in "Fourth Prose" with even more force than in *The Noise of Time*. The notion of poetry as a *verbal* art is not new for Mandelstam. In *The Noise of Time* he describes the risk of losing one's voice in the increasing chill of the post-Revolutionary winter. In "An Army of Poets" Mandelstam describes the voice as a poet's chief tool: "Of course, the voice is a working tool; it is inconceivable without a tune, like a carpenter's plane. Poets work with the voice, the voice." Mandelstam's fascination with the voice led to a related interest in the parts of the body that function in speech production. "The mouth works, the smile nudges the line of verse, cleverly and gaily the lips redden, the tongue trustingly presses itself against the palate," he continues. "The inner form of the verse is inseparable from the countless changes of expression flitting across the face of the narrator who speaks and feels emotion."[30]

In an era when the written word is increasingly subject to confiscation, oral poetry's essential freedom becomes especially important and the poetry recital becomes the best way for poets to unite voice, word and audience. The recital becomes a magical moment when poet and audience enter into a form of communion mediated by the poet's voice and the words of the poem as they pass through the air. Mandelstam's own commentary on this in "Conversation about Dante" is almost shocking: "Poetic material does not have a voice. . . . It is devoid of form just as it is devoid of content for the simple reason that *it exists only in performance. The finished poem is no more than a calligraphic product.*"[31] The notion that poetry is empty unless it is spoken aloud, while an overstatement to those who conceive of poetry as an act of writing, is absolutely central for Mandelstam. For him, poetry is an act of communication: Poetry demands an audience, and it is really alive only when charged with all the richness of sound as a voice turns it into speech and a listener responds. Judging by the accounts of his contemporaries, Mandelstam's own recitals were powerful confirmation of the need for poetry to come alive through the poet's voice. Nikolai Khardzhiev describes a recital in November 1932 where Mandelstam recited for two and a half hours, covering his entire poetic output for two years and concludes: "They were such terrifying exorcisms that many people took fright."[32]

Recognizing the importance of a word's sound leads directly to the realization that a poet must be able to hear as well as speak. When a poet loses one of these faculties (hearing or speech), poetic speech disappears. Mandelstam goes so far as to suggest that a poem's life begins with sound, so that even before a single word is formed, "the poem can already be heard. This is the sound of the inner image, this is the poet's ear touching it." A poet's ear is revealed immediately in poetry, and in trying to stamp out an insurgence of bad poets in "An Army of Poets," Mandelstam draws attention to their lack of sensitivity to sound: They shout rather than speak, they "are stupefied by the sound of their own voices," they sing in nasal voices, or they mumble. To succeed as a poet, Mandelstam insists, one must learn to listen to one's own words.[33]

The poet isn't the only one whose ability to listen makes poetry viable. A good listener is the other essential part of meaningful poetry, and Mandelstam pondered the listener's role from his early days as a poet. In "On the Addressee" (*O sobesednike*, 1913) Mandelstam argues that the Symbolists lost touch with their audience, neglecting the "mutuality" of the poetic word to focus only on the poet's role as a kind of musical instrument. "But a piece of music has its own independent existence regardless of the performer," he continues, and the music itself will reach out and generate a response that the musician cannot always control or even imagine.[34] Mandelstam recognizes the need for poems to exist within a loosely structured semantic space that allows for dialogue with the listener. The reader/listener ends up with a significant role in the interaction.[35] Above all else the poet must resist the temptation to violate this space and box in the listener/reader, Mandelstam says. The poet who faces this temptation most powerfully is the one who knows his or her audience and tries to steer poetry along specific channels. "Aiming" at a listener cripples poetry, Mandelstam writes. But a poet who clings to the belief that there *will be* a worthy reader at some point in the future will create lyrics that retain an eternal freshness, an element of surprise. Mandelstam himself demonstrates how to act the role of audience in "Conversation about Dante," where he becomes that surprise reader whom Dante could never have anticipated and who must now treat Dante honorably in the act of reading and listening.

Freeing the audience is only one side of poetic creation. The other part is liberating the word. Again Mandelstam approaches his idea by referring to errors made by the Symbolists. In "The Word and Culture" (*Slovo i kul'tura*, 1921) he argues that the Symbolists "enslaved" the word by creating "automatic" metaphor linkages: "What can be done when a word is fettered to its denotative meaning: doesn't this amount to serfdom?" he asks. In the late 1920s the Soviet state started to encroach on the word's sovereignty from the other side, attempting to reign in language, to define and contain it. These efforts led steadily toward a "literature of fact" that would avoid the dangers of metaphor and multiple meanings altogether. The very essence of poetry, its indirect complexity, provides the most urgent reason for its containment. The notion that a word is free, that its reception by a listener can't be strictly controlled even by the speaker, constitutes a threat to state authority. Theorists from LEF (the Left Front of Art) recognized this threat and tried to move ever further from metaphor, hoping that the newspaper would prove the ultimate bastion against the uncertainty of symbolic speech. The worker correspondent, a writer content to report only verifiable facts without aspiring to literary greatness, became LEF's ideal Soviet writer.[36] For Mandelstam, who believed strongly that the Russian language has an "ontological function," these attempts to limit the freedom of language were offensive and terrifying. Any form of violence against language becomes an act of violence against Russian history itself, a "sacrifice of language" for ulterior motives.[37]

Mandelstam's own perspective is quite different. For him, the word is an unrestricted free agent. "The living word does not designate an object, but freely chooses for its dwelling place, as it were, some objective significance," he says in "The Word and Culture." Much later Mandelstam repeats the same fundamental concept in "Conversation about Dante": "Any unit of poetic speech, be it a line, a stanza or an entire lyrical composition, must be regarded as a single word" because poetry departs from the poet's lips with meanings "sticking out of it in various directions" and the reader cannot simply attach a preformed meaning to it: This would be the same as performing a "semantic abortion," he argues.[38] In an environment where the state seeks to control expression and limit independent voices, it is easy to see how Mandelstam's absolute resistance to predetermined meanings would inevitably lead to confrontation.[39]

There is an essential aloneness in the act of poetic creation. When the sounds of a new poem were taking shape in Mandelstam's mind, he needed to separate himself from others in some way. When he could, he walked his way through the birth process, wandering the streets and mumbling to himself. If he was visiting at a friend's apartment, he sometimes wrapped a blanket or jacket over his head and retreated into a mental cocoon—anything to create some personal space, some separation from life's distractions, so that he could hear the sounds that signaled the emergence of a new poem.

Mandelstam also recognized a larger scale and more abstract separation between the genuine poet and the mass of nonpoets. This awareness lay at the root of his passionate attempts to keep idlers away from poetry, and of his opposition to all those who tried to turn "poet" into just another job title. When the Formalists described the poet as a technician, or the Proletkult set up how-to workshops for barely literate workers, Mandelstam spoke out on behalf of poetry as an art. The cultural capital accumulated by poetry over more than a century should not be abandoned just to satisfy the demands of new political masters. It was important to him that the designation "poet" was not scattered about carelessly, but granted only to those with a genuine gift.

In between these two realms of isolation—the micro level of creation, and the macro level of cultural institution—Mandelstam could easily see himself as a part of the broader community, at least until the mid-1920s. He was a part of Russian culture and history in its broadest sense, and felt close ties to his chosen "family" of Russian literature. He identified himself as an Acmeist and was quick to criticize the excesses he saw in the Symbolists, Futurists and other poetry schools. But he could recognize genius wherever he saw it, regardless of affiliation. Even in *The Noise of Time* Mandelstam sensed a bond with most of his colleagues in Russia's literary family as they faced the prospect of the cold State's growing appetite.

In "Fourth Prose" the middle ground disappears. The poet's isolation, already established on the personal and societal levels, now becomes absolute as the intermediary space for collegial literary relations turns into a battleground. The poet now stands alone. Literature itself has risen up against him, and he is faced with a stark choice: Give up and be subjugated in the most humiliating manner, or stand alone and resist to the last breath. In "Fourth Prose," Mandelstam recognizes that his alienation is now complete, but he also recognizes that poetry needs a champion. If no one else will stand up for poetry and the poet against the relentless onslaught of State-dominated literary figures, he will fight on his own.

The alienation experienced by the poet-narrator of "Fourth Prose" is both externally and internally imposed. Mandelstam has been pushed out of literature by the new high priests of culture, but he also flees on his own because he cannot bear to identify with the new literary ethos. This dually imposed alienation offers an almost ideal example of what Nathan Rotenstreich calls the two potential psychological effects of alienation: either an emotional elevation, or a sense of "subjugating estrangement."[40] The unusual feature of "Fourth Prose" is that not just one but both of these tendencies manifest themselves in turn; the result is an emotional tone that shifts back and forth between two very different moods. At times Mandelstam's outbursts are palpably, even cruelly, hostile when he addresses the subjugating literary figures who have transformed his beloved cultural space. But there are other passages that project a kind of "alienation sublime," a sense of ecstatic purpose that carries him into a state of emotional exaltation. With all the cards except one in the hands of his opponents, he turns isolation into the ultimate trump card and cherishes it ferociously.

Mandelstam's sense of alienation is similar in nature to the sense of exclusion that Lee Upton describes as a "muse of abandonment" experienced by American poets like Charles Wright.[41] But while Wright and other American poets take principle-based stands to oppose contemporary cultural trends like radical consumerism, American poets (fortunately) do not face this isolation with the same sense of frantic urgency experienced by Russian poets like Mandelstam. For Mandelstam, the alienation was accompanied by a real and tangible sense of potential doom. The deaths of both recent (Sergei Esenin, Nikolai Gumilyov) and long ago (Alexander Pushkin, Mikhail Lermontov) precursors made Mandelstam keenly aware that the poet's essential aloneness was too often fatal. The increasingly hostile literary climate only reinforced this sense of foreboding.

In "Fourth Prose" Mandelstam picks a particularly volatile analogy when he returns to his Jewish heritage to depict his sense of exclusion. His approach this time is radically different—and considerably more complex—than it was in early poems or in *The Noise of Time*. This time there are actually two streams of Jewish identity that flow through the text, and the sharp differences between them have drawn conflicting responses. Charles Isenberg and Jane Gary Harris describe the Jewishness in "Fourth Prose" as a very positive element, something that anchors Mandelstam's "moral perspective" as he reclaims his identity and wields it as a badge of honor against his persecutors.[42] But Mandelstam's pejorative descriptions of some characters in "Fourth Prose" as "Yids" have led scholars like Gregory Freidin to see a real anti-Semitic flavor in the work.[43]

There is no easy way to tiptoe along a *via media* that would resolve this volatile issue: Mandelstam's outbursts against several figures are directly linked to their Jewishness, but his decision to resist is just as firmly rooted in an explicit affirmation of his Jewish past. The only way to start addressing this contradiction is to recognize that Mandelstam is creating a distinction between genuine Jewishness and compromised Jewishness, and that this metaphor is less relevant as a link to his own blood heritage than as a metaphoric representation of his primary allegiance to genuine literature, and especially poetry. It is not Jewishness in general that becomes an impelling moral force, but a special "remnant" Jewishness that is contrasted to "assimilating" Jewishness to form a paradigm of identity. Mandelstam becomes a shifty Jew of ancient pedigree, someone who traces his roots back to kings and patriarchs, and who resists all efforts to force him into the docile tribe of assimilating Jews.

Above all, the Jewish identity adopted in "Fourth Prose" functions on a symbolic level. It is a happy coincidence (perhaps also a complication) that Mandelstam is Jewish by birth, but this is almost beside the point. As Clare Cavanagh aptly puts it, in "Fourth Prose" "the true Jew . . . is not necessarily Jewish."[44] The key element in Mandelstam's discussion is an association that is sometimes voiced but sometimes stays on the level of metonymic association: Jewishness functions as a representation of literature. The true Jew evades authority while becoming a genuine writer/poet; the false Jew is unmasked as a literary impostor who actually subverts and deforms literature while hunting down and subjugating all those who resist.

Gornfeld, Mandelstam's accuser in the Ulenspiegel scandal, enters the text of "Fourth Prose" as a Jew who has sold himself wholly to the literary establishment. Mandelstam accuses Gornfeld of following the directives of the state and willingly turning himself into a literary assassin: Gornfeld's written attack on Mandelstam is just as deadly as the bullet that George d'Anthès fired to kill Mandelstam's great poet-ancestor Alexander Pushkin. For Mandelstam, the whole Ulenspiegel experience has been a bitter confirmation of the power of the word, and Mandelstam considers Gornfeld's actions a fitting gesture for someone who would dare (as Gornfeld did) to publish a book entitled *Torments of the Word*.[45] Rather than stoop to this betrayal of literature, Mandelstam suggests, Gornfeld should have contented himself with crying into the "pure literary Jewish waistcoat of Mr. Propper." Another reference to Jewishness comes earlier, when Mandelstam uses the pejorative "Yid" in reference to a character who is closely tied to a sinister editor/coffin maker. This editor is a terrifying figure, an "illiterate horse doctor of happening, deaths and events" who is delighted "when the black horse blood of the age spurts forth in a gushing fountain." An editor who is illiterate, who delights in reporting the fatal events of the age, who rejoices at the spurt of blood and then promptly inters the victims in the morning edition: This is a repulsive portrait and a terrible indictment of not just newspapers but the entire publication industry.[46] Descriptions like these show how much aversion Mandelstam feels for these "accommodating Jews."

The positive side of Jewishness is acknowledged by most who comment on "Fourth Prose," but its depths—and its links to the Avvakum story line—have not been adequately recognized. I would argue that Mandelstam's search for a positive Jewish model takes him deep into Jewish sacred history, where he finds an ideal match for the poet's role in the image of an Old Testament royal priesthood. This is a completely different hypostasis of the Jew, a form of Jewish identity that cannot tolerate assimilation, and Mandelstam embraces it wholeheartedly in his search for a Jewish identity that has not been sullied by the stigma of accommodation. Officially sanctioned literature "is incompatible with the honorary title of Judean, of which I am proud," asserts Mandelstam. As collateral to add credibility to this "honorary title," Mandelstam offers the weight of true heritage and ancient pedigree, a lineage of "sheep breeders, patriarchs and kings."[47] The term that I have given in English as "honorary title of Judean" [*pochetnoe zvanie iudeia*] has been translated variously: Clarence Brown uses "honorable title of Jew," Charles Isenberg uses "honorable title of Hebrew," and Jane Gary Harris uses "honorable calling of Jew." I have used the terms "honorary title" and "Judean" because both are important for the central Jewish theme of "Fourth Prose." The word *iudei* was much less common than the more stylistically neutral *evrei* (Jew), and Clare Cavanagh is quite right to point out the Biblical overtones of the term *iudei*.[48]

Before exploring the significance of the term "iudei" in "Fourth Prose," I should note that this is not the only occasion where Mandelstam uses this word. Perhaps the most notable examples of his usage are in the "Bookshelf" and "Judaic Chaos" sections of *The Noise of Time*, but *iudei* also appears several times in his early poetry. In these passages it is hard to see any substantive distinction between Mandelstam's use of *iudei* and *evrei*, and both terms can be rendered "Jew." But between *The Noise of Time* and "Fourth Prose" everything changed for Mandelstam. The most basic terms of reference for his relationship to Russian culture had to be completely reconsidered, and the cultural assimilation that he described in *The Noise of Time* is no longer a worthy goal, but a moral degradation. With such a shift in outlook, it is not surprising that a corresponding distinction would enter Mandelstam's linguistic framework.

It is this personal realization that leads to Mandelstam's much more careful use of the term *iudei* in "Fourth Prose." In Jewish history Mandelstam finds a pattern of assimilation and resistance that corresponds perfectly to his own sense of alienation from his own kind, and his proud assumption of the title *iudei* shows clearly that his Jewishness is radically different from the Jewishness of his tormentors. The term *iudei* comes from *Iuda* (Judah), the tribe of Israel that gave the biblical tradition both King David in the Old Testament and Jesus Christ in the New Testament. In "Fourth Prose" Mandelstam evokes both of these figures as part of his honorary lineage, but initially his focus is on David.

In the Old Testament history of the people of Israel, after David's son Solomon died there was a struggle for succession. As a prophet had predicted, eleven tribes joined the breakaway kingdom (Israel) and only the tribe of Judah remained loyal to the house of David. For centuries the Hebrew people remained split between the two kingdoms, and fierce wars broke out periodically between them. David's descendants ruled in the kingdom of Judah, and Judah remained generally faithful to the Hebrew

God. The kingdom of Israel, however, is referred to over and over in the biblical text as a land of apostasy, idol worship, and accommodation to the religious practices of the surrounding peoples. David is constantly held up as the standard of what a king should be, and although the kingdom of Judah had occasional rulers who led them away from the Hebrew God, there was a constant return to the faith of the patriarchs.[49]

When Mandelstam refers to himself as an honorary Judean, then, he associates himself with Judah, the loyal remnant of David's kingdom, and places himself into an ancient historical pattern that continues into the present. The Old Testament struggle between an apostate majority and a loyal remnant finds a clear parallel in the story of the archpriest Avvakum's refusal to submit to a religious betrayal from within, and Mandelstam brings the story into the post-Revolutionary age with his casting of the literary elite as false priests and himself as an outcast true believer, a lone priest of the poetic word. Just as the kingdom of Judah remained the symbol of faithfulness while the other tribes betrayed their faith, so Mandelstam depicts himself as a faithful holdout for true faith (genuine literature) against the majority that has lapsed into the apostasy of state control (permitted literature). Where *The Noise of Time* showed Mandelstam trying to escape from his Jewish roots entirely and gain entry into an "alien" culture, "Fourth Prose" shows a very different perspective: Here assimilation signifies betrayal, and Mandelstam needs a model that will both demonstrate integrity and provide the moral basis for defiance.

Mandelstam's reference to sheep strengthens the link to Judah, and also reinforces Mandelstam's identity as a chosen one. King David is the Old Testament's best-known shepherd and comes immediately to mind when we start to look for the roots of Mandelstam's claim of the shepherd's mantle. But Mandelstam's recurring references to goats indicate that sheep are important for another reason as well, and the combination clearly refers to the gospel binary of "sheep" versus "goats" that Mandelstam has deployed previously. In "The Word and Culture" Mandelstam makes his most explicit comment on this pattern of opposition when he says that people are "either friends or enemies of the word. Literally, sheep and goats."[50] Mandelstam is clearly one of the elect, since he is tied to sheep (the chosen) rather than goats (the rejected). Throughout "Fourth Prose" we see this opposition extended with repeated references to goats; invariably, they are associated with the dark side of the literary world.

The moral courage gained from recognition that he is part of an honorable tradition, that he is one of the few remaining loyalists, becomes one of Mandelstam's main weapons against the dominant majority. Certainly he cannot triumph physically, for the traitorous "accommodating" Jews have allied themselves with the broader antipoetic tribe of gypsy writerdom and together they persecute the loyal Jew. The most grisly sign of inhumanity in this writers' tribe is not its willingness to prostitute itself by following orders that keep subjects meek and pliable for their superiors. Terrible as that may be, it is writerdom's willingness to "help judges execute reprisals against doomed men" that Mandelstam describes with most abhorrence, and with the intensity of one who has himself suffered from these reprisals.

The text of "Fourth Prose" describes these reprisals as an escalating pattern of violence against Mandelstam, with the first ritual reprisal coming in the form of an attempted "literary circumcision" carried out at the initiative of the elders of the writers' tribe. "In a certain year of my life," writes Mandelstam, "grown men from that tribe which I despise with all the strength of my soul, and to which I neither wish to belong nor ever shall, conceived the intention of jointly performing on me an ugly and repellent ritual. The name of this ritual is literary circumcision or dishonoring."[51] The word that I translate here as "circumcision" has more frequently been rendered as "pruning" or something equally metaphorical, but I would argue that Mandelstam uses "circumcision" here quite deliberately. The links between this passage and the next step in the increasingly violent aggression make the reasons for my conclusion clear. This second reprisal is even more horrifying, for Mandelstam describes it as a deliberate castration attempt, again carried out by the tribal priests: "grown men with beards and wearing horned fur caps brandished a flint knife over me, with which they meant to castrate me. Judging by the evidence, they were priests of their tribe: they smelled of onion, novels, and goat meat."[52]

The links between these two events have received no attention, but I consider them to be a central part of the work's complex Jewish treatment. First, they show the increasing levels of violence that the literary "false priests" or elders are willing to adopt. If they cannot coerce the "honorary Judean" into the tribe of false Jews by forcing him to undergo the initiatory rite of circumcision, they will do something more extreme. The act of castration will simultaneously subjugate and sterilize this rebellious poet, eliminating any chance that his thirst for individual creativity will be passed on to a new generation. And both acts, of course, are a perversion of the Jewish rite of circumcision. Circumcision was intended to serve as commemoration of the covenant between God and his people. Forced circumcision becomes a tool of subjugation, of forcing someone into the tribe against his will. Castration is simply the next and most extreme step. Within this broader thematic structure, it becomes clear that Mandelstam's first reference must be seen as a clear indication of circumcision, but in a corrupted form that is deformed even further by the literary leadership's desperate attempt at castration.

The fundamental rottenness of the writers' tribe is vividly conveyed through its description as a group of prostitutes living in the "yellow" districts, named after the yellow tickets given to registered prostitutes in tsarist Russia. It is no coincidence that Mandelstam is careful to note that the writers have their headquarters in the *"yellow* building on Tverskoy Boulevard," or Herzen House. And it is here, right at the source, that Mandelstam initiates the final confrontation between himself and the literary priests.

Again Mandelstam returns to the theme of the "honorary title" that allies him with the tribe of Judah; this, time, however, the line of succession through the tribe of Judah does not stop at David but leads all the way to Jesus. A solitary Jew is betrayed, taken before the council of Jewish priests, and charged with blasphemy: If we substitute literature for religion, it is easy to see the correspondence between Mandelstam's Ulenspiegel ordeal and the Passion story of Jesus. The congruence must have appealed to Mandelstam and perhaps even reassured him, because he would be sure of ultimate triumph if his own narrative were to include the resurrection story that followed Jesus's crucifixion.

Mandelstam's retelling comes complete with his own Judas (Gornfeld) and the clink of the betrayer's silver coins, and the entire episode fits seamlessly into the picture of a spiraling Jewish plot against the Jewish poet/messiah: First these literary priests tried to circumcise him; when that failed they attempted castration; finally, they have appointed a Judas to betray him. But although the scenario clearly leaves Mandelstam wearing Jesus's robe as potential martyr, Mandelstam rewrites the story's ending. Where Jesus accepted the betrayal by Judas and went with his captors to face trial and eventual execution, the poet Mandelstam determines to make a final burst for freedom and casts aside his literary fur coat to run into a brutally cold winter night.

By returning to the motif of the fur coat that started the entire Ulenspiegel scandal, Mandelstam turns this story into an intensely personal one. Most obviously, the reference revisits the wording of Gornfeld's original accusatory letter about Mandelstam, but there is also another and more carefully coded reference here that recalls the concluding pages of Mandelstam's earlier autobiography *The Noise of Time*. There, Mandelstam ends his account by associating the increasingly hungry Soviet state with the deep chill of winter, and he leaves the reader with a grim image of literature as a furry beast threatened by the state as furrier. In "Fourth Prose," literature is no longer a friend, and the "fur coat" of literature is a threat rather than a buffer against the cold of the Soviet winter. Mandelstam no longer wants any part of it. Not content to wait passively, Mandelstam becomes his own furrier, "skinning" himself as he throws off his fur coat. Literature has shifted its allegiance so completely that he can no longer hope—as he did in *The Noise of Time*—to find a haven there. It no longer offers warmth against the increasing wintry chill, and the true poet is better off without its deceptive promise of shelter.[53] Mandelstam recognizes that the consequences may be deadly (he calls it a "fatal chill"), but the attempt must be made. Defiance in the face of external pressure is the only honorable course—anything else would be a betrayal of true poetry.

This new defiance by Mandelstam did not go unnoticed, and Boris Pasternak was quite alarmed when he saw it emerging in Mandelstam's poetry of the 1930s. Where "Fourth Prose" concludes with the conviction that confrontation is inevitable and the poet must not back down, Pasternak's *Safe Conduct* (written at about the same time as "Fourth Prose") has a radically different perspective. For Pasternak, defiance like Mandelstam's can only lead to death in the increasing terror of Stalin's Russia; the poet's only hope of preserving Russian culture is to find some way to live within the system without cooperating actively with the state. In Pasternak's view, the maximalism of Mayakovsky or Mandelstam is a trap from which there is no escape: Once the poet accepts the mantle of the poet-hero, there is nothing ahead but the inevitability of death. For the poet who stands up to the forces that attack individual artistic expression, it will be either physical or artistic death, and both lead to the same eternal silence. For the poet who accepts the mantle of state Poet, it will be a moral death as the essential uniqueness of the poet's voice is overwhelmed by the state's peremptory demands.[54]

In Pasternak's personal poetic economy, then, the willingness to become a poet-hero is the path of least resistance because it absolves the poet of having to deal with moral shades of gray. Defiance of the kind expressed in Mandelstam's "Fourth Prose" is an either/or stance: One capitulates, or one fights. Pasternak's perspective does not trivialize the courage of the moral stand taken by Mandelstam, but rather attempts to find a loophole somewhere, a way to preserve life—and thus continue the struggle to preserve culture. This path is filled with moral quandaries and invites attack both from those who demand more subservience to the state, and from those who demand complete separation.

In "Fourth Prose," Mandelstam discards any notion of this middle ground. Instead, his commitment to resistance and absolute separation compels him to race defiantly into winter's chill—but his position is not quite as hopeless as it might at first appear. Even if he fails to escape, even if he does suffer the same fate as Christ, he clings to the secret conviction that he too will live on in a resurrected noncorporeal form. A secret weapon will eventually rise to justify him, and that weapon is the essential tool of a poet in a hostile world—the voice.

When Mandelstam returns to the theme of the poet's voice in "Fourth Prose" there is a sense that this time the stakes are much higher than they've ever been. He has been fascinated with the process of speech production and with a poet's verbal power since his earliest days as a poet, when his first published poem in the collection *Stone* began with the words "A sound, cautious and muffled. . . ." His fascination with speech continued throughout his early poetry and became an important part of his identity formation in *The Noise of Time*. Mandelstam was never primarily a "paper" poet, but in "Fourth Prose" he abandons paper—and writing—absolutely. Now sound and the production of sound become the ultimate weapons in his poetic arsenal because of their fundamental unpredictability.

Here we find a narrator who embraces his identity as a poet and openly acknowledges the vast forces massed against him since violence is always just below the surface of this text, even when it is not directed actively against the poet. The entire culture has been so permeated by violence that it becomes an automatic response to any offense. The descriptions in the text are chilling: A coachman's young son has offended a more privileged boy and a crowd gathers, helping the young dandy beat the poor boy senseless. A cashier's accounts are slightly out of balance: kill her, comes the response. A peasant hides some grain: kill him, is the solution.

Fighting this culture of violence, alone and armed only with the most unconventional of weapons, is the poet. The poet has only the word, but the word offers a powerfully humane response to counter the brutality of the state. Mandelstam quotes from a poem that he introduces as a kind of talisman, something that can be used to ward off the violence and "dispel evil spirits," as he puts it. This is poetry come alive, poetry with a human face, the word against oppression. It is a line from a poem by Sergei Esenin, who wrote: "[I] didn't shoot the wretches in the dungeons."[55] The contrast between the poet and the state is absolute. The state kills. Poetry pardons. For Mandelstam, the state's grotesque, exaggerated response has tremendous personal significance, since his own "offence" (the Ulenspiegel scandal) has generated a massive and potentially deadly reprisal. By sentencing a writer to the ranks of the unpublishable, the state effects a sentence of slow and bitter death. Mandelstam recognizes this and knows that the scandal threatens his existence as a writer.

Mandelstam's answer is to redefine the entire notion of a poet's identity. First, he creates a new division in the realm of literature: "I divide all the works of world literature into those written with and without permission. The first are trash, the second—stolen air." The presence or absence of permission becomes a litmus test for literature: Writers who receive permission are a disgrace to the title "writer," while anything written without permission becomes—by its very existence—a challenge to the state, for it exists as stolen air. Mandelstam goes on to explain what he means by "stolen air." A publication ban means nothing, Mandelstam asserts, because "I have no manuscripts, no notebooks, no archives. I have no handwriting because I never write. I alone in Russia work from the voice while all around the bitchpack writes. What the hell kind of writer am I!? Get out, you fools!"[56]

There is no clearer articulation of Mandelstam's position anywhere in "Fourth Prose." The mass of writers with their written and published work produce what in the Soviet state is, ipso facto, "permitted" literature. Any work that acknowledges the state's authority to grant permission is easy to control: Manuscripts can be seized, publication can be banned, entire print runs can be destroyed. A work's very appearance in print means that it has passed through the gauntlet of state censorship, and this alone disqualifies it in Mandelstam's eyes. A true writer, he says, will resist any attempt at external control. The voice, on the other hand, is fundamentally unpredictable. To recall Mandelstam's words from an early essay, "the living word . . . freely chooses" its own objective significance; the spoken word is the most independent of all, leaving the poet's lips with a range of potential meanings that even the poet can no longer control as it wafts through the air.[57]

The only way to establish absolute control over this kind of verbal art is through physical removal of the speech organs or complete elimination of the speaker.[58] In Avvakum's *Life* Mandelstam read about tortures that functioned as such ultimate acts of censorship, so he knew that "losing one's voice" could be much more terrible and permanent than when he used that expression in the last pages of *The Noise of Time*. In these new and increasingly alarming days, such reprisals are no longer unthinkable. But the bottom line remains that speech is—must be—unsanctioned. It is an extension of the voice, and since the fate of the *poetic word* is Mandelstam's most pressing concern, only an independent voice can ensure the word's survival. In a state that attempts to control every facility, every social group, every aspect of life, even the air within the state's boundaries comes to be seen as "state air." The poet's voice steals this air and in concert with the voice it becomes a new, free work of unwritten literature. Mandelstam has created another of the oxymorons that he likes so much: a non-writing writer. This poet is a nonconformist par excellence.

The notion of "permitted" versus "independent" literature in "Fourth Prose" bears more than a passing resemblance to Pasternak's discussion in *Safe Conduct* about literature that functions under a system of state "sponsorship."[59] But Pasternak's personal stance on the "sponsorship" of literature is more restrained: He states that the patron will always be deceived because art can never be produced precisely to order. Art comes to life in ways that even its creator cannot always predict, and sometimes subtly, sometimes openly, contradicts the authority that sanctioned it. Mandelstam is much more extreme. There is no discussion of subversion from within, no subtle counterattack. Instead, resistance is overt and all-consuming. The poet becomes a literary guerilla, stealing wherever possible and making no concessions in the attack on an entrenched enemy.

"Fourth Prose" itself becomes an embodiment of Mandelstam's argument that the only true literature is that written without permission. It is filled with verbal games and rapid register switches; it includes passages that seem to have no semantic thrust and exist only for the sound of the words. Those critics who considered Mandelstam's Russian to be substandard or "idiosyncratic" (a term they used in a deliberately pejorative sense) would have been delighted to read "Fourth Prose" and would have considered it a vindication of their criticism.[60] What Mandelstam achieves, though, is a style that puts him in the tradition of Avvakum's earthy, universally accessible Russian. Blatantly and defiantly he calls attention to his status as a writer without permission. The style of "Fourth Prose" counters in every way the "authorized" literary style then gaining currency in Soviet literature, and becomes a physical manifestation of the new literary ideology it proposes.[61]

There is another good reason for Mandelstam's sudden virulent opposition to the notion of writing. Viktor Krivulin notes that the words "writing" and "to write" took on a very menacing new significance in the Soviet context of the late 1920s and 1930s, since "writing" became a synecdoche for political accusations. "Idioms like 'They wrote on him' (the word 'accusation' is left out) started to appear," says Krivulin. "'Writing' became the most important attribute of the coercive and repressive machine. The 'sounding' word remained the last sanctuary of freedom. The Saussurean dichotomy 'langue-parole' took on a politico-ideological tone in Russia on the eve of the Great Terror."[62]

"Fourth Prose" ends with a return to the notion of work as Mandelstam asserts that no matter what superhuman feats of physical strength he might perform, he will never become a worker. His work, he notes, is taken only for mischief or lawlessness, but "it is a question of how you look at it. What I prize in the doughnut is the hole. . . . Real work is Brussels lace, the main thing in it is what holds the pattern up: air, punctures, truancy."[63] What Mandelstam really values is the space that the doughnut cannot fill, the air that reveals the finery of the lace. It is a transparent reference to the "stolen air" of genuine literature, and a sign that his work will never be appreciated because his working instrument is his voice, something impossible to fully circumscribe.

This short autobiography draws to a close with the final words: "And in Armavir on the city coat of arms it is written: the dog barks, the wind carries."[64] The final phrase is a common Russian expression that can refer to the harmful use of words as gossip, or alternatively to a word's impotence to change the course of events. Charles Isenberg leans toward the first context, suggesting that the "dog" referred to here is really the

Writers' Federation and that the phrase functions as a "final denunciation."[65] At the same time this may be Mandelstam's last subversive act in the text: a reminder that when a voice (whether a dog's, or an accuser's, or even a poet's) emerges it takes on a life of its own and the air carries it away in an unknown direction, to an unknown audience, where the word will present itself in an unknown way. It is a final sally to attack the notion that the state can ultimately control the voice and its product, the poetic word.[66]

After rhetorically freeing his voice and expelling his personal demons in "Fourth Prose," Mandelstam found himself once again able to write poetry. One might expect that after the total defiance of "Fourth Prose," the poetry that Mandelstam wrote in the 1930s would be unequivocally directed against the state. What we find, though, are numerous poems where Mandelstam's words are more ambivalent, including the notorious "Stalin Ode" which has often been interpreted as Mandelstam's attempt to seek approval from on high. Anna Akhmatova recalls that Mandelstam once told her that this poem was an "act of sickness," while Alexander Kushner suggests that the all too common "Stalin hypnosis" swept Mandelstam off his feet when he started to work on the ode.[67] Other scholars see a subtext that is less conciliatory. My point here is not to revive this debate but merely to point out that even after the defiance of "Fourth Prose," ambiguity and pressure still had an impact on Mandelstam. He still had to live in a world where survival demanded various degrees of compromise. Gregory Freidin surveys the available evidence and suggests that even at this late stage, Mandelstam still hoped at least to coexist with the revolutionary moment.[68]

The despised literary machine was something else, though. A fear of being absorbed into the world of "official" literature continued to trouble Mandelstam through the early 1930s, when he lived in a state of uneasy tension with the literary community. One telling sign of this tension was Mandelstam's hypersensitive response to Pasternak's well-meaning congratulations when Mandelstam was unexpectedly and incredibly granted an apartment in 1933. Pasternak saw the apartment as a release from domestic anxiety and an opportunity to concentrate more on art. Mandelstam saw it as a temptation. By moving into this apartment, was he giving up the personal autonomy that meant so much to him? Was he losing the moral basis for his opposition? The implication that he was "worthy" of the apartment threatened to undermine the very sense of exclusion that gave force to his cries of protest. It seemed to render him indistinguishable from those privileged members of the writers' tribe who had treated him so brutally only a few years earlier. And just as important, an apartment and a desk are not necessary for a poet who doesn't write, who composes his poetry on the move.[69]

It was this sense of constantly being on the move, of forever dodging, that gave Mandelstam such a strong sense of kinship to poet precursors like Dante Alighieri. How many pairs of shoes did Dante wear out while he wandered the hills and composed his verse, Mandelstam wonders in "Conversation about Dante." Dante never exchanged his personal honor for acceptance and comfort—he remained someone whom the "honorary title of Judean" would fit until the end. The stigma of conformity or a lapse into complacency are the only things that can silence a true poet, and Mandelstam recognizes in Dante a fellow poet who avoided both. Mandelstam's increasing sense of connection to Dante makes itself felt not only in the moving "Conversation about Dante," but also in many poems from his so-called second Voronezh notebook. Mandelstam turns repeatedly to the poet's verbal production, and sees Dante as a poet who continued to sing no matter how hopeless his cause seemed. "Alighieri sang even more powerfully / When his lips were exhausted" Mandelstam wrote in the 1937 poem "I hear, I hear the early ice" (*Slyshu, slyshu, rannii led*).[70] Even the recognition that he, the twentieth-century Russian poet Mandelstam, is able to read Dante and still appreciate the Italian poet's verbal power becomes a reassurance that genuine poetry survives every attempt to destroy it. The poet's body may cease to exist, but the voice continues.

By 1937 Mandelstam recognized with increasing clarity that his days were likely numbered. Although his first cycle of arrest and exile was officially over, Mandelstam knew that his status was tenuous at best, and with the nationwide clutches of Stalin's Great Terror reaching further and further, a combination of factors induced him to write several poems which suggest that not even he was immune to "Stalin fever." But he also wrote other poems which some argue carry within themselves the semantic subversion of the more conciliatory verse, making any attempt to use these poems to define Mandelstam's deepest orientation a very complex endeavor. Through it all, Mandelstam recognized that his previous case could be reopened at any time and a suitable pretext found for another arrest. A year later, in May 1938, the order finally came, and by the end of the year Mandelstam had perished in Siberia.

In the movingly titled 1937 poem "I sing while my larynx is moist and my soul is dry" (*Poiu, kogda gortan' syra, dusha sukha*), Mandelstam acknowledges his own mortality while simultaneously asserting the essential immortality of his art: "Already it is not I who sing, my breath is singing." He continues by refocusing attention completely from the poet to the poet's song, underlining his deepest hope for posterity: "An unselfish song is its own praise: / A comfort for friends and rebuke to enemies."[71]

This defiant side of Mandelstam, the side released by "Fourth Prose," remains present and still dominant despite the temptation to lower his guard in a personal reconciliation with reality. In some poems his rebellion is quite open, as in the fateful "We live without sensing the land underfoot" which eventually led to Mandelstam's death. In others, his nonconformity takes a curious and even perverse form, as Clare Cavanagh notes: Now that the world has become decidedly non-bourgeois, it becomes rebellious to take up the "bourgeois" cause of world culture, and Mandelstam does so in a variety of poems.[72] The old marks of complacency become the new signs of agitation, and one might paraphrase Tsvetaeva's formula from *The Poem of the End* to say that "In this most socialist of worlds, Poets are the bourgeois."

Ultimately, Mandelstam paid with his life for the stance that he articulated so eloquently and forcefully in "Fourth Prose," and which he continued to express regularly in the poetry of the 1930s. His early attempts, described in *The Noise of Time*, to find an identity by moving away from his Jewish heritage and into Russian (even world) culture had to be reconsidered in light of the drastic changes in Soviet Russia. The new voice of defiance acquired in "Fourth Prose" was his personal artistic liberation, but also his death sentence. It is a tribute to the poet's courage that he could make this decision by "signing with both hands" even though he knew what the stakes were. Poetry, for Mandelstam, needed a defender and he was not one to count personal safety or immediate risk when it came to a defense of poetry. Where Pasternak might look for larger, strategic patterns in the war for Russian culture, Mandelstam saw an immediate battle that had to be fought despite the odds against him. He faced the challenge with the moral conviction that he was one of a small remnant of "honorary Judeans" called to defend poetry's sacred cause.

In the end, it is some consolation to realize that Mandelstam's voice ultimately did triumph, that it was resurrected as he had hoped. The prophecy from his 1935 poem "Yes, I lie in the ground" (*Da, ia lezhu v zemle, gubami shevelia*) did eventually start to come true: "Yes, I lie in the ground, with my lips moving / But what I will say, every schoolboy will learn by heart."[73] "Fourth Prose" marks a critical stage in the defense of poetry not so much for its own immediate impact—it started to circulate only years after it was written—but for the new poetic insight and inspiration that it gave to Mandelstam. It became a personal declaration of independence that led him to take up the role of "poet guerrilla" in a struggle with the literary establishment, and it proved to be the moral catalyst for some of his most moving lines in the 1935 poem "Having deprived me of seas" (*Lishiv menia morei*):

> Having deprived me of seas, of land and air escapes
> And having given only violent earth for the foot's support,
> What have you achieved? A brilliant result:
> Moving lips you could not take away.[74]

5

The Poet's Birthright

If anyone could match the intensity of Mandelstam's "Fourth Prose" it was Marina Tsvetaeva. When she turned her attention to autobiographical prose in the 1930s, Tsvetaeva approached it with the energy and passion of her best poetry. The result was a prose so essential, so much a renunciation of all superfluity, that no less a critic than Joseph Brodsky said that Tsvetaeva achieved a sharpness of focus greater "than anyone in Russian and, it would seem, world literature."[1] Like Mandelstam and Pasternak, Tsvetaeva used her autobiographical writing to consider what it meant to be a poet in an age when poetry had gone dangerously out of fashion. Tsvetaeva's circumstances were rather different, however. As an émigré, Tsvetaeva was separated physically from the literary convulsions that threatened poetry in the Soviet Union, and in the late 1920s Tsvetaeva was able to publish poetry that solidified her reputation within the Russian exile communities in Berlin, Prague, Paris and beyond.

But that is only part of the story. Like Pasternak and Mandelstam, Tsvetaeva found that politics and life have a way of breaking into a poet's world and forcing change. By the early 1930s, she was caught up in a complex blend of government and literary politics that made it increasingly difficult for her to publish her poems. The exile community in Paris included representatives from many of the political and literary movements that had jostled for space before the Revolution and their displacement in a shared exile did not miraculously resolve their differences. Tsvetaeva understood this complexity fully but had little patience for it. She never tried to ally herself with any movement, either literary or political. Instead, she considered it her responsibility to seek justice and to express compassion for the weak and falsely accused, regardless of their political affiliations.

Tsvetaeva's sometimes blatant disregard for the political implications of what she said and wrote caused consternation and even resentment within the exile community, whose members were both divided and defined by political allegiance. She was impossible to categorize politically, and this ambiguity—together with the kind of poetry she wrote—helped keep her an outsider in the émigré community. Her poetry was considered too "difficult" for easy consumption, especially by the many journal editors for whom literature was only a secondary interest. As a result, Tsvetaeva felt herself increasingly cut off in a dual exile, isolated from her homeland and ignored by most of the substantial Russian émigré population.

Prose became a form of survival for Tsvetaeva, something that she could still publish as a way to earn money and to make her family's desperate financial situation at least temporarily tolerable. "The emigration is making a prose writer of me," she wrote to her friend Anna Tesková in November, 1933. "Of course, the prose is also *mine*, and the best in the world after poetry. It is lyrical prose, but still—*after* poetry. . . . Those are my literary affairs. When I receive the Nobel Prize (*never*)—I will write poetry. The same as others taking an around the world cruise."[2]

Certainly this was not what Tsvetaeva had anticipated when she left the Soviet Union in 1922. As the wife of White Army volunteer Sergei Efron, her future in the new Soviet state would have been tenuous at best and when she finally got news that her husband was alive in Europe, Tsvetaeva started looking for ways to join him with their surviving daughter. Her last poems before leaving the USSR show that the decision to seek a new life in Europe was far from painless. Moscow, even in its post-Revolutionary upheaval, was still her home and she felt an overwhelming sadness for all the blood that had been shed. And although Tsvetaeva identified with her husband's side in the conflict, Viktoria Schweitzer is quite right to conclude that Tsvetaeva pitied all the fallen, not just the Whites, and that her departure from Moscow was not marked by a farewell condemnation but by an expression of forgiveness.[3]

Starting over in Europe was difficult. Tsvetaeva was finally reunited with her husband in Berlin, where her eventful six-week stay included a poetry reading just three days after arriving. From Berlin, Tsvetaeva and her daughter Alya moved on to settle in Prague with Efron, who was attending school there. Life in Czechoslovakia was not easy for the family. Efron's studies took him away from home frequently, living conditions were difficult, and the relationship between Tsvetaeva and her husband was strained almost beyond repair when Tsvetaeva entered into a lengthy affair with another man.[4]

Looking back, however, this was probably the most "literary" life that Tsvetaeva ever had. Despite all the difficulties, she had numerous outlets for her poetry, she began to take on the role of critic for some of the local publications, and she produced a torrent of new poems, including some of her very best. It was, as Schweitzer puts it, the only time that she had the chance to live "inside literature."[5] Knowledgeable editors listened to her opinions, took her seriously, and published her poetry even if she did not share their political orientation.

But the grind of daily life grew increasingly harsh, especially when their son Georgy (or Mur, as Tsvetaeva always called him) was born in 1925. By then the center of gravity for Russia's émigré literary community had shifted to Paris, and Efron and Tsvetaeva started to think about moving there. By November, Tsvetaeva and the children had set off on an exploratory trip to France. It was the last time she ever saw Prague.

The most immediate reasons for Tsvetaeva to go to Paris were to give a public poetry reading and to make publication arrangements for a book. Her reading was a tremendous success, and she was invited to travel to London for a similar reading there. She also started to get involved in some of the new journals being established in Paris, publishing both poetry and prose. It was one of these early prose works, an essay called "The Poet on the Critic" (*Poet o kritike*), that set the tone for many of Tsvetaeva's literary encounters during her years in Paris.

Published in January 1926, less than three months after her arrival, the essay's scathing attack on the state of contemporary literary criticism elicited a storm of indignation. Tsvetaeva didn't hesitate to scold even the most popular of the Russian émigré critics, but a careful look at her text shows that her aggressive tone was not prompted by a desire to settle any personal scores. Instead, Tsvetaeva's battle instincts flared up when she sensed that poetry was being used as a pawn in some larger game and not being taken seriously on its own terms. These critics don't actually care about poetry for its own sake, she argues, but pay most attention to a poet's political allegiances. That kind of criticism demeans both poetry and poet.

The article also contains Tsvetaeva's passionate defense of genuine poets in the face of a threat from poet-dilettantes, and her vigor immediately calls to mind the remarkably similar outrage in some of the articles that Osip Mandelstam was writing at about the same time. Like Mandelstam, Tsvetaeva describes the process of poetic creation as internal and largely aural. Something "sounds in me," she writes, an inner essence that sometimes points the general direction, and sometimes commands absolutely with "an aural path to the poem: I hear a tune, I don't hear the words. I seek the words." These words are not part of some programmatic function, but rather part of the unified internal compulsion that inexplicably drives a genuine poet. "Why do I write? I write because I can't not write," says Tsvetaeva, using one of her frequent rhetorical questions to make her answer even more powerful. "The work, while it is being written, is its own purpose." Then, in a mood like the indignation voiced by Mandelstam in his "Army of Poets" (*Armiia poetov*), Tsvetaeva goes on to deny that poetry can be taught as a trade. "Poetic schools (a sign of the age!) are a vulgarisation of poetry," she says, and lead to a mind-set that treats art as a kitchen, a place where the right recipe will produce reliably good art. If critics think that their writing about poetry can have this kind of didactic function, they are sorely misguided, she concludes: "There is only one teacher: your own labour. And only one judge: the future."[6]

Tsvetaeva's rhetoric was offensive on many levels. Not only did she identify leading figures of the émigré literary community by name and then take them to task for poor judgment or lack of artistic insight, but she wrote in an altogether too personal style, something that offended the sensibilities of many readers. And then there was her insistence that poetry should remain disconnected from politics, that it has a human core, an individual essence incompatible with any sort of program. In a literary community where political identity formed the distinguishing characteristic of many leading journals, this deliberate denial of a political function for poetry could only alienate her from the very editors who would soon be asked to publish her poetry.

The vehemence of the response to her article caught Tsvetaeva slightly off guard, but in one sense it only reinforced what she had said in her article. The wave of indignation provided a living confirmation of the article's depiction of the "lofty poet" surrounded by small-minded critics, notes Lily Feiler.[7] Claiming that no one defended her and that she was completely alone, Tsvetaeva wrote to her confidante Anna Tesková: "I am totally content."[8]

Examined more closely, this claim of contentment seems more an article of faith at the deepest level of self-identity than a real description of Tsvetaeva's emotional state. An increasing alienation characterizes much of Tsvetaeva's correspondence in the late 1920s and early 1930s. Time after time she writes about feeling cut off from any meaningful social and intellectual engagement, tied to her increasingly cheap and inconvenient string of Paris-area lodgings by the drudgery of daily life and a chronic shortage of money. Housework constantly demands her attention because she is trying to support the family virtually on her own, it seems.[9] Daily life left her too exhausted to listen to her muse, too excluded from literary life to have a sense of belonging.

But exclusion is only part of the story. Certainly the accounts of desperate poverty ring true, and memoir accounts by acquaintances confirm the numbing demands that wore Tsvetaeva down: the endless laundry, shopping, cooking, washing up, hauling firewood and coal. Tsvetaeva's description of desperate social isolation, though, is less readily confirmed by her contemporaries. Elena Izvolskaya, who lived near Tsvetaeva in 1930, calls her a well-liked member of the émigré community, someone who constantly had people sitting in her kitchen as guests.[10] Tsvetaeva's own correspondence is at times contradictory. On vacation in 1935, she writes to Tesková that she and Mur are social outcasts: "The Russians are boycotting us." Only two months later, though, she sums up the summer's events quite differently, describing a series of "pleasant acquaintances" and one "genuine friendship" that were formed during the summer months.[11]

I mention the different accounts and memories here only because I believe that they are integrally connected to Tsvetaeva's conviction of what it means to be a genuine poet. Reading Tsvetaeva's letters, her articles, her poetry, there is no avoiding her insistence that a genuine poet is always marked for isolation. In a 1932 letter to Tesková she writes:

> You get the sense that ... there's no place for you. ... But maybe this is all because I don't want to be *liked* by anyone and (because of that)—am not liked, maybe it's *because of me*. ... And I'm separated from the Russians—by my poetry, which no one understands, by my way of thinking, which some take as Bolshevism and others take as monarchism, and still others—as monarchism or anarchism. ... .[12]

In the 1932 essay "Epic and Lyric of Contemporary Russia" (*Epos i lirika sovremennoi Rossii*), Tsvetaeva describes the poet's "lonely path" as an essential part of what it means to be a genuine poet. In "The Poet and Time" (*Poet i vremia*), also written in 1932, she is even more explicit, writing that "Every poet is essentially an émigré, even in Russia. Émigré from the Kingdom of Heaven and from the earthly paradise of nature. Upon the poet—upon all who belong to art, but most especially upon the poet—there's a particular mark of discomfort, by which you'll know him even in his own home."[13]

Tsvetaeva never had the luxury of living in relative comfort as an adult, so we will never know how that "mark of discomfort" might have shown itself if her material circumstances had granted her ease, not destitution. But her sense of a poet's lot in life included the conviction that a poet was inevitably separated from the crowd of non-poets. Given her own unshakeable conviction that she *was* a poet, it was quite consistent for Tsvetaeva to emphasize her isolation from others even when the people around her perceived the situation quite differently. What mattered to Tsvetaeva was not just social contacts and pleasant conversations with acquaintances, but something much more intense. Her craving for all-consuming relationships, relationships characterized by passion and powerful attraction, prompted her husband Sergei Efron to remark in a letter that "she is like a huge stove that needs wood, wood and more wood to function."[14] When the relationship was exhausted and Tsvetaeva moved on, she inevitably felt anew the sensation of being alone, and it was while sensing loss so powerfully that she created some of her best poetry. As a result, the linkage between "aloneness" and "being a poet" was reinforced.

If we return, then, to Tsvetaeva's assertion that she was completely alone and therefore "totally content," it becomes clear that the linkage between "aloneness" and "contentment" is inextricably linked to Tsvetaeva's sense of identity as a poet. This is a contentment that defies mere material and social circumstances because it is tied to a deeper allegiance, a loyalty to poetry itself. Here we can easily see the similarity between Tsvetaeva's and Mandelstam's views on the essence of being a poet for there is an essential compatibility between the two.

For Mandelstam, though, the embrace of aloneness, of outsider status, was a profoundly and deeply political stance by the time he composed "Fourth Prose," since it placed him defiantly outside the reach of the incestuous literary-political alliances that had come to dominate Soviet literature. Tsvetaeva's sense of aloneness was built on a different foundation, and can be seen as political only in a more oblique way, in the way that a deliberate nonalignment can be construed as a political stance. It was this sense of nonalignment that led to many of her conflicts with the émigré community in Paris, but her unwillingness to conform politically was evident even before she left Moscow. One dazzling example of her refusal to mouth the expected platitudes came at a poetry reading for an audience comprised largely of Bolsheviks. Confounding expectations, Tsvetaeva included a tribute to White soldiers in her reading. The result was unexpectedly positive as the power of the poet's voice and rhythms transcended even the words of the poems themselves. After the reading a young Communist approached her and said, "None of this matters. You're a revolutionary poet all the same. You've got our tempo." In describing this encounter from the vantage point of her new status as an unwelcome Russian poet in Paris, Tsvetaeva concludes: "In Russia they forgave me everything because I was a poet; here, they forgive me for *being* a poet."[15] Michael Wachtel's investigation of the relationship between poetic form and content helps to explain the encounter that Tsvetaeva described, for as he puts it, "the non-semantic elements of language are what prove to be most persistent."[16] Tsvetaeva's unorthodox syntax and rhythms seemed an organic fit for the turbulence of the post-Revolutionary age, at least in the ears of listeners like the young Bolshevik who heard her poetry in Moscow.

At a more essential level, though, Tsvetaeva already knew that political developments in the Soviet Union made it unlikely that a poet could survive as an artist within the Party's good graces. When she was only thirteen, Tsvetaeva had asked an old revolutionary: "Is it possible to be a poet and also be in the Party?" and was told, without any reflection, "No." Years later she remembered this exchange while considering the tragic fate of Vladimir Mayakovsky and she had to agree with the old revolutionary's assessment. Just as Lenin and his colleagues assumed that the poet Alexander Blok could not really be on their side, this unnamed man recognized that the genuine Russian poet demands the right to resist and rebel, and this demand can never be granted within the Party's system. Yes, Tsvetaeva reflects, the Party was founded on the principle of rebellion, but it demands a conformity-in-rebellion that a poet cannot accept. Eventually the poet's need to find his or her individual voice will triumph, and the poet will veer away from the Party line. This near certainty of individual revolt is too threatening for the Party to contemplate, and a real poet will never last long within its ranks.[17]

What Tsvetaeva discovered in Paris, though, is that this fierce and unpredictable loyalty to one's individual sense of right and wrong is disconcerting almost everywhere. In the 1929 narrative poem "Perekop" (*Perekop*) Tsvetaeva provides a sympathetic account of the White Army's last stand at the town of Perekop in the Crimea, but it was rather poorly received by her audience in Europe. In the 1932 essay "The Poet and Time" Tsvetaeva analyzes the unenthusiastic response to "Perekop" and concludes that the poem really fits young Soviet listeners better than the White Russian audience of the emigration: Soviet youth would understand its underlying passion, even if the subject was politically wrong. "If only no politicians stood between poet and people!" she writes.[18]

Tsvetaeva had the deep conviction that for Russian poets, and especially for her, the times—and also places—were deeply out of joint. "There [in the Soviet Union] I wouldn't be published, but I would be read," she wrote. "Here I'm published—and not read." The emigration was concerned with looking backward to its artistic roots in some far-removed past, Tsvetaeva said, and the senior members of the emigration's literary elite still related to figures like the seventy-year-old poet Konstantin Balmont as a twenty-year-old youth, either struggling against him or "forgiving" him the way one might an errant grandson. But dwarfing everything else was Tsvetaeva's sense that émigré life was built around an artificial base from which it was impossible to escape. In Paris she found hermetic literary groups, small halls and listeners self-satisfied with a sense of their own significance. The scale was just not right, Tsvetaeva felt, and she longed for the arenas, multitudes and anonymous but eager listeners of Russia. The smallness, even pettiness, was a constriction that made her long for Russia's vastness: "In Russia, as in the steppes and on the sea, there is a place to speak from and into. If they'd let people speak."[19]

These words offer one of Tsvetaeva's most succinct summaries of the frustration she felt as a poet in Paris. Those around her kept trying to pin her down and identify her, with some claiming that she was a Bolshevik and others accusing her of being a monarchist. As Simon Karlinsky puts it, Tsvetaeva "confused and irritated the moderate and liberal Russians in Paris. She was somehow too far left and too far right at the same time."[20] But they were all missing the point, Tsvetaeva said. A poet transcends politics, and it is a mistake to measure a poet against a political yardstick. A poet who gets directly entangled in partisan politics risks the loss of artistic credibility, something that Tsvetaeva saw demonstrated most vividly in the person of Vladimir Mayakovsky. Like Pasternak, Tsvetaeva considered Mayakovsky's party loyalty a detriment to his status as a poet. Yet she never stopped respecting him as a great poet, even after he had denounced her in the Soviet press. When Mayakovsky held a poetry reading in Paris, Tsvetaeva gave an appreciative account of the event in her husband's journal *Eurasia* (*Evraziia*) and went so far as to conclude that real strength lay "over there"—a conclusion that brought a swift and harsh response from her scandalized fellow émigrés.[21] Her remark had been an assessment of poetic vitality (and shows just how little she really knew about the rapidly declining conditions for poets in the Soviet Union), but her readers mistakenly assumed that her words had a political slant. Not long after this uproar, Mayakovsky's death in 1930 proved the catalyst for another scandal in Paris, with one group of émigrés mourning the loss of a great artist and another group seizing the opportunity to criticize Mayakovsky as both a poet and a political figure. Tsvetaeva's allegiance was obviously with those who mourned the artist, and the commotion even prompted a powerful cycle of poems dedicated to Mayakovsky's memory. The intensity of the dispute, however, reinforced Tsvetaeva's sense that a poet must stand alone.

When she decided to turn her attention to autobiographical prose in the 1930s, then, Tsvetaeva was writing within cultural, political and literary contexts in which she clung to her identity as a poet—and associated this identity with an essential independence, of being set apart from the crowd around her. This consciousness pervades her autobiography, where poetry and the figure of the poet are the central features of the text. This is also true of Mandelstam's "Fourth Prose" and Pasternak's *Safe Conduct*, of course, but there are significant differences in Tsvetaeva's prose. Her self-depiction features nothing like Pasternak's narration of a search for identity that eventually led to the realization that he was a poet, and Tsvetaeva is much more direct in her assertions than Mandelstam was in his nuanced depiction of a poet's childhood in *The Noise of Time*. Instead, Tsvetaeva describes herself as knowing from childhood that she was a poet, and her account is the story of one who clings to this identity despite all the efforts to tear it from her.

As in Mandelstam's "Fourth Prose," a conflict is frequently the center of Tsvetaeva's autobiographical writing. But while Mandelstam describes a struggle against powerful literary forces that want to silence him, Tsvetaeva's battle is fought against someone much closer to home. Indeed, it would be more accurate to describe Tsvetaeva's struggle as a battle fought *at home*, since the most powerful force of opposition that Tsvetaeva encounters, the one opponent against whom she has to test her resolve from birth itself, is her mother. The intensity of this opposition—at least as it is remembered by Tsvetaeva when she turns to her autobiography in the 1930s—is powerfully introduced in the opening words of Tsvetaeva's "Mother and Music" (Mat' i muzyka), where she writes: "When, instead of the longed-for, predetermined, almost preordained son Alexander, all that was born was just me, Mother, proudly choking back a sigh, said: 'At least she'll be a musician.'"[22]

These words set the stage for Tsvetaeva's entire relationship with her mother, and they also define the autobiography's central conflict. Just as her mother resolves to turn her into a musician, Tsvetaeva resolves not to succumb to her mother's relentless pressure. Instead, the pages of the autobiography reveal that contrary to her mother's expectations and efforts, Tsvetaeva has been born—or chosen, as she wrote later—to be a poet. The relationship between mother and daughter has frequently been given a central place in autobiographies by Russian women; as Barbara Heldt puts it, many of them consider that "understanding one's mother is . . . the preface to self-understanding."[23] This concern is not unique to Russian women, of course, and Bella Brodzki notes that for many western women the compelling need to enter into discourse with one's mother is often the "pre-text for the autobiographical project" itself.[24] Because Tsvetaeva emphasizes her mother and her mother's family, the text becomes a world populated primarily by women and its narrative style departs dramatically from the masculine narrative mode, note scholars like Natasha Kolchevska, Stephanie Sandler and Beth Holmgren. Tsvetaeva focuses on her female rather than her male progenitors and describes her mother as "the troubling, demanding source of her genius," writes Holmgren.[25]

Readers hoping to find a triumphantly woman-centered text will be disappointed, though. Tsvetaeva had no explicitly feminist agenda and was irritated by those who seemed to expect one from her. In one widely cited expression of exasperation, Tsvetaeva writes: "Ever since my birth I have had an aversion to all that is marked by some kind of female (mass) separateness, somehow: women's courses, suffragettism, feminism, the completely notorious woman question. . . . There is no woman's question in creativity: there are women's answers to human questions." The same convictions inform Tsvetaeva's autobiography but emerge much less vehemently. In one particularly poignant passage she writes almost wistfully of her longing for an androgynous world, a place where simple but absolute descriptors like "she" and "he" would be completely irrelevant: "How much a human being loses with the acquisition of a sex . . . !"[26]

For Tsvetaeva this "loss" started at birth, when her mother had to bite back disappointment at not having borne a son. From that point on, the relationship between the two carries the strain of two determined people, one pushing and the other resisting. So while Holmgren is quite right to point out that Tsvetaeva acknowledges her mother's gift of lyricism as a fundamental element of her poetic nature, the passage in question does not stop with Tsvetaeva's recognition of her mother's significance in motivating her to become a poet. Instead, she concludes by explaining *why* she felt as she did, and we find that the recognition is based not on acceptance, but on fierce rejection: "After a mother like that I had only one alternative: to become a poet. To expurgate her gift to me, a gift that would have suffocated me or turned me into a transgressor of all human laws."[27] This is a gift that could only be realized by resisting the crushing force of obligation that was intended to accompany the gift, and it was in the act of resistance that Tsvetaeva found a creative locus within which her gift for poetry could flourish. Her resistance is much more localized than the almost universal resistance proclaimed by Osip Mandelstam, but its effect is just as important for her as a fledgling poet: The poet gains strength by walking a solitary path, and by fighting the external pressures that seek to mold or influence.

It is this insistence on the centrality of poetry that forms the crucial core of Tsvetaeva's autobiography, rather than an attempt to fight against a patriarchal order by filling her pages with female figures who proved influential. Despite the overwhelming number of females in the world described by Tsvetaeva, following the path of gender criticism too closely would obscure some of the critical encounters with men that influenced her. One of the most important of these was an event that she remembers in "The House at Old Pimen," when she describes how her "step-uncle" (the half-brother of her father's first wife), Sergei Ilovaisky was the first one to encourage her poetry writing: "[He], I think, was the one person during my whole childhood and adolescence, who didn't laugh at my poems (mother—got angry), who didn't use them, like the red cloth and the bull, to lead me into the temptation of rage . . . accept my gratitude for that big-headed, short-haired, plain little girl that nobody liked, from whose hands you so carefully took the notebook. With that gesture—you gave her to me."[28] I mention this episode not to suggest that we should look for unacknowledged indications of a male-dominated frame of reference in Tsvetaeva's autobiography, but rather because it reminds us that at the heart of Tsvetaeva's thinking, even more central than her thoughts on gender, was poetry. Tsvetaeva's understanding of poetry and her identity as a poet were the foundation stones on which she built her sense of self, and her comments on poetry sometimes reveal an almost startling reverence: "The realm of the poet is the soul. The *entire* soul. Above the soul is the spirit, not needing poets, but if it needs anything, it needs prophets. Prophecy in a poet is like an accompaniment [*soprisutstvie*], not like essence, as poetry is in a prophet. 'Which great poets are prophets [?]'—to speak like that is to cheapen the prophet. 'What great prophets—they are poets!': to speak like that is to exalt the poet."[29]

The following pages, which look at the way Tsvetaeva carefully structures her autobiography as the account of a young poet's progress, will show how the narrative's constant return to her struggle with her mother functions as a surrogate for the more current struggles that she faced to maintain her identity as a Russian poet in Paris. First, a few words about the nature of Tsvetaeva's autobiography project are in order. Unlike Pasternak's *Safe Conduct* and Mandelstam's *The Noise of Time*, Tsvetaeva's autobiography was never published as a completed work. Instead, she published prose segments in various journals, sometimes with severe cuts by journal editors. As a result, scholars continue to debate which of these prose pieces should be considered central elements of Tsvetaeva's autobiography, and there is no easy way to resolve the question. It is tempting to establish a hierarchy within the various pieces of Tsvetaeva's autobiography, especially if that hierarchy tends to support a particular interpretive vector. My own discussion here will focus primarily on three of the "long chapters" that typically receive most scholarly attention: "Mother and Music," "The Devil" (*Chert*), and "My Pushkin" (*Moi Pushkin*). I will mention the fourth extended chapter, "The House at Old Pimen" (*Dom u Starogo Pimena*), and the shorter segments only briefly, but only because they do not concentrate attention as directly on Tsvetaeva's calling as a poet.[30]

Tsvetaeva took her autobiography project very seriously in the mid-1930s, partly as a pragmatic realization that prose was easier for her to publish than poetry—an important consideration given the family's poverty at the time. However, another important element in her concentration on this project was a sense that it was time to establish a lasting self-portrait that differed in several important ways from the portrait that emerged in her lyric poetry. In her correspondence, Tsvetaeva described her autobiographical writing as a kind of family chronicle, and questioned family acquaintances closely to learn what they remembered about her relatives and her family's dwellings. Clearly, she wanted to present a fact-based account of her childhood that would include verifiable information about her past and she saw this project as quite different from the poems where she recounted similar experiences.

One indication of how she approached prose and poetry differently can be found in the self-disclosures that Tsvetaeva makes in each literary mode. She took it as self-evident that reality must be transformed through poetry (what we might crassly call "lying"), and wrote: "And how can I / Not lie,—when my voice is more tender,— / When I lie . . ." As Jane Taubman observes, this kind of confession does a lot to explain Tsvetaeva's attraction to personal mythmaking, but "[w]hile this was essential for her poetry, it often had a disastrous effect on the human relationships which were its most frequent subject. Tsvetaeva acted as if *her* reality were the operative one."[31]

When it came to prose, Tsvetaeva's initial approach suggests that she truly wanted a firm historical base for her autobiography. But her search for facts about the past proved troublesome because she started to realize how much her own memories diverged from the memories of others. In a letter to Vera Bunina in which she requests help piecing together her family's history, Tsvetaeva admits that she can't remember events and details completely accurately, since "I saw only—my own." But after she started to receive information from Bunina and saw how much her own memory conflicted with Bunina's "facts," Tsvetaeva appears to have opted to follow her own memory, imperfect though it may be: "I will write as I remember," she decides.[32]

But that is not quite the end of the story. In the text of her autobiography Tsvetaeva returns again to an emphasis on "facts," providing what was almost certainly an unintended echo of the "literature of fact" that had helped to push poetry aside in the Soviet Union only a few years earlier. Tsvetaeva's claim to authenticity is more properly a link to the disclaimers that had once been a commonplace in autobiographies, but which had disappeared almost entirely in the twentieth century. "I will not tell anything that didn't happen," she writes, "for the whole aim and value of these notes is in their identity with what really was, in the identity of that, I admit, strange but *factual* child with her own self."[33] A statement like this shows a rather different orientation than we find in Pasternak and Mandelstam, who cared little even for the appearance of complete verisimilitude. Instead, Tsvetaeva's claim brings her closer to much earlier poet-autobiographers like Gavrila Derzhavin and Afanasy Fet, who asserted their objectivity so frequently that the repetition seems irresistibly to invite further scrutiny. The same skepticism could be prompted by Tsvetaeva's claim, and when her sister Anastasia depicts a rather different childhood than that found in Tsvetaeva's writing, the discrepancies are disconcerting if one hopes to see a "reliable" biography in Tsvetaeva's text. But if we return to Lydia Ginzburg's formulation about the relationship between autobiography and authenticity, we realize that Tsvetaeva does indeed describe the facts of her childhood (specific events that provide the "authenticity" of the orientation), yet structures and presents them according to aesthetic or other criteria.

For the purpose of this study the *presentation* of these childhood "facts" is most interesting, for in the arrangement and interpretation of her childhood memories Tsvetaeva, showing just how vital poetry is to her entire concept of self-identity, traces events that she feels were formative in shaping her growth as a poet. In the process she helps to extend a personal self-construction that had already taken shape through the powerful mythmaking of her poetry and other prose. While other scholars have looked at how Tsvetaeva created a personal mythology in her poetry and interpersonal relations, much less has been done on the area which will receive my attention here, namely the way she used these techniques in her defense of poetry and the notion of the poet.[34]

When Tsvetaeva began her autobiography she knew already that she was a major poet, even a great poet. Even though her public status seemed to be declining by the 1930s, she remained unshaken in her commitment to her "calling" as a poet, and to the "special destiny" that this calling implied, as Lily Feiler puts it.[35] These become the recurring threads that tie Tsvetaeva's autobiographical prose pieces together, and although there has been a recent increase in scholarly discussion of Tsvetaeva's autobiographical prose, relatively little attention has been focused on the way she constructs a portrait of herself as a poet in this prose and how this relates to the personal and political circumstances in which she lived. In the three pieces that I will examine closely, we find two central characters and one recurring pattern. The characters are the child Marina and her mother, Maria Aleksandrovna; the pattern is the opposition that Tsvetaeva sets up between two opposing forces in each work. In "Mother and Music" the primary opposition is between Tsvetaeva and her mother; in "The Devil," the main conflict is between Tsvetaeva's savior devil and her mother; and in "My Pushkin," the opposition is largely between Pushkin and Tsvetaeva's mother.

Even when it is not on the dominant plane of the narrative, though, Tsvetaeva's uneasy relationship with her mother lurks in the background, emerging regularly in digressions and subplots. Unlike Tsvetaeva's father, who is almost entirely absent in these texts and whose presence seems to require only formal acknowledgment from time to time, Tsvetaeva's mother demands passionate engagement. Attention from her mother provokes a supreme battle of wills and it is in the crucible of her mother's home and under the force of her mother's gaze that Tsvetaeva feels herself growing stronger as a poet.

In "Mother and Music" the conflict between Tsvetaeva and her mother functions as the central theme, and Tsvetaeva writes about herself as a young child who is assailed by two seemingly irresistible forces: her mother and music. Music becomes an agent of Maria Aleksandrovna's will, and by saying "At least she'll be a musician" after swallowing the disappointment of Marina's birth, she is really saying "I will create her to be the person I choose." The remainder of the account (and in many ways the remainder of Tsvetaeva's prose autobiography) is a description of Tsvetaeva's resistance to this pronouncement by her mother. This work is completely encircled by a sense of gender, from Tsvetaeva's first words describing her "failure" at birth (arriving as a daughter instead of the longed-for son), to an encounter that she describes near the end. At a stopover in Munich on the way back to Russia, Maria Aleksandrovna begins to play the piano. Everyone present is affected by the beauty of the music, but for one young boy the sounds prove to be truly overwhelming: Seemingly powerless to resist, he is drawn toward the piano until he literally collapses at Maria Aleksandrovna's feet. Watching her mother's tender response to this unknown boy, Tsvetaeva senses instinctively that her mother is responding to a "what-might-have-been" scenario: This is the son Alexander who should have been born, the child who is both male and musical and thus fulfills those most basic needs that Tsvetaeva will never be able to meet for her mother. "I will never forget my mother with that boy who belonged to someone else," says Tsvetaeva. "In all my lifetime that was the deepest *bow*."[36] This sense of absence, of being replaced by another, or perhaps rather by two qualities that she could not control (gender and musicality), was a part of Tsvetaeva's consciousness throughout her childhood. Sometimes her inadequacy was only implied, as in Berlin; at other times she was reminded of it very directly.

In its essence, Tsvetaeva considers her entire childhood a drawn-out examination, a continuous testing period that her mother used to mold and make her into the image that Maria Aleksandrovna wanted her to become: "Mother did not bring us up—she tried us out: she tested our strength of resistance: would our rib cages fall in? . . . Mother gave us drink from the opened vein of Lyricism, . . ." Tsvetaeva was shaped by her mother's testing, which became her "good fortune" by teaching her endurance. This passage illustrates the ambivalence that always characterizes Tsvetaeva's response to her mother. Although the troubles are extreme, she finds something positive within the experience by identifying a sense of Lyricism as the legacy of her mother's testing; on another occasion, she remembers her mother's lesson about the importance of standing "one against many." What her mother doesn't say, but Tsvetaeva grasps intuitively, is that for herself as a young child it is her *mother* who is the "many." The lesson that Maria Aleksandrovna teaches Marina is turned against her own dominating presence in a desperate struggle to avoid subjugation: "After a mother like that I had only one alternative: to become a poet. To expurgate her gift to me, a gift that would have suffocated me or turned me into a transgressor of all human laws." There is a kind of monstrous tonality surrounding Tsvetaeva's mother here, but at a deeper level this is also Tsvetaeva's way of repaying a debt of gratitude: Without the superhuman willpower that her mother first helped to instill in her, and without her mother offering a kind of "ideal Other" against which to direct and perfect this will, Tsvetaeva might never have become the poet that she was. In a sense, her mother offered herself as an unwitting sacrifice, a force that needed to be overcome, and remained completely oblivious to the fact that all her efforts were reinforcing Marina's determination to flee music for poetry: "Did Mother know (about me—the poet?). No, she went *va banque*, she bet on the unknown, on herself . . . on the unrealized son Alexander. . . ."[37] Maria Aleksandrovna bet everything on her ability to shape her daughter into a musician, resisting to the end any recognition that young Marina's true realm was poetry.

Music becomes the primary venue for the struggle between mother and daughter in "Mother and Music." "Mother used music to wear me down," Tsvetaeva writes. "Mother deluged us with music. . . . Mother flooded us like an inundation. Her children, like those poor people's shacks on the banks of all great rivers, were doomed from their inception." The beautiful music that pours out of the piano under her mother's hands seems to mock the cruder sounds that come from her own playing, and Tsvetaeva reflects, "And how could I not feel repulsion for it? A born musician would have subdued it. But I was not a born musician." Indeed, young Marina is a *created* musician, the product of her mother's continual efforts to shame her to higher and higher levels of achievement. But there is a force within Tsvetaeva that simply rebuffs all this pressure: She has a different destiny. It is hard to know whether it is the precocious child subject or the wiser adult narrator who displays such a clear sense of identity when Tsvetaeva writes that her mother "demanded from me—herself. From me, already a writer, never a musician."[38] Not only was she "not a born musician," but she had always been a writer, formed for the word rather than for the note.

Eventually, Tsvetaeva feels a kind of sympathy for her mother: "Poor Mother, how I embittered her and how she failed ever to realize that all my 'unmusicalness' was nothing more than *another* vocation!"[39] This "other" vocation begins to occupy an increasingly important place in the text as Tsvetaeva creates a dialogue between literature and music: She is capable—even gifted—in music, but is pulled instead toward the Word, where she finds a freedom that she cannot find in music. The notion of comparison, of a push/pull relationship between music and literature, is a recurring theme. Where Pasternak's early music career was the result of a pull toward music, Tsvetaeva's musicality is portrayed as unnatural from the outset. It seems fitting, then, that while Pasternak depicts himself as discovering that he is a poet only after passing through several phases of discovery, including music, Tsvetaeva describes herself as a poet from birth, but a poet who must overcome a series of obstacles that prevent her from displaying her true identity.

The opposition between Tsvetaeva's writing and Maria Aleksandrovna's music is a power struggle, with music securely in the dominant position. One indication of music's power and authority is the enormous presence of the piano in the text. There is nothing random about this, for Tsvetaeva herself refers to this seemingly inanimate object as "the main *dramatis persona* of my childhood." Gradually she recognizes that this is no mere piece of furniture, but a near-sacred shrine. Its dominating power is made clear when she describes how objects of the word—books and newspapers—are figuratively forced to bow before the piano: "You must not put anything on it, not only feet but even books. As for newspapers—Mother, with the undefined, lofty persistence of a martyr, every morning, without saying a word to Father, who invariably and innocently put them there, took the newspapers off the piano—swept them off."[40] There is a clear contrast between her parents that follows the distinction between writing and music: Tsvetaeva's father doesn't appreciate the sacred nature of music, and her mother doesn't appreciate the value of his books. Tsvetaeva ends up in the middle, with her musical ear helping her to form the verbal music that is poetry.

When young Marina allows herself to forget that the piano is sacred, that it is a *piano*, it takes on a variety of other manifestations. It might remind her of an underwater world as she sits beneath it, looking at the plants behind the piano and imagining the music as a watery wave of sensations, or she might see a horror, "a set of teeth, huge teeth in a huge cold mouth stretching to the ears." A consuming force lies just under the piano's alluringly smooth and shiny surface, and if Tsvetaeva ever succumbs to the forbidden temptation of clouding the piano's mirror-like surface with her breath, it is "as if the piano had taken my mouth—and swallowed it." The precision of the picture—the adult narrator's consciousness shimmers around the observations of the young child at times like this—is striking, for the piano is precisely the object that threatens to swallow her poetic speech. The young poet is much more comfortable with the piano at a safe distance. While up close the piano "entered into my fancy as a petrified, bestial monster," backing away from it changes the perception completely, and it becomes a beautiful dragonfly on the wing. In this way, she reflects, the piano actually helps lead her to poetry because she learns how something ordinary—even her own face—could be seen in new and unexpected ways: "The piano was my first mirror and my first awareness of my own face was through blackness, through its translation into blackness, as into a language dark but comprehensible. That is how it was my whole life: to understand the simplest thing I had to plunge it into poetry, to see it *from there*."⁴¹

The piano, then can be overcome and can even function as a catalyst leading into the magical realm of poetry. The metronome, though, is something else entirely. This most odious element in her musical universe is an implacable force that ignores rebellion and wears down resistance. Tsvetaeva's description of her attitude toward the metronome shows a profound psychologist at work:

> as soon as I was *subjected* to its methodical click, I started hating it and fearing it until my heart beat faster, until I felt faint, until I turned cold . . . Someone is standing over your soul and hurrying you, and holding you back and not letting you take a breath or swallow, and will go on hurrying you that way and holding you back when you go away. . . . The lifeless over the living, that which has not existence over that which does. . . . It was truly Death itself standing over a soul.⁴²

The metronome becomes a Mother-machine, keeping her in line when her mother cannot be there to watch her practice at the piano. As the metronome attempts to constrain and inhibit her, she resists and resents it with all her might. "If ever I wanted to kill someone—it was the metronome," she remembers. "And my eyes have never ceased sending out that look of voluptuous revenge that I presented to it when I had played my way to freedom."⁴³

Her response to these two dominating musical objects reveals a fundamental incompatibility with the path that her mother is forcing her along, but it is her response to music itself that most clearly reveals Tsvetaeva's poetic—not musical—nature. Music for music's sake is completely alien to the young Tsvetaeva, a violation of her inner being. Describing her attempts at reading sheet music, Tsvetaeva can only explain her perplexity by referring to her poetry: Her mind, she realizes, is cut off from music and functions only in terms of poetry. If she plays the piano by ear or by heart, she shows promise. When she tries to *read* music, she is hopeless. "Reading" and "music" are incompatible constructs for her. The same frame of reference governs her perception of the piano as a musical instrument. What Tsvetaeva likes about the piano are the keys as symbols, for she imagines the emotions or meanings they contain as pure potential. She loves the possibility of the unexpected and links her love for the chromatic scale with her natural affinity for the romantic and dramatic. Describing the concept of "top" and "bottom" in a musical scale, Tsvetaeva writes that she was always confused about the common way of referring to the right hand as "top" and the left as "bottom." There is something intuitively wrong about this, but why? Suddenly, language and reading give her a flash of insight: Her instinct for the "top" and "bottom" of music runs parallel to the notion of "beginning" and "end" in reading. Just as reading moves from left to write and from top to bottom (in languages like English and Russian, at least), she links the left end of the keyboard to its beginning. Literary experience confirms instinct.

Indeed, one of Tsvetaeva's most inspiring musical memories is actually connected more to words than to notes. She finds that the graphical representation of the treble clef (𝄞), which in Russian has the wonderfully evocative name *skripichnyi klyuch* (literally, violin key), signifies something very special about music. For Tsvetaeva, the *skripichnyi klyuch* elicits a response primarily because of the sound and sight associated with the symbol itself. It is the visual signifier as an element of language and form that catches her interest and fires her imagination: The clef is a key that unlocks the world of the violin; it is a swan swimming in telegraph wires; it is a swooping stream of water that accelerates from a gentle stream to a deadly torrent. Tsvetaeva's response highlights her fundamental incompatibility with "real" music: She is not drawn to the music that is symbolized by this "violin key," but revels instead in the poetic associations that are evoked by it. The bass clef (𝄢) provokes an equally intense but opposite response: She doesn't like the look or the sound (*basovyi klyuch*) of it, and grows to hate it because it is an ear with holes "stupidly" punched beside rather than through the ear. Remembering her obsession with copying a row of treble clefs, Tsvetaeva reflects: "But that was graphic, scribal, writer's ardor. I had—and it's time to say it—no musical ardor."[44] Facing the competing claims of music and writing, she never has any doubt about writing's preeminent claim.

Tsvetaeva concludes "Mother and Music" with a final return to her mother. Here, in a reminder of the metronome's "lifelessness," Maria Aleksandrovna is present only as a shade from the past, a ghostly addressee who still haunts her young daughter's consciousness. If her mother were still alive, Tsvetaeva reflects, she would inevitably have attended Moscow's Conservatory and emerged "a fair pianist." She was "saved" from this fate only by her mother's death—making the death a highly ambivalent event in her memory. While depriving Tsvetaeva of the mother whose approval she sought, this ultimate threshold event meant the end of life for the parent and a chance for new life for the daughter.

Even with her mother physically removed, Tsvetaeva's departure from music is gradual. Her motivation for playing had always been a mixture of fear and a desire to please; now both of these are meaningless, since it was her mother who was the locus for each one. As she slowly frees herself from the demands of her mother, music recedes and its place is taken by poetry. Poetry has always been there, latent, gaining strength and asserting itself more and more; now it emerges as conqueror.

In "The Devil," started almost immediately after "Mother and Music" was finished in October 1934, Tsvetaeva takes the nebulous power of poetry and gives it shape, creating for herself a demonic other who does not stand against her but rescues and claims her for Poetry. Tsvetaeva knew that it would be a controversial work; letters to her friend Anna Tesková in 1934 reveal a combination of defiance and desperation when she says in October that after "The Devil," "the emigration will renounce me completely, if only from their deep hypocrisy." Tesková herself was probably not surprised at the direction Tsvetaeva's writing had taken, for earlier in the year a letter from Tsvetaeva showed her sifting through connections between art and the demonic: "For the Greeks, 'demon' and 'genius' were the same thing," Tsvetaeva writes, providing a capsule guide to what would eventually become "The Devil." Increasingly, Tsvetaeva felt the need to establish her legacy, to communicate her essence in a form that would remain long after her own disappearance. In November she writes to Tesková: "These days I keep wanting to write my testament. In general, I would like not to be. I walk with Mur [Tsvetaeva's son] or without Mur, to school or to get milk—and from within, all by themselves—the words of the testament. Not of things—I don't have anything—but something that I need so that people would know about me: *an explanation*. To settle *accounts*."[45] There is an ominous tonality here, and even those inclined to see this text as evidence of Tsvetaeva's capacity for hyperbole cannot ignore the thinly veiled death wish that prompts this sudden rush to shape her testament. Precisely what form this "testament" was to take is not clear; what we do know is that Tsvetaeva was at that very time actively working on this autobiographical prose in a direct engagement with her past. The pieces of her autobiography may indeed have been the intended form of this testament, since in them she focuses her attention very clearly on her formation and development as a poet.

"The Devil" is an extension of the childhood account that began in "Mother and Music." Even the cast of characters is similar, with one critical exception: The piano, identified in "Mother and Music" as the main *dramatis persona* in Tsvetaeva's childhood, is replaced here by an enigmatic, alternately frightening and inspiring, devil. This peculiar devil is visible only to females—but never to Tsvetaeva's mother, Maria Aleksandrovna. There is something about him so alien, so completely incompatible with her vision of the world, that she could never see him. Using the pronoun "him" to describe this devil is possible only with reservations, for although the word is grammatically masculine in Russian (*chert*), the physical description shows a blend of seemingly incompatible characteristics: part dog-like (specifically, like a Great Dane), part like a female lion, but with no fur, just a steely gray skin. The devil's most dominant features, though are its eyes, and Tsvetaeva's description of them ("colorless, passionless and merciless") suggests pure, elemental power. Perhaps the most striking aspect of Tsvetaeva's account, though, is her instantaneous, unthinking acceptance of this devil: "He sat, I stood. And I—loved him."[46] From complete absence to complete possession requires only a heartbeat, because, as Tsvetaeva explains later, a space within her had been prepared just for this devil: She had merely been waiting for her appointment with destiny.

Tsvetaeva's most dramatic encounter with the devil comes in a fantastic dream, where the role of this creature in her life suddenly becomes clear. She dreams that she is drowning or has perhaps already died in the Oka River. She starts to see other wraithlike drowned figures but is then suddenly lifted out of the river's deadly flow and *from the first instant*, from the first sensation of lift, she knows that it is her devil who has come to rescue her. There is no hesitation: The totality of her response is one of the most powerful signs of the bond she feels between them. The description of clinging to her rescuer has unmistakably erotic overtones, and when she is safely deposited on the riverbank, she hears him say: "And someday you and I will get married, the devil take it!" The dream is a tumbled complexity of sensations and perceptions, reflecting an adult and child consciousness both striving to emerge in the retelling. The child's curiosity and the adult's eroticism merge into a confusing blend of wide-eyed admiration and sensual fascination, and the marriage proposal is momentarily forgotten even by the rescued girl. But then the realization comes: He is courting me, "without any request from me."[47]

As J. Marin King has observed, the links that bind the watery world of "The Devil" to the metaphors of "Mother and Music" show that ultimately the devil is a poetic force saving Tsvetaeva from the clutches of her mother's music.[48] The "devil versus Mother" opposition developed here leads to a significant shift in the power relationship between Tsvetaeva and her mother; previously, Tsvetaeva resisted the combined forces of mother and music alone, learning to match her own resistance against the force of her mother's will; she survived, and gave some of the credit to her mother for providing an opportunity to learn the power of human resolve. In "The Devil" Tsvetaeva gains something new, a defender-devil who rescues her from the depths of her mother's musical world, who becomes her champion, her lover—and even her parent. "He didn't even know that I have a mother," Tsvetaeva writes. "When I was with him I was *his* little girl, his devil's-own-waif."[49]

The conflict between the devil and Tsvetaeva's mother leads finally to the devil largely supplanting Maria Aleksandrovna, but that comes later. Initially, Tsvetaeva hopes that her encounter with the devil might actually lead to closer mother-daughter ties. But when she recounts a tamer version of the dream that does not actually name the devil, her mother's disgust is unmistakable:

"Congratulations! . . . I've always said it! Good children are led across the abyss by angels, but children like you . . ."

Afraid that she would guess and name him this minute, and by doing that cut it all off forever, I say hurriedly: "But they—honest!—*were* drowned, as drowned as drowned can be, blue . . ."

"And you think that's—better?" said Mother ironically. "Nasty thing!"[50]

In the dream, and especially in the retelling of it, the Oka becomes Tsvetaeva's personal Rubicon: This is a crossing from which she will never return, because if any doubt had lingered in Tsvetaeva's mind about surrendering herself to the devil that is Poetry, surely this renewed censure would have swept it away.

This inversion of the biblical salvation story is alluded to in the other major sections of Tsvetaeva's autobiography. In "My Pushkin" there is an unmistakable reference to the devil's rescue when Tsvetaeva writes about the longing in her soul for some unreachable place like the far bank of the Oka, someplace where she will be the only and best-loved daughter, not Marina but something else—Katya, perhaps. Or—best of all—perhaps she can be reborn as the longed-for boy Alexander. And it turns out that these unattainable dreams, these "far banks of the Oka," *can* be realized. These are no ordinary human crossings, though; to become Katya, to come to new life as Alexander, means crossing first to an "otherworld' in her imagination, a land where poetry destroys all barriers. To get there she need only surrender herself to the devilish arms of poetry, to accept the union that this diabolic force proposes.

There is one more heavily marked allusion to Tsvetaeva's night crossing into poetry. It appears in "The House at Old Pimen," another chapter of her autobiography in which she recounts a conversation between herself as a seven-year-old and her "step-uncle" (the brother of her father's first wife, therefore not a blood relation) Sergei Ilovaisky. Here she receives her first direct encouragement to write poetry when Sergei asks whether she would copy out some of her poems for him, and her answer is a clear response to her devil ("Well, of course, the devil take it!"). Here she appropriates the words as her own, taking control of these crucial signifiers and thereby asserting her own authority as an independent agent in the discourse of poetry, a fully formed poet who needs no intermediaries in language or expression.

In "The Devil," though, the young girl has not reached that level of maturity. Instead, like "Mother and Music," "The Devil" portrays a young poet-in-process who is both *already* a poet, and *still becoming* a poet. She senses that she is no longer her mother's child, that she is becoming her devil's when she is with him ("I was *his* little girl, his devil's-own-waif"), but she also contributes a special receptivity that is crucial for the union's success. This is how Tsvetaeva avoids the implication of complete passivity. She has been born to a calling, and the very formation of her character attracts the devil's attention. Her statement that "the first mark of *his* chosen ones is complete detachment, from the first and from everything—exclusion" is already true in her life before the devil claims her.

This sense of combined exclusion and exclusiveness provides a clear linkage between the tenor of Tsvetaeva's autobiography and her life at the time of writing, when remarks about being completely alone and bearing a "mark of discomfort" were a regular feature of her conversation and correspondence. Given the symbiotic nature of writing as both reflection and creation of life for Tsvetaeva, it would be pointless to speculate about which of these realities (childhood or adulthood) had a greater impact on the development of the isolation motif in her autobiography, but the overwhelming sense of rejection in her autobiography is unmistakable. One of the most compelling of Tsvetaeva's memories shows her pain at invariably being the least favored child, the one called on last. Tsvetaeva describes how her mother used to read to the three youngest children, turning every new story into a didactic experience and grilling the children about a story's theme or significance. Tsvetaeva describes her growing frustration as Maria Aleksandrovna always asks her stepson Andrei first, then turns to her youngest child, Anastasia, and finally, almost as an afterthought, deigns to notice the eager Marina. The pattern is repeated anew with every question to reinforce the hierarchy: First comes the son (even though he is not *her* son); next comes the youngest (the favorite); and last comes the precocious Marina, whose talent and will are a challenge—and therefore a threat—to the mother. On one occasion, Tsvetaeva writes, even though Maria Aleksandrovna deliberately passed her by and was about to stop reading because the other children could not answer a question, Tsvetaeva would not be denied. "Green is—*der Teufel* [the Devil]" she bursts out with the correct answer. Instead of approval, her mother is disgusted: "Why is it always *you* who knows, when I am reading to *all of you*?"[51]

This rejection even in success must have been devastating, but here the blow is transformed into a positive sign of calling. While Tsvetaeva's letters of the 1930s reveal that her frequent sense of profound loneliness led to bouts of deep emotional unhappiness, in this semi-mythical "life of the young poet," detachment—even rejection by such a crucial figure as her mother—becomes a badge of honor for the poet. Again, the devil is the figure who allows her to transform loss into gain, because emotional exile is a secret sign of calling: "The first mark of *his* chosen ones is complete detachment, from the first and from everything—exclusion."[52]

In the concluding section of "The Devil"—deleted from the original publication by journal editors who worried about reader response—we find another side to the devil-child relationship. Here Tsvetaeva ascribes all her failed loves, all her "divine pride," all her "unseemly" courage, all her uniqueness, and all her sympathy for the downtrodden, to her devil. And most of all, she says in addressing her devil directly, "if you condescended in the form of a doggish nanny to me, a little girl, it was only so that she [that is, Tsvetaeva] would afterwards for her entire life be able to cope by herself." Here the address to the devil is more vexed, but Tsvetaeva remains resolute to the end, concluding: "If one wants to search for you, then it can only be in the solitary confinement cells of revolt and in the attics of Lyric Poetry."[53]

The importance—and inevitability—of poetic isolation is developed further through the metaphor of card games, especially a childhood favorite called Black Peter in which the players try not to be left holding the jack of spades. Tsvetaeva's account reveals the complexity of her growing identity, for although she is secretly thrilled by the conviction that she alone has a special connection to the eternally outcast Black Peter, she must doubly dissemble during the game: Not only must she pretend that she does not *want* to be left with Black Peter, but she must use all her wiles to get rid of him. Remembering the circumstances of Tsvetaeva's writing (increasingly ostracized and unwanted by the Russian emigration in Paris), these passages surely reveal a dual "orientation to authenticity," to use Lydia Ginzburg's phrase. We hear the defiance of the writing consciousness expressed through the parallel experience of the child when Tsvetaeva writes: "In that game I proved myself his real daughter . . . It was once again my secret and his, and never, perhaps, did he feel me so much his own as when I so cunningly and dazzlingly gave him away, got rid of him, once again concealed my secret and his, and perhaps the main thing, once again was able to get along—even without him."[54] The complexity that marks these layers of attraction and rejection, the claim that loyalty sometimes shows itself most profoundly in apparent betrayal: These are elements that demonstrate an essential ambivalence to commitment. Tsvetaeva connects this to an assertion of the poet's need to revolt. A poet's isolation is tied to a defense of the oppressed, she writes, highlighting both the development of the poet as a child and the very real experiences of Tsvetaeva in the 1930s. In the act of writing, then, she not only reinforces her authority within the poetic tradition, but also stakes out the moral basis for remaining aloof from all the intrigues of Parisian émigré life: The poet's identity is singular and based on compassion, not on party affiliation or externally imposed values. A poet must stand apart, or cease to be a poet.

The essential isolation of the poet takes on almost religious overtones in Tsvetaeva's writing, and one senses on several occasions that her devil is really a religious—and not an antireligious—figure. In hierarchical terms, he is at least an archpriest if not a divine (anti-divine?) being. The pervasive juxtaposition of terms and concepts shows how foundational elements of the Christian story are inverted: Instead of Christ as the savior figure, the young child is saved from drowning by a devil. At one point Tsvetaeva directly associates her devil with God, and is both frightened and fascinated by the juxtaposition "God-devil," with its sense of breaking taboos and entering forbidden territory. ("Maybe it was the poet's inborn passion to juxtapose," she writes.) She carries this as an underlying theme throughout "The Devil," having earlier suggested that the devil transformed himself into a bookshelf Tree of the Knowledge of Good and Evil, just like the one that tempted Eve in Eden. Just as Eve and Adam shared their guilty pleasure and hid from God, Tsvetaeva greedily devours the forbidden literature and hides her secret knowledge from her mother. The tightly bound relationship between good and evil is a recurring theme in Tsvetaeva's poetry as well as her prose, and in one especially telling passage from "My Pushkin" she describes the possibility of following Pugachev, the rebel leader from the time of Catherine the Great, farther than caution would allow, "into the very thickets of good and evil, to that place in the thickets where they are inseparably entwined together and, *in the intertwining, make the shape of real life*."[55] Here Tsvetaeva reveals that one *needs* to stand within the conflicting force fields of good and evil, since that is where one becomes truly alive.

There is one manifestation of poetry that Tsvetaeva will never outgrow, and it is this figure that she turns to in "My Pushkin," her final piece of autobiographical prose. Here, more than anywhere else, Tsvetaeva as the writing subject imposes her presence on the text and the result is a constant temporal dialogue, a comparison between "then" and "now" that makes "My Pushkin" her summa.

Could this be the "testament" that Tsvetaeva referred to in her letter to Anna Tesková? It would be a natural choice on many levels, even though it is written in prose and not in verse. Could Tsvetaeva hope to improve on a testament that demonstrates a profound kinship, even a spiritual and creative union, with Russia's poetic father?[56] The repeated references in the text to the Pushkin monument on Tverskaya street lend support to this notion, since any Russian would instantly associate the juxtaposition of the words "Pushkin" and "monument" with Pushkin's own lyric testament "I Have Created a Monument Not Made by Human Hands" (*Ia pamiatnik sebe vozdvig nerukotvornyi*). But Tsvetaeva can do even more—she can actually improve on an association that would limit her association with Pushkin to just the man who wrote poetry. For her, the concept "Pushkin" is much more than just the human genius who happened to be a man. In Tsvetaeva's conception of the poetic universe, "poet" includes not just the poet's corporeal presence but also everything that the poet has ever written ("In order to understand my poetry, you have to know everything that I have written earlier," she asserts in "The Poet and Time"). "Pushkin," then, includes both the man and all that he created; for Tsvetaeva, this provides an opportunity to create a gender-neutral equation where the male Pushkin is balanced by his great female creations and inspirations.

But there is another presence that lurks around the edges of this text. Between the time when Tsvetaeva finished "The Devil" in mid-June 1935 and when she began "My Pushkin" in 1936, Tsvetaeva had the chance to see Boris Pasternak. For years she had corresponded with Pasternak and for a time guarded their relationship with a lover's jealousy, even though their contact was only epistolary. Pasternak's physical absence allowed Tsvetaeva to construct a semi-mythical Pasternak in her mind and through her correspondence; when everyone else seemed determined to isolate her, she felt stability in her connection to another great poetic spirit.[57] The connection was more than just poetic for Tsvetaeva, though, and she sought a totalized relationship that implicitly acknowledged an absolute affinity between them. The degree to which she succeeded in constructing this image of the relationship in her mind, and the degree to which Pasternak's thoughts about the relationship differed from hers, can be understood from a letter that Tsvetaeva wrote to Anna Tesková after hearing that Pasternak had left his wife for another woman: "For years I lived because of a dream that I would see him. Now I feel empty. There is no one for me to go to in Russia. A wife, a son—that I respect. But a *new* love—I move out of the way. . . . Because I considered him, despite his family, to be completely alone: mine."[58]

Their response to each other as poets was more even, and each held the other's poetry in extremely high regard. Tsvetaeva's response to Pasternak's poetry anthology *My Sister, Life* (*Sestra moia—zhizn'*) was almost ecstatic, and she wrote to him that after opening its pages, "For ten days I lived by it—as on the high crest of a wave: letting myself go, I yielded and did not choke."[59] Pasternak's early response to Tsvetaeva was more cautious, but in 1926 he credited one of her poems as the force which gave him new determination to continue as a poet, and in his last autobiography he singles Tsvetaeva out as the one poet with whom he would most like his name to be linked.

After Mayakovsky's death in 1930 and the outrage that greeted Tsvetaeva's words in his defense, she thought even more about Pasternak and wrote two powerful essays that considered Pasternak and the broader status of poetry in the Soviet Union. Tsvetaeva had no way of knowing exactly how badly poetry was being undermined at the time, but she had enough information to be very concerned and recognized the dangers that inevitably accompany a centralized demand for artistic production. "Does a political party—even the most powerful, even the one with the biggest future in the world—represent the whole of its time, and can it present its command in the whole of it?" she asks in "The Poet and Time." The very concept troubles her, and she answers "No." A political command to a poet has the wrong addressee, she writes, since the poet responds to much larger issues than those limited by any party's political agenda. If the leaders of the proletarian literary groups really respected poets, they would abandon their pedantic teaching mission and allow poets to have their passions—and pens—aroused by events around them. But Tsvetaeva continues in a way that suggests that she understood at least the fundamental elements of the Soviet literary conflict (and which by 1932 had been all but won by the politically dominant literary forces). Allowing poets to respond to events around them could be risky, she implies, if those events do not reflect well on the state; in that case the poet's efforts could be turned against the very forces that demand subservience. And if the state goes on to control or quell the elements that inspire the poet to write, then the resulting collapse of freedom will either silence the poet, or ensure the poet's resistance. Tsvetaeva then returns to her own initial question and changes her answer. Yes, there is after all one demand that a state can make of its poets, she reflects: "Do not write against us, for you are a force." But this command/prohibition is simultaneously a tribute and an acknowledgment of the poet's power, since a demand for silence is an implicit admission of weakness before the strength of the poet's voice.[60]

By 1932 it had been a decade since Tsvetaeva had personally faced the demands of the Soviet state. But she remembers her own attempts before leaving the USSR to depict the emotional truth of the age without bowing down to demands for careful political correctness, and she knows from personal experience that this same kind of pressure is applied forcefully in émigré life as well, only from the opposite side of the political spectrum. As a result, Tsvetaeva realizes that a poet cannot be tied too closely to time, that poetry can only serve its time if this temporal element provides a link to a much more important eternal essence. In this sense Tsvetaeva recognizes that poetry could very well have a political function, but only apart from a partisan political battle. Anything political in poetry must be linked to the eternal struggle for justice and liberty, to which the true poet will inevitably be allied.

In a later afterword to "The Poet and Time" Tsvetaeva describes coming across a proclamation by Soviet cultural authorities that they had shifted their attention to the "poetry front." Noting that a major conference had been convened to debate the function of poetry in the Soviet Union, Tsvetaeva quotes Pasternak's remarks to the delegates. First, she says, Pasternak noted that not everything had been destroyed by the Revolution, and then he went on to state that "Time exists for man, not man for time." For Tsvetaeva, this is an almost magical confirmation of the kinship that exists between her and Pasternak: "Boris Pasternak over there, and I over here, across all the spaces and prohibitions, external and internal, . . . not consulting with each other, are thinking of the same thing and saying the same thing."[61] For Tsvetaeva, this complete union of minds proves that she has chosen the poet-path.

Tsvetaeva's second major essay of 1932 has a much narrower focus, for she uses "Epic and Lyric in Contemporary Russia" primarily to examine the different poetic trajectories of Pasternak and Mayakovsky. She respects each one as a great poet, although if she had to choose one over the other she would choose Pasternak. But that is not the point, for Tsvetaeva wants to examine the way time and place influence a poet's destiny. These are two poets who are almost diametrically opposed, Tsvetaeva shows: Mayakovsky reveals while Pasternak conceals; Mayakovsky shouts to the masses while Pasternak whispers to the solitary individual; Mayakovsky says "I am in all" while Pasternak says "All is in me"; Mayakovsky is real while Pasternak is magic. These are only a few of the dozens of contrasts that Tsvetaeva presents, but they are enough to show the essential nature of her response to each poet. In Tsvetaeva's judgment, the Revolution formed a crucial juncture in the career of each poet: Mayakovsky gained, while Pasternak lost. When lyric poetry had been pushed aside in the late 1920s and only the epic remained a viable poetic genre, Pasternak wrote the epic poems *Lieutenant Schmidt* and *The Year 1905*. Tsvetaeva laments both his decision, and the historical circumstances that forced him to consider the switch from lyric to epic:

> who knows how far Pasternak might not have gone, to what depth he might not have dug down, were it not for this involuntary mediumistic attraction to the communal cause: to Russia's, the century's, history's present hour. I give all that's due to *The Year 1905*, to Pasternak's genius in *The Year 1905*'s image; but I have to say that Schmidt would still have been Schmidt without Pasternak, Pasternak would still have been Pasternak without Schmidt—and with something other than Schmidt, with something that has no name, he'd have gone further.[62]

Leave this compulsion to tell a story, to record the age in verse, for someone who doesn't have your gift for lyricism, she would like to tell Pasternak—and she did suggest to him in correspondence that this poem did not really show him at his best. But she also recognized the bind that Pasternak faced because he could not extricate himself from his age and place. "If in Russia now the hour is favourable for a poetic career—for a poet's external travel and arrival—for a poet's lonely path it is unfavourable," she writes. One could make a *career* as a poet—the state was looking for a "national poet" who could become a larger-than-life figure in the national consciousness, and even offered the role to Pasternak. To his credit, he recoiled in dismay: Like Tsvetaeva, like Mandelstam, Pasternak recognized that a poet can only *remain* a poet on the "lonely path." But there was no escaping the bitter conclusion that the Revolution cost Pasternak a great deal. "Pasternak would have gone on growing and growing . . .," Tsvetaeva writes. "Pasternak, like every lyric poet, feels restricted everywhere but within; he feels restricted in the whole world of action, especially in that very locus of world action—present-day Russia." Her sympathy for Pasternak's plight is accompanied by her recognition that he had to face the Revolution as he did, sparring and evading in the search for ways to keep his inner, poetic, essence intact.

A few years later, when there were actions—like the poems to Stalin, or translations of odes by Georgian poets who sang Stalin's praises—that showed Pasternak bowing to the pressure of his time and place, she attempted to understand these lapses without abandoning the conviction that a poetic essence remained.[63] No matter how tempting it may be to judge Pasternak, or Mayakovsky, or other poets for some of the things they did or said, Tsvetaeva asserts that "No one has the right to stand as judge over the poet. Because no one knows. Only poets know, but they will not judge." Irina Shevelenko points out that Tsvetaeva's reference here is to an ethical or moral judgment and argues convincingly that although Tsvetaeva may have experienced personal discomfort or disappointment over the poetic acts of another poet, this was a disappointment prompted by recognition of differences in character or thought, not a disappointment as a poet.[64]

This rich poetic and personal history provided the framework for the 1935 meeting between Tsvetaeva and Pasternak in Paris.[65] Nothing could have prepared Tsvetaeva for the reality, though, because the meeting was a disaster. Pasternak was in a very fragile mental state and was already hovering on the brink of a breakdown when he was forced to join the Soviet delegation at an international writers' conference in Paris that was being billed as an antifascist defense of culture. On the way he stopped briefly in Berlin, where his sister warned him to be particularly judicious in his comments because Hitler's regime would respond to criticism with an attack on their parents, who were then living in Germany. The actual meeting of Pasternak and Tsvetaeva was unsatisfactory for each of them. Pasternak later expressed bitter regret at his failure to warn Tsvetaeva more directly about the peril of returning to the USSR; Tsvetaeva was shocked to discover that Pasternak had been coerced into attending the conference, that he had responded out of fear. Not only did she not appreciate the extent of Pasternak's illness, but she could not imagine the extent to which political terror had gripped the Soviet Union, and the way that political pressure had started to wear down even the country's most renowned poet.

The memory of this meeting was still fresh in Tsvetaeva's mind when she began "My Pushkin" and her thoughts about the fate of Pasternak and other fellow poets in the Soviet Union may help to explain why there are several deliberate political allusions included in this text, in contrast to the apolitical character of the earlier sections of her autobiography. Tsvetaeva's defense of the poet becomes a restatement of the poet's cultural authority and can stand as an implicit contrast to the signs of weakening that she saw in Pasternak's behavior during these years. Her disappointment at the "non-meeting" with Pasternak in Paris reminded her that separation is a poet's customary lot, but also focused her attention on poetic linkages that exist longitudinally (historically through time) rather than laterally (contemporaneously). The approach to Pushkin, then, is not an attempt to gain allies or support. Rather it is a combination of testament and genealogy, for one of the central motifs in "My Pushkin" is Tsvetaeva's assertion of a poetic birthright based on the claim that she is no one if not Pushkin's daughter.

A filial relationship to Pushkin has profound implications for Tsvetaeva's attitude toward her biological parents, and undercurrents of Tsvetaeva's troubled relationship with her mother recur throughout "My Pushkin." When young Marina witnesses a visit by the great poet's son but finds her attention diverted by a star on the man's chest when she was supposed to be looking at his face, her mother is appalled: "A star! As if no one else had a star on his chest! You have some special gift of looking in the wrong direction and at the wrong thing." The structure of this exchange reminds us of the eternal conflict between the poet and everyone else: Tsvetaeva's (poet's) vision is scorned by her mother because it is different—but this is inevitable. The key phrase here is "special gift": Tsvetaeva's mother has unwittingly paid her the ultimate compliment by naming the poet's essence. It is an essence that Maria Aleksandrovna can't hope to understand, though; Tsvetaeva realizes this, and is almost gentle when she relates this instance of her mother's uncompromising nonpoetic demands. When Maria Aleksandrovna witnesses yet another example of Marina's inability to provide the expected answer to a question, she becomes "menacing": "Mother didn't understand; Mother heard the meaning, and, perhaps, was rightly indignant. But she did not understand—rightly." Tsvetaeva asserts her own higher privilege when she continues by saying that her words were based on a *poet's* sensibility, which she shares with "all poets—and Pushkin first."[66]

"Pushkin first" is a very literal description of how Tsvetaeva begins her poetic journey, for he is her first great poetic encounter. Even the structure of "My Pushkin" reinforces this impression, as Tsvetaeva begins her account by describing how Pushkin's death engendered the birth of her own poetic consciousness. The suggestion of an initiation rite is unmistakable here as Tsvetaeva becomes a novice passing through stages that eventually provide access to the most revered talisman of a secret society. There is a secret room, and in that room is a secret cabinet, and in that secret cabinet are the forbidden poetic fruits that will—for the true poet, at least—lead to the knowledge of good and evil. But to get to the room and the cabinet and the book, one must first pass through a gateway whose function is filled by a "secret" picture of Pushkin's fatal duel. The child's perspective that structures the description is filled with the clear-cut binary oppositions that are found so frequently in Tsvetaeva's prose: The picture is black and white (although the original was in color), the conflict is obvious (poet versus non-poet, without any of the complicating third parties of history), and the result is clear (Pushkin is carried away, while his opponent in the duel, d'Anthès, walks).

One of the most interesting juxtapositions is Tsvetaeva's statement that "Pushkin is—a poet, and d'Anthès—a Frenchman." Here she creates a new transnational identity, or, even better, with this simple verbal juxtaposition she establishes a "land of poetry" that all true poets share. This description of the duel is also a return to the theme that she develops throughout her autobiographical prose, the theme of the poet as an individual set apart from—and opposed to—the "dark mass" of the non-poets, the crowd. The allusion to Pushkin's "The Poet and the Crowd" (*Poet i tolpa*) is clear, and returns us to Tsvetaeva's own circumstances in Paris where she, too, was surrounded by a mob who wouldn't, or couldn't, appreciate her poetry; instead, like the mob in Pushkin's poem, they demanded poetry that was understandable and useful.

Like her encounter with the devil, Tsvetaeva describes her connection to Pushkin as instantaneous and absolute. Her first gaze upon the picture with the dying Pushkin was a threshold moment: "From then on, yes, from then on . . . I have divided the world into the poet—and all of *them*, and I have chosen—the poet, have chosen the poet to be among those I defend: to defend the poet—from all of *them*, however they all are garbed, however they all are named." Like her meeting with the devil, Tsvetaeva's encounter with Pushkin in the painting is merely the *confirmation* of a preexisting affinity, a relationship that exists already, latent and simply waiting to emerge at the appointed time: "Before Naumov's *Duel* there was another Pushkin, a Pushkin when I didn't know yet that Pushkin—is Pushkin. Pushkin not a memory, but a state of being. Pushkin—forever and fromever."[67] And only when the child has passed this trial of initiation, only once she has *understood* Pushkin, can she finally see what is in that secret cabinet of "forbidden fruit," as Tsvetaeva describes it. Again, the connection to her devil deliverer is quite obvious and shows why

Tsvetaeva's sense of moral transgression makes the act of reading Pushkin infinitely more alluring than reading some bland "permitted" literature.

The conflict between Tsvetaeva and her mother reemerges when Tsvetaeva attends a children's evening at her music school and she describes her attraction to Pushkin's greatest creations (Tatyana and *Eugene Onegin* [*Evgenii Onegin*]) rather than the more "appropriate" *The Mermaid* (*Rusalka*). Immediately she feels her mother's wrath. Maria Aleksandrovna refuses to believe that a young girl could understand the complex blend of emotion and desire in *Eugene Onegin* and tells Marina "You're an utterly foolish girl and more stubborn than ten mules!" before turning to the school director and saying: "There isn't one child in the world who would like 'Tatyana and Onegin' out of all they saw, they'd all prefer [*The Mermaid*] because it's a fairy tale, something comprehensible. I really don't know what I'm to do with her!!!"[68] The scolding continues all the way home.

Later Tsvetaeva turns again to a discussion of her mother and we find one of the only passages in these chapters where Tsvetaeva expresses a real emotional connection with her mother. The connection is *not reciprocal*, though: It is a retrospective comment of the adult narrator, trying to see *why* her mother acted as she did. Revealing that Maria Aleksandrovna had been inspired by the example of Tatyana to sacrifice a youthful romantic dream and instead "elected the most burdensome fate" of marriage to a widower twice her age (with small children, yet!), Tsvetaeva writes: "Thus, Tatyana not only had an influence on my whole life, but on the very fact of my life: if there had been no Pushkin's Tatyana, I would not have come into existence."[69] Tsvetaeva is repaying a debt of gratitude here, and although much of her response is directed toward her deceased mother, she simultaneously extends the credit for her very existence to Tatyana, and thus back to Pushkin himself. In the most important way of all, then, Pushkin really *is* her true father.

Even though Pushkin is the work's central figure, the women who populate this text become important parts of Tsvetaeva's broader context and have sometimes been identified as a collective female counterbalance to what might otherwise become a male-dominant account. Contrary to some who read this as an attempt to make the text more "gender neutral" or tip the scale to the female side, I would suggest that Tsvetaeva is not so much concerned with raising the status of women in the text, or attacking the patriarchal order, or trying to create a precariously balanced sexual state, as she is with escaping the bonds of gender altogether, of slipping into a state where notions of male and female simply become irrelevant and all that remains is poetry.[70] It seems appropriate in this context to recall Tsvetaeva's description of her "devil of poetry"—part female, part male, and wholly other. In that encounter with poetry, there was already a hint that poetry can transcend sexual identity. In "My Pushkin" we sense an almost palpable longing for a complete and eternal "out of gender" experience when Tsvetaeva writes: "My God! How much a human being loses with the acquisition of a sex . . . And how cruelly mistaken we are, designating it—*that way*, and how we were *not* mistaken—then!"[71]

This longing for a return to pre-sexual identity cannot, of course, be fully realized, but it shows the deep-rooted intensity that emerges when Tsvetaeva grapples with this question. Indeed, Irina Shevelenko traces the roots of Tsvetaeva's attempts to escape the constraints of gendered sexuality all the way back to 1918–1920, arguing that by then Tsvetaeva's sense of being a social outcast was accompanied by a similar uneasiness concerning her sex. "Men and women are not so much equally close to me as they are—equally distant," Tsvetaeva wrote in August 1918, and Shevelenko notes that there are numerous similar passages in Tsvetaeva's notebooks during this period. "It's not only impossible to separate automythologizing from Tsvetaeva's real psychosexual peculiarities, but it's unproductive," Shevelenko concludes. Instead, she suggests, it's important to recognize that this ambivalence was a constituting factor in the formation of Tsvetaeva's literary "I" and that it conditioned her sense of alienation.[72] Alyssa Dinega sees a similar disruptive role played by gender and writes that for Tsvetaeva, gender "forges a wedge between the demands of poetry and the demands of life" that conspires to keep them eternally separate.[73] It is this powerful sense of gender as separator that continues to influence Tsvetaeva in "My Pushkin." If she could sidestep gender, could these worlds of poetry and life merge? Tsvetaeva understands that the question is moot but the energy that it unleashes provides the impetus for examination of parallel injustices. She will stand not just with those oppressed by gender-based inequity, but with those assailed by any form of discrimination and repression.

The defense of the oppressed in "My Pushkin" is first of all a defense of the Poet, but Tsvetaeva's compassion and sense of justice (here "poetic justice" becomes the highest and most absolute justice possible, far removed from any notion of "they had it coming") embrace a much broader spectrum of the downtrodden and oppressed, the underdogs of society. As we have seen, it includes women forced to conform to paternal demands, but it also includes daughters who are subjected to the absolute control of their parents (mother or father). Again she turns to Pushkin for inspiration, and finds in his African heritage an important support for her attraction to the marginalized. "The Russian poet—is a Negro," Tsvetaeva writes. "The poet—is a Negro and the poet—was struck down. (Oh God, how it all came together! What poet among those that were and those that are, *isn't* a Negro and what poet—hasn't been struck down and killed?)"[74] Once again Tsvetaeva shows her unhesitating and constant identification of poets with the minority, with the oppressed. Poets are the eternal outsiders in her poetic worldview, as in the famous formulation of poetic identity from her 1924 *Poem of the End* (*Poema kontsa*):

> Life—is a place where it's not possible to live:
> The Jew—ish quarter.
>
> So would it not be a hundred times better
> To become the Eternal Jew?
> Since for everyone who isn't scum,
> A Jew—ish pogrom
> . . . .
> Ghetto of the chosen ones! Wall and ditch.
> Mer—cy don't await!
> In this most Christian of worlds
> Poets are yids.[75]

In "My Pushkin" the original formula ("Poets are Yids") is reformulated to become "Poets are Negroes" but the underlying message is the same: The poet is an outcast, misunderstood, rejected.

There are several moments like these where "My Pushkin" shows signs of a deep-rooted passion for contemporary justice, for not only does Tsvetaeva look at the persecution of poets, but she also allows politics to enter her work in a way that was for her extremely rare. Where Mandelstam can discuss the Revolution's aftermath in *The Noise of Time* or shriek at the injustice of the contemporary Soviet state in "Fourth Prose" and Pasternak can at least allude to the similarities between contemporary Soviet literary policies and the horrors of literary persecution in ancient Venice in *Safe Conduct*, Tsvetaeva typically remains aloof from political commentary. In "My Pushkin," though, politics enter her autobiography, at least obliquely. Commenting on Pushkin's ability to render things as minor and seemingly "factual" as a bird so that they take on a different type of reality through poetry, she remarks: "It would be interesting to know what the sober school children of Soviet Russia think about that bird." Later, writing about Pushkin's *Poltava*, she describes her inability to understand the concept of a "denunciation" being delivered to Peter: "If they had explained, I would not have understood, would not have inwardly understood as even now I don't understand the possibility of writing a denunciation."[76] These were the realities faced by poets like Pasternak in the Soviet Union, trying to keep poetry alive in an environment where metaphor had become a threat to socialist reality, and where the act of writing had become more frequently life-threatening than life-affirming. Tsvetaeva's defense of the poet appears to have stirred something in her that demanded justice far beyond poetry.

The essence, the beauty, the power of poetry, Tsvetaeva shows, is that it can make the world *different*. Just as Wallace Stevens' blue guitarist does not play things "as they are," Tsvetaeva allies herself with Pushkin in claiming the right—even the responsibility—to create a world that is different through poetry. Describing Pushkin's lines about a "little bird" that should really be understood as a butterfly, Tsvetaeva remarks that no one has ever thought to question whether it was a bird or not. The power of the "poetic melody" was too strong, since "once it is stated that way—it *is* that way. That way—in *poetry*. That little bird is a poetic liberty." In the same way, Pushkin's "To the Sea" (*K moriu*) forever changed Tsvetaeva's understanding of what a sea *is*. What Pushkin was able to capture was a notion of the sea's absolute freedom, its paradoxical combination of formlessness and constancy. Later, Tsvetaeva connects her image of the sea (received through Pushkin) to her other great poet-interlocutor, Boris Pasternak, whose own Pushkin-inspired poem she quotes toward the end of "My Pushkin." She describes a community of poets linked by this "free element" but also by poetry, and there is a sense of satisfaction in Tsvetaeva's conclusion to "My Pushkin."[77] Musing on the "illiteracy" of her childish assumption that Pushkin's use of the word "element" (*stikhiia* in Russian) had to be connected to lyric poetry (*stikhi* in Russian), Tsvetaeva concludes that it may have seemed to be just a misunderstanding based on limited vocabulary, but actually "proved to be prophetic insight: the 'free element' proved to be poetry and not the sea; poetry, that is, the one element with which there is no parting—ever."[78]

There could hardly be a more fitting conclusion to Tsvetaeva's autobiography. Whether she is thinking about her own isolation as an unappreciated poet in Paris or about the threats facing poets in the Soviet Union, the sense of an unbreakable link to poetry provides a consolation and sense of belonging that transcends all else. And although it may be tempting to dismiss such an absolute assertion as hollow rhetorical bravado, the overall emotional tenor of Tsvetaeva's autobiography stands behind the intensity of this claim. In Paris she may be criticized for being too Red, too White, too indifferent, too different—but none of that matters in the realm of poetry, the one place where she can move about with absolute authority.

And that is the core of Tsvetaeva's autobiography. This is not primarily a story of gender rebellion or assertion, or a story of generational conflict with mother against daughter. Instead, this is a story about poetry and about poets: Where does a poet come from, and how does she realize her destiny to be a poet in the face of determined opposition? Tsvetaeva answers that question with a tale of individual determination and a poetic birthright that can be traced directly to Pushkin himself.

Joseph Brodsky once wrote that for Tsvetaeva, autobiographical prose was "just a breather," but if he is right then these works must rank among the most intense "breathers" ever written. The style, the sheer force of verbal creation, and the emotional depth combine to form a memorable autobiographical work. As Tsvetaeva describes the story of her childhood and youth, we see a young girl who knows that—no matter what others around her may say, or how much they may try to make her conform to their plans for her—she is destined to be a poet. Through the eyes, ears, and impressions of Tsvetaeva in her dual incarnation as author and subject we see that poetry is a force so elemental (the *stikhiia* that reveals *stikhi*) that no obstacle can stand in its way. Whether it develops through instinctive resistance, through the intervention of a *diabolus ex machina*, or an alliance with another great poet, the reality of poetry will never be swept aside. Much more than any other poet discussed here, Tsvetaeva makes poetry and her identity as a poet the very core of her autobiography, the absolute center of her being, and "the one element with which there is no parting—ever."

6

A Survivor's Story

Boris Pasternak's second autobiography, written in 1956 only a few years before his death, is a rarity whose true value has never been adequately appreciated. It isn't just that the slim *People and Propositions* (*Liudi i polozheniia*) is one of the only significant autobiographies written by a poet in the years immediately after Stalin's death, or even that this second account offers an intriguing insight into the way Pasternak's priorities shifted from the time of *Safe Conduct* to the later work. These are both important points, but the greatest significance of this second autobiography is even more basic: Pasternak survived to write it. He was not the only poet of his generation to outlive Stalin (others, like the officially discredited Anna Akhmatova, lived even longer). But Pasternak's fate was more precarious. After Vladimir Mayakovsky's death he was the most gifted poet to live directly in the public eye and in the Stalin era this was the most dangerous place to be. Countless Soviet politicians, artists and writers found that fame and success brought no immunity in the purges that regularly swept the nation. Instead, greater recognition seemed more likely to precede eventual disaster. Pasternak recognized the tenuousness of his position and there were numerous occasions when he thought that arrest was imminent. Still, he survived. He dodged attempts by others to reshape him into the new national poet after Mayakovsky's death and he remained just aloof enough when controversy swept through the Soviet literary establishment. Judiciously timed assertions of independence were interspersed with occasional efforts to fit in. And when cornered by authority that he could not ignore, Pasternak gave ground as slowly as possible.

As a result, Pasternak was still alive to write his second autobiography long after poets Paolo Yashvili (1937) and Marina Tsvetaeva (1941) had been hounded to the point of suicide and Osip Mandelstam and Titsian Tabidze were arrested and taken to their deaths during the Great Terror of the late 1930s. Poets were consumed all around him and when Pasternak turned again to autobiography after a quarter-century gap he had both the long view of the survivor and the incredibly focused vision of one who knows that for him, too, the end may not be far off. The result was a terse account that covers ground similar to that explored earlier in *Safe Conduct* but with a distinctly new emphasis and a sharply different tone. The spiraling impressionistic narrative style of *Safe Conduct* is replaced by a laconic directness that openly rejects the earlier autobiography. No more flights of fancy, Pasternak says with this shift in style. Instead, the sober tone fits completely with the new text's function as a commemoration of the many poets lost and as a literary monument to the author himself.

This new approach was not a sudden shift, but the result of a long personal evolution as Pasternak observed and adapted to a steady stream of changes in the country's political and literary structure, right from the time when the final installments of *Safe Conduct* appeared in 1931. Today's western reader has a double handicap when trying to understand these changes, since the passage of time and the distance of separation conspire with a natural inclination to look for narrative continuity. It's relatively easy to choose a series of key events and construct a smooth narrative arc of the Soviet state's life span, moving from the chaos of revolution to the brutally efficient terror of high Stalinism, then on to the decay of Brezhnev's era before passing through the final euphoria of glasnost and ending in complete collapse. The benefit of hindsight and our passion for convenient capsulization obscure the messy realities which made daily life much more complex than this convenient story line would allow. We easily forget that the times were not just unnerving and often frightening, but also very confusing for Pasternak and his contemporaries.

Even the 1930s, which seem to invite a narrative thread that runs smoothly from the clampdowns of the cultural revolution to the terror of the purges at the end of the decade, were filled with events that sent contradictory messages about the country's future. The years 1930 and 1931 offer an excellent but not unique example of how unpredictable these years were for Pasternak. In the fall of 1930, trade and professional associations of all kinds were mobilized to demonstrate their indignation at the crimes of the still untried defendants accused of sabotaging the country's first Five Year Plan. As Lazar Fleishman puts it, "Failure to express the most active support for punitive measures began to be interpreted as duplicity and, by extension, as sympathy for enemies of the Soviet regime. These months witnessed the forging of a new political phenomenon: Soviet unanimity, the principle of unconditional support for any and all steps taken by the Soviet leadership, no matter how contradictory."[1] Pasternak tried to separate himself physically from places where he could be drawn into the campaign, but even this small move of resistance was dangerous. Then things seemed to change in early 1931 when the final installments of *Safe Conduct* were published in the journal *Red Virgin Soil* and there were signs that could be interpreted as a political thaw: Boris Pilnyak was allowed to travel to America and Stalin gave a speech in which he suggested that the proletarian writers did not have enough literary finesse to meet the country's expectations.[2]

Pasternak responded to the changes with a poem that indicated a willingness to enter into conversation with the rulers of this new age. The poem "A Century and a Bit" (*Stolet's lishnim*) paraphrased several lines from Alexander Pushkin's famous "Stanzas" (*Stansy*) in which Pushkin adopted the role of interlocutor and advisor to Tsar Nicholas I, urging Nicholas to show mercy to the Decembrist plotters as a sign of true nobility and imperial wisdom. Pasternak knew that his readers would instantly seize on the poem as an indication that he was stepping into a similar role in relation to Stalin and he probably anticipated that it would generate controversy. Some have interpreted the poem as capitulation. Others wonder whether it anticipates positive changes or perhaps warns that Pushkin's optimism is out of place in the new century. At the very least, the poem shows Pasternak's belief that the poet's function has not been eclipsed and that a poet's intercession makes a difference. That conviction alone demonstrates Pasternak's continuing hope for brighter days.

But there were other poems and experiences that create a contrasting impression. Also in early 1931 Pasternak wrote the poem "To a Friend" (*Drugu*) (originally titled "To Boris Pilnyak" [*Borisu Pil'niaku*]) in which he recognized the dangers that lay in wait for any poet who became too closely identified with the state. In June Pasternak was sent to the Ural mountains to witness the enormous construction projects undertaken to support the Five Year Plan. The trip did not lead to the kind of propaganda triumph that the organizers had hoped for, though. Pasternak came home early, depressed by the toll that the Plan was exacting on the people.

The trip to the Urals was followed by another, very different, journey. In the fall of 1931 Pasternak went to Georgia, where he met Paolo Yashvili, Titsian Tabidze, and other poets who inspired him with their vitality and passion for great art, something that he had seen too seldom in Moscow's more politically charged cultural circles. Life in Georgia seemed better—socialism seemed to have left fewer brutal traces on the people and their entire way of life. When he returned to Moscow, Pasternak shared his impressions at several literary gatherings and was moved even to the point of extremely risky comparisons, reportedly telling one group of writers that in the south not all literature had been "destroyed" by the revolution.[3]

The shifting political fortunes of individuals and entire movements continued to alternately raise and dash hopes in the following years. At the beginning of 1932 Pasternak found himself targeted by the proletarian writers who led RAPP (the Russian Association of Proletarian Writers) when they launched a series of articles and speeches that attacked *Safe Conduct*'s idiosyncratic and allegedly bourgeois style. This campaign came at a time when Pasternak's domestic life was in turmoil: He had left his first wife, but did not break completely with her while already living with the woman who would eventually become his second wife. The complications in his literary and private affairs brought Pasternak so low that he attempted suicide in the spring of 1932.[4]

The next shift in the cultural balance of power was so swift and so dramatic that it took almost everyone by surprise. In April 1932 the Central Committee of the Communist Party issued a decree that called for a complete reorganization of literary organizations. RAPP was officially dethroned and some of those who had been actively haranguing Pasternak only weeks earlier now found themselves the targets of even more ferocious denunciations. At first glance the demise of RAPP should have been welcomed by the non-proletarian writers and poets who suddenly found themselves returned, almost by default, to places of greater prominence in Soviet culture. In Pasternak's case, his return to favor was signaled by the publication of a new collection of his poetry, *Second Birth* (*Vtoroe rozhdenie*), and by the approval of an extended trip of his own choosing. But these positive results obscured a deeper and rather chilling shift. With the instantaneous and complete transformation of RAPP from hunter to hunted, the Party sent a powerful message: The era of relative laissez faire literary politics had ended. No longer would literary groups compete with each other for the opportunity to dominate literature. From that point on the Party intended to take complete and open control of literature.

In 1933 no one knew exactly what the Party intended, though. The return of several political prisoners suggested a "definite relaxation" on the political front, writes Lazar Fleishman, and the delay in establishing a new literary authority left a power vacuum that could also have been interpreted as a loosening of official controls. When Pasternak returned to Georgia in late 1933 he ruffled numerous local feathers by not devoting an appropriate portion of his attention to the politically correct poetry that state officials urged him to promote. Instead, he took advantage of what seemed to be the start of a new period of increased freedom and sought out poets whose more independent lyric voice kept them off the state's list of "reliable" poets.

It seems inconsistent, then, that soon after his return from Georgia Pasternak was a key figure in what can now be identified as the beginning of the Stalin personality cult that would soon engulf the entire country. The primary ingredient in this campaign was an almost worshipful article about Stalin that appeared in a January 1934 issue of *Pravda*. The article, "Architect of Socialist Society" by Karl Radek, was accompanied by Pasternak's Russian translations of two similarly laudatory odes by Georgian poets. Why would Pasternak allow his name to be associated with such an obvious effort to create a superhuman Stalin? The poems were from a special anthology of poems about Stalin commissioned by Lavrenty Beria in Georgia, where Beria was one of the region's major political forces before moving to Moscow to take over the secret police. Pasternak certainly knew about the anthology project and about Beria's status as local strongman, and there were whispers and even outright assertions that his translations signaled a new stance of political alliance with the regime. Given his recent actions, though, such an absolutist judgment is hard to support. Fleishman and others are closer to the mark when they argue that Pasternak's involvement was primarily a gesture of support for Georgian poets and secondarily a sign of hope that the era of terror was ending. The "hyperbolic formulas of glorification" in the poems were part of Georgia's literary tradition and Pasternak translated them in that spirit, writes Fleishman, although the translations themselves still represented political compromise.[5]

It was also in 1933 that Pasternak learned of another Stalin poem, but a poem with a completely different orientation. This was Mandelstam's poem depicting Stalin as a bloodthirsty "Kremlin mountaineer"; after Pasternak heard Mandelstam recite it he uttered the now famous (and ultimately prophetic) verdict that this poem was not really a literary artifact but rather "an act of suicide." Subsequently Mandelstam was arrested, attempted suicide, was sent into exile, released, then eventually rearrested and sent off to his death. After Mandelstam's first arrest Pasternak did what he could to help, writing and calling on people who might be able to secure Mandelstam's release, and he even received a special telephone call from Stalin to discuss the Mandelstam affair.[6] Whatever else the disagreement over Mandelstam's poem may indicate about the way the two poets approached contemporary life, it also shows that each one recognized the risks inherent in composing and even knowing such a poem. In other words, even if Pasternak may have been hoping for a political relaxation, he (like Mandelstam) harbored no illusions about what was possible and impossible for a poet to say safely in 1933. Poems could very literally be the source of life and death and this must have been a terrible thing for Pasternak to contemplate.

The following years continued the cycle of repression and relaxation. The 1934 Writers' Congress instituted a new literary hierarchy and although he was the target of some criticism during the congress, Pasternak was elected to the Board of Directors. And while the official exhortation to follow the tenets of state-approved socialist realism showed an alarming willingness to limit the writer's creative freedom, the new policy could also be interpreted as a partial democratization of literature, especially in light of Maksim Gorky's emphasis on maintaining aesthetic standards.

Then came the assassination of Sergei Kirov in December. A new cycle of political arrests began and Pasternak fell into what he called an internal crisis that lasted through much of 1935. His condition left him almost immobilized at times, and it was precisely at this time that he was coerced into attending the Paris conference of writers where his fateful "nonmeeting" with Tsvetaeva took place and where he was expected to represent Soviet literature in a denunciation of German fascism's attack on the arts. Later in the year the political climate changed yet again: The country was said to be on the verge of receiving a liberal new constitution and Pasternak was given a prominent place as one of only two poets (the other was his Georgian friend Titsian Tabidze) featured in the special 1936 New Year's issue of *Izvestia*.

Soon after the New Year, though, any lingering doubts about the Soviet Union's political direction and its cultural policy were removed. On January 28 *Pravda* published an intensely personal attack on composer Dmitry Shostakovich, accusing him of artistic malfeasance in the creation of his opera *Lady Macbeth of the Mtsensk District*. In February the board of the Writers' Union—of which Pasternak was a member—met and began to compare Pasternak and Mayakovsky, evidently following up on Stalin's 1935 statement that Mayakovsky was the best example of a Soviet poet and that indifference to Mayakovsky could be considered a crime. Pasternak was both criticized and defended at the meeting and a follow-up gathering was called for March. On each occasion Pasternak defended both himself and others who were now accused of wildly varying political and aesthetic misdeeds. Indeed, aesthetic failures were interpreted as politically based and deemed indicative of either political ignorance or insubordination.

The literary campaign against Pasternak and others started to fade but soon the cultural establishment was caught up in the countrywide furor stirred up by the trial of Lev Kamenev, Grigory Zinoviev and fourteen other defendants accused of terrorist crimes against the state. There was severe pressure on all major unions and organizations to issue official statements against the accused, and each new statement reached a higher level of intensity as no one wanted to risk being perceived as weak when it came to the officially proclaimed fight against terrorism. Calls for the execution of the accused overlooked the seeming technicality that they had not yet been tried, and the Writers' Union was also expected to denounce the accused. On August 21, in the middle of the trial, a statement entitled "Wipe Them Off the Face of the Earth" was published in *Pravda* and signed by the entire board of directors—including Pasternak. Did he authorize the inclusion of his name? Readers, both in the USSR and abroad, assumed that he did. Fleishman points out the practical obstacles that would have had to be overcome to get Pasternak's agreement before the inclusion of his name with the letter; Christopher Barnes confirms that Pasternak had not authorized the use of his name, and adds that under great pressure, Pasternak "agreed not to remove his name at the proof stage."[7] Barnes's clarification actually casts the entire incident in a more somber light, though: If Pasternak did indeed know about the inclusion of his name in advance and if it really would have been possible to remove his name before publication, then it follows that his inclusion is at least partially volitional. We will never know what threats were made to dissuade him from removing his name but they found their mark and his name was still there when the paper went to press. Pasternak's reluctance was noted, though, and even this tacit support for the official anti-terror campaign did not prevent a new wave of accusations against him in December, when French writer André Gide published a book critical of the USSR and Pasternak refused to join in condemning it.

In 1937 the purges and terror escalated dramatically and Pasternak saw the political deterioration cut even more tragically into the literary community. Boris Pilnyak was arrested. Nikolai Bukharin, one of the few Party leaders who cared about literature as an art form, was arrested. Georgian poets Paolo Yashvili and Titsian Tabidze both perished, one by suicide and the other in the prison system. No one knew who would be next, and it was clear that past support for the Party was no guarantee of safety—indeed, such support might be more a liability than a surety. Some of the most vocal and energetic leaders of RAPP, including the formerly dominant Leopold Averbakh, were arrested and executed.

The cases of Yashvili and Tabidze were particularly troubling, not just because they were close friends but because their inclusion in the list of victims underlined the seeming irrelevance of past actions. Yashvili had been a prominently featured contributor to the 1934 anthology in Stalin's honor, and had participated actively in many of the 1936 denunciations. Less than a year later Beria suggested that Yashvili should think carefully about his past actions and the Federation of Georgian Writers took this as an authorization to lash out at Yashvili. After being relentlessly attacked at a series of special meetings Yashvili looked for a way out, confessing to a broad array of ideological errors and mistakes in judgment. But his pursuers proved relentless. Yashvili's official expulsion from the Federation was scheduled to take place at the July 22, 1937 meeting of the writers' presidium but he preempted the action by taking an even more drastic step. In the middle of the proceedings Yashvili pulled out a gun and shot himself in front of his fellow writers.[8]

Tabidze may not have shown the same kind of zeal in supporting the regime during the 1936 trials, but he had demonstrated support for the new order in previous years. When the Georgian writers reorganized their Federation in the early 1930s, Tabidze participated on a five-member panel that heard the cases of 110 writers at a 1931 meeting; the panel voted to expel nearly a fifth of them on the grounds of "ideological and creative" shortcomings.[9] Even his featured appearance alongside Pasternak in the special 1936 New Year's edition of *Izvestia* did not help. Clearly there was no way to predict where or when the dreaded knock on the door might come, but Tabidze had no illusions of security. He made no public concessions, and in one of his last known poems wrote that even if the poet's throat would be "slit ear to ear," immortality would still be conveyed in the atom of the poem itself.[10] For years Pasternak clung to the hope that Tabidze had somehow survived in the prison system and he learned only much later that Tabidze had been killed soon after his 1937 arrest.

The death toll continued to mount in the following years. In 1938 Mandelstam was arrested and taken to his death. In 1939 Tsvetaeva returned to the Soviet Union from France and discovered for herself how bad the conditions were: Her husband was arrested and then shot, and her daughter was arrested, tortured and sentenced to an eight-year imprisonment. The outbreak of World War II interrupted this cycle of arrests and accusations and it was something of a shock when the state initiated a broad cultural mobilization to support the national war effort. There were even signs of artistic rehabilitation: Anna Akhmatova suddenly regained national prominence with lyrics in the most important national newspapers, a series of triumphant public readings, and an anthology that ended years of complete exclusion from publication. Pasternak returned to lyric poetry after a lengthy silence. Taken as a whole, the war years offered a greater degree of freedom than poets had witnessed in more than a decade, but news of Tsvetaeva's suicide in 1941 provided a bleak reminder that not everyone shared equally in the state's goal-directed tolerance.

When the war ended in triumph many thought that the relaxed artistic atmosphere would continue into a new era. Instead, the end of one war merged almost seamlessly into the start of the new cold war and wartime cultural gains were quickly negated. Akhmatova and Mikhail Zoshchenko became the first victims of the literary onslaught known as Zhdanovism, named for the Party functionary who provided its most recognizable face. When Pasternak responded to the new campaign by isolating himself more and more from the world of official literature, his absence was interpreted as a dangerous show of independence and he was finally stripped of his directorship in the Writers' Union. It was therefore a surprise when an edition of his poetry was approved for publication in February 1947; more understandable was the subsequent decision, however belated, to rescind approval and to destroy the entire print run of 25,000 copies. Pasternak turned away from poetry and spent most of the next decade devoted to the prose work that had come to dominate his hopes and his imagination—*Doctor Zhivago.*

I offer this skeletal summary of the events that surrounded Pasternak from the 1930s to the 1950s because an understanding of the era's constant anxiety, of the recurring cycle of raised hopes dashed by further repression, and of the steady disappearance of poets and others who meant so much to him, is essential to appreciate Pasternak's narrative strategy in *People and Propositions.* Even the most cursory look at the new autobiography shows some significant changes from the text of *Safe Conduct.* Perhaps most obvious is the brevity of the new work, which is only about half the length of its predecessor despite the fact that Pasternak was almost twice as old as he'd been when he wrote *Safe Conduct.*

One reasonable explanation for this discrepancy is that *People and Propositions* was originally written as an introductory essay for a proposed new anthology of Pasternak's poetry and thus faced concrete space limitations. A deeper reason for the change, though, is that the new, shorter narrative reflects Pasternak's changed attitudes to literary creation, both in poetry and in prose. By the 1950s he had shifted largely from poetry to prose and was consciously cultivating a simpler style in both modes. The desire for simplification becomes a recurring theme in his conversations and letters and is frequently accompanied by expressions of frustration at being cut off from contemporary life. This sense of estrangement had been growing steadily even before a new series of literary reprisals started in 1946, he told Nikolai Smirnov in April 1955, and although initially it was his own doing it soon became clear that he was being pushed out of the literary mainstream. As a result, Pasternak says, he values Smirnov's opinions as someone still in touch with contemporary life. In a December 10, 1955 letter to Nina Tabidze he expresses himself even more directly, writing that "I could be happy, in my very closest circle all is well. . . . But now there are so many reasons and attempts to disturb my isolation, to draw me into public activities! And then misfortunes begin for me. There is so little in common between me and people who consider me their own. . . . I want something very different than what they want. . . ."[11]

There is a curious juxtaposition at work here: Even as Pasternak senses himself increasingly removed from contemporary life, he moves ever more deliberately toward a style that will be accessible to the broadest range of readers. This is one reason why Pasternak showed such anxiety about his newest work and the way it would be received. The April 5 letter to Nikolai Smirnov (cited above) reveals a mixture of satisfaction and apprehension about his work on the second part of *Doctor Zhivago*: Pasternak describes his work on the novel as something that both provides and expresses profound joy and inner satisfaction, but also indicates that he has been writing with a kind of "dullness and naivete which I permitted myself and forgave." In another April 1955 letter to Smirnov, Pasternak repeats this renunciation of ornamentation and says that he is writing "modestly, without special effects and stylish coquetry."[12]

The simpler, more direct style that Pasternak strove for in his novel was carried over into *People and Propositions*, and the enormous Zhivago project effectively bridges Pasternak's approach to the two autobiographies. During the years that he worked on *Doctor Zhivago* Pasternak spent relatively little time on poetry, and found himself oriented more and more toward prose. When he was approached by an admirer for advice on whether to pursue a literary career, Pasternak responded with a rather brusque reluctance to offer concrete advice, telling the young man that people do not appreciate that "I don't like 'verse in general,' that I don't grasp poetry the way it is commonly understood, that I am no judge, no connoisseur in that sphere." After recommending that his young reader take up history, or better yet one of the natural sciences, Pasternak claims that he is absolutely set apart from those who write, read and discuss poetry and states that he has never even claimed the title "poet" for himself.[13]

This statement is rather disingenuous, since Pasternak clearly recognizes himself a poet even if he will not label himself one directly. And despite his disclaimers, one cannot escape the sense that Pasternak is consciously assessing his place in literature during these years. In a practical sense poetry had its limits in the contemporary age, he remarked to Olga Carlisle in a 1960 interview: "I believe that it is no longer possible for lyric poetry to express the immensity of our experience. Life has grown too cumbersome, too complicated. We have acquired values which are best expressed in prose." But he still saw an inherent value in verse, for he deliberately made poetry the central thread in *People and Propositions* even while seeming to move away from the lyric mode in his other creative work and in his statements to correspondents and friends. Indeed, even the shift to prose represented by the monumental *Doctor Zhivago* can easily be misconstrued as a sharp turn from poetry until we remember that this entire story is a *poet's* story, and that it is the protagonist's poetry that constitutes the work's most powerful defense of moral and aesthetic values. In his conversations with Carlisle, Pasternak even suggested that the poems served as a kind of essentialist reprise of the entire work because "the plan of the novel is outlined by the poems accompanying it."[14] Clearly he isn't referring to the novel's plot, so even while Pasternak considers poetry unsuitable for capturing the full "immensity" of contemporary life, it retains the ability to capture life's elusive essence.

It is in this broader sense of poetry's cultural value that *People and Propositions* fits so logically and naturally into Pasternak's artistic vision of the 1950s. While *Doctor Zhivago* tells the fictionalized story of an alter ego poet, *People and Propositions* functions as Pasternak's personal and "real life" poetic retrospective, with the impression of verisimilitude enhanced dramatically by the shift to a simpler and more direct style. Pasternak actually mentions many of the same people and events that appear in *Safe Conduct*, but the new treatment is quite different. Christopher Barnes captures the dispassionate tone quite well when he describes the work as a "distant and almost serene look at the author's past life,"[15] but there is a deep sense of emotional restraint, of an emotional depth that rarely surfaces directly. When Pasternak wrote *People and Propositions* the figures of his tragic poet-martyr Yury Zhivago and of the suffering Lara must have been always before him, and I would argue that their influence helps to explain why in this second autobiography there is no mention of ambivalence or delay in Pasternak's coming to poetry.

But Zhivago's experiences connect to *People and Propositions* on even more fundamental levels. Zhivago's personal struggles provide a context for Pasternak's greater inclination in this autobiography to depict the poet's life as a *redeeming* life. The development of the fictional character Zhivago gave Pasternak a chance to construct a workable model for the relationship between poetry and prose as Zhivago searches for a way to capture for posterity those inner forces that demand expression. Zhivago finds his immortality in the poems that survive him and that for many readers have become (perhaps not altogether foreseen or even intended by Pasternak himself) the most treasured part of *Doctor Zhivago*. The inclusion of these poems in the text offers eloquent testimony to the fact that Pasternak still recognizes poetry's ability to communicate differently than prose; there may be ways in which prose can "express values" best, but poetry offers a timeless way to express the ineffable thoughts that sometimes lie even *beyond* what we might try to define as "values" or even "ideas." Just as Zhivago dies but leaves behind a poetic legacy that will never be erased, Pasternak in *People and Propositions* prepares for his own eventual death: He provides a framework within which people can interpret his life as a poet and understand the poetry that will serve as *his* legacy. In this way, I believe, Pasternak's autobiography becomes a prose version of the "Exegi monumentum" poems that great poetic predecessors like Gavrila Derzhavin and Alexander Pushkin used to define their own places in history.

As already noted, Pasternak's style in *People and Propositions* is quite different from the style that characterized his work in the 1920s and

1930s. The turbulence of *Safe Conduct*, where every individual object seems to be in perpetual motion as an actor in Pasternak's poetic universe, gives way to a more restrained, modest style. Again, *Doctor Zhivago* is the primary mediating force here. The stylistic "lapses" or plot implausibilities in *Doctor Zhivago* are part of what makes Pasternak's later prose "more obvious," to use Angela Livingstone's term. She attributes this quest for simplicity to Pasternak's desire to make his writing more comprehensible to the broadest possible audience. "There is a peculiar generosity in this attempt of Pasternak's to pin down and exhibit the elusive flights of his own creativity," writes Livingstone. "Often it meant giving up flying for walking."[16] But this quest for "simplicity" is not the same as a desire for "accessibility" as it was understood by the Soviet literary hierarchy; instead, says Victor Erlich, Pasternak was actually going directly against the ideological mainstream, even if he was moving toward the more normative aesthetic mode. It was an attempt to achieve maximally effective communication, a sense of moral urgency, and Erlich notes that Pasternak himself claimed to be striving for an "unnoticeable" style with no gap between idea and representation.[17]

In the end Pasternak's shift in style had no impact on the readers he hoped to find because the autobiography was not considered suitable for publication. When Pasternak submitted his first draft to the editorial offices the text contained nothing about the revolution. Editor Nikolai Bannikov considered this omission to be a serious problem and at his insistence Pasternak agreed to rework his draft. He returned with an additional section called "My Sister Life" in which the Revolution was discussed, but this was also judged unsatisfactory and the autobiography was again turned down. Eventually, *People and Propositions* was translated into Georgian and included in a Georgian publication in late 1956; an English-language version appeared in the west in 1959, but after a plan to print the autobiography in the December 1956 issue of *Novy mir* fell through, publication in Russian was delayed almost a decade until 1967.

In some ways *People and Propositions* is very like *Safe Conduct*. Christopher Barnes points out a number of the similarities: the lack of coherent narrative after the revolution, the absence of a domestic life, and the looming silence about many events that took place after 1930.[18] And there are other areas of overlap as well. Poetry and poets are again the dominant topics in *People and Propositions* and many of the same events are related in both accounts, although in *People and Propositions* they are generally presented more succinctly and always more matter-of-factly.

There is one overwhelming and fundamental difference between the two, though, and this difference influences the entire style, structure, and contents of *People and Propositions*. The question that Pasternak wrestles with here is very nearly the opposite of the question that faced him in *Safe*

Conduct. If the first autobiography was an attempt to define a space and mode for a poet to *live*, then *People and Propositions* might be summarized as an attempt to discover how a poet should prepare to *die*. This work is an attempt to help define and shape Pasternak's legacy, to show how he would like to be remembered. I will briefly examine the text of *People and Propositions* to show how the work's style, its organization, and its protagonists help Pasternak to build his case.

The very first sentences of *People and Propositions* establish its stylistic parameters when Pasternak writes that his earlier autobiography, *Safe Conduct*, was "spoilt by unnecessary affectation, the besetting sin of that period."[19] The acknowledgment announces an abandonment of pretentiousness and also serves as the first admission in what will become a very confessional narrative. In stylistic terms this work is almost eerily quiet, especially when juxtaposed with *Safe Conduct*. One of the best ways to point out the essential shifts in Pasternak's narrative style from the first autobiography to the second is to look at how Pasternak takes the same event and treats it quite differently in the new work. Here is a short excerpt from the passage in *Safe Conduct* where Pasternak records his first impressions of Mayakovsky:

> What was natural in his case appeared to be supernatural. The reason was not his stature, but a more general elusive quality. To a greater extent than with other people, his whole being was there in his personal manifestation. He contained within him all the expression and finality which are lacked by the majority, who rarely emerge from the murk of their half-brewed intentions and barren conjectures—and then only do so when particularly jolted. He seemed to exist as on the day after completing some immense spiritual life that had been lived through already in reserve for all future occasions, and everyone now encountered him wreathed in its irreversible consequences.[20]

In *People and Propositions*, the first encounter is described like this:

> There sat before me a handsome, saturnine young man with the bass voice of a precentor, the fists of a boxer, and an inexhaustible, deadly wit—something between a mythical hero from Aleksandr Grin and a Spanish toreador. You could see at once that while he was handsome, witty, and talented—perhaps supremely so—these were not the most important things about him: his main characteristic was his iron inner self-mastery, a set of rules or principles of honour, a sense of duty, which meant that he could not let himself be other—less handsome, less witty or less talented—than he was.[21]

The differences are dramatic. While both passages convey Pasternak's immediate admiration for Mayakovsky and the powerful impression of their first meeting, in *Safe Conduct* Pasternak attempts to capture

Mayakovsky's intangible essence by surrounding him with descriptions and associations that cannot be fixed or pinned down: "His whole being was there in his personal manifestation," he "seemed to exist as on the day after completing some immense spiritual life," he was "wreathed in its irreversible consequences." The description conveys sensation without concrete detail, and Mayakovsky could be perceived only as an enormous essence.

In the passage from *People and Propositions*, the description immediately conjures up a living individual: He has a certain kind of voice, a certain kind of fist, a certain kind of face, and his character is clearly and simply delineated. Pasternak's eloquence remains, but now it comes through in language that is simple and concrete: "the bass voice of a precentor," "fists of a boxer." One could find a virtually limitless supply of passages in each work that would make the same point. The hyperbole of *Safe Conduct* ("It was one of those nights that found it hard to reach the nearby fence and hung above the earth, dazed with exhaustion and with all its strength spent") gives way to more seemly moderation and a much more straightforward style ("silver frost and golden birches lay on [the land] like a modest decoration").[22] The restraint of *People and Propositions* is an essential element in Pasternak's overall objective, for the clarity and brevity offer implicit reinforcement for the narrative's plot as it sets out to create a sense of order in Pasternak's life and work.

These attempts to atone for earlier lapses in style (lapses, at least, in Pasternak's new hierarchy of aesthetic values) are accompanied by a confessional streak that seeks to atone for lapses in character. The admission that his elaborate style was an "affectation" is soon followed by other exercises in self-criticism.[23] Describing his break with music, Pasternak is quite expansive in listing the pragmatic factors that made this career unsuitable: his lack of real skill at the piano, brought on by adolescent arrogance; his lack of discipline; and his perverse conviction that he could not succeed without perfect pitch. There are also literary confessions. With the wisdom of years, he describes a poor translation that he submitted for publication ("my work was immature and dull"), and regrets that because "fair-mindedness, modesty, gratitude, were things not appreciated by young people in the artistic circles," he did not send a note of thanks for the improvements made by an unknown editor but instead sent an angry letter to Maksim Gorky in protest. His shame is exacerbated by the realization that came much later when it finally dawned on him that the editorial improvements were made by Gorky himself and he exclaims in chagrin: "I complained to Gorky about Gorky!" Pasternak relates the pretentiousness of "affecting a Berlin accent" while living in Berlin for a year, and says that what others took for originality in his early poetry was really "utter helplessness and tongue-tiedness." He calls the title of his book *Twin in the Clouds* "idiotically pretentious" and admits that an acquaintance was right when she predicted that he would eventually regret publishing it. These comments, and others like them, present a side of Pasternak that remains almost unseen in *Safe Conduct*, where the only hint of this self-revelation is Pasternak's self-deprecating description of his involvement in the poetry group Centrifuge (*Tsentrifuga*). In *People and Propositions* Pasternak appears to be looking for a way to make amends, and also to anticipate critics who will someday take him to task for the very lapses that he himself reveals here in a series of preemptive strikes. His apologies are both literary and moral/ethical, and together they convey the sense that Pasternak is very deliberately searching his soul as he writes, trying to rectify errors in his past.[24]

Another problematic element of *Safe Conduct* that Pasternak seeks to "rectify" in *People and Propositions* is the structure. Leaving the spiraling narrative and Bergsonian time shifts of *Safe Conduct* behind, Pasternak's new autobiography is emphatically chronological, perhaps even too chronological. The conventional elements of classical autobiography are all present: The day of his birth is carefully recorded, his earliest sensations and impressions are noted.[25] The narrative moves forward with almost pedantic emphasis on its chronological structure. Here we have an extreme simplification, a refutation of the Modernist style with its "provisional nature of the text" and its demand that the reader exercise a "creative sensibility," as Olav Severijnen puts it. Where Pasternak earlier demanded that the reader "fill in the gaps" with events like his fall from a horse, in *People and Propositions* he relates the event in detail, effectively shifting much of the reader's responsibility to the author. The painstaking emphasis on linear chronology becomes another means to renounce *Safe Conduct*'s modernist pedigree because chronological narration does not correspond to the movements of consciousness and subconsciousness that characterize Modernism.[26] In Pasternak's case, the chronological sequencing is virtually unbroken. He explicitly draws attention to this careful arrangement by breaking the chain at one point with a digression about Alexander Blok's visit to Moscow, and then apologizing for the break: "But I have run on ahead, and must return to the story where I left it, in the far-off 1900s."[27]

The emphasis is almost *too* strong, it seems: Why make this such an issue? Perhaps one reason for this insistence is that at one very crucial juncture, Pasternak reshapes time to conflate two events and bring into focus his central theme. The events that Pasternak conflates—his presentation of a paper on art, and the death of Leo Tolstoy—must be seen in combination, for it is the interaction between them that Pasternak wants to emphasize. The paper, entitled "Symbolism and Immortality," is a success, Pasternak reports. Upon his return home after the discussion, he learns that Tolstoy has died and leaves with his father for the Astapovo train station where Tolstoy spent his last days. In the real world of dates and "facts," though, the events were apparently three years apart: Tolstoy died in 1910, while Pasternak's paper was given in 1913.[28] How does the artificial juxtaposition of these events affect our understanding of them? On one hand, not at all. If Pasternak wants to construct a text in a certain way, the reader is left with the task of trying to understand what the juxtaposition accomplishes. On the other hand, if Pasternak is trying to create a sense of reliability and order by emphasizing his trustworthiness as a narrator, this slip hurts his credibility. For our purposes, the discrepancy is a useful reminder that this is still a constructed text, and that elements in the text are more carefully arranged than Pasternak wants to admit.

With that in mind, it is worth examining this passage more closely because it becomes one of the central elements in Pasternak's subtly developed central theme and reveals the function of *People and Propositions*. The full text of "Symbolism and Immortality" has not survived, but Pasternak summarizes its central thesis in his autobiography:

> whenever an individual person dies, he leaves behind a fragment of immortal, racial subjectivity. . . . The main aim of my paper was to suggest that this highly subjective, universally human corner or portion of the soul was perhaps the everlasting arena and chief content of art. And furthermore, that although an artist was of course mortal like everyone else, the joy that he experienced in his existence was something immortal, and could be experienced by others centuries after his death, through his works, in some approximation to his own first, intimate, personal appreciation of it.[29]

The sight of Tolstoy's body, first perceived by Pasternak as "Mt. Elbrus" and then later acknowledged as "no mountain" but rather "a little, wrinkled old man," is an immediate confirmation of Pasternak's thesis. Both sides of the great artist are juxtaposed: The immortality that carries on through his works creates the metaphoric association of mountain-like immensity, but the physical mortality that inevitably robs one of life is there as well, in all its nonmetaphoric concreteness. This realization of the contrast between the immortality of one's work and the mortality of one's body is the issue that Pasternak wrestles with in trying to shape and present his own legacy in this text. If a reminder is needed, Pasternak provides one a few pages later when he recalls the "last, *immortal* document" of Mayakovsky, *At the Top of My Voice* (*Vo ves' golos*). The careful reader will remember that in *Safe Conduct* Pasternak described this work as still speaking to him "from beyond the grave"; its reappearance here a quarter century later proves the timelessness of real art.[30]

The relevance of Pasternak's focus on death is obvious when one notices that his text contains a virtual society populated almost entirely by dead poets—Pasternak is one of the only poets still living. At one point he stops his account to try to understand this: What drove so many poets to commit suicide? He lists Mayakovsky, Tsvetaeva, and Yashvili, and slightly later he discusses Esenin. In trying to understand the suffering of these poets who took their own lives, he declares a figurative moment of silence in tribute to their memory and their suffering. The passage sums up Pasternak's attitude toward other poets in *People and Propositions*, for despite occasional references to poets whose work he doesn't understand or particularly care for, a sense of appreciation—sometimes tempered by judicious words of critique—dominates here. No longer concerned with finding a spot apart and knowing that he is inevitably moving closer to a meeting with these poets beyond death's threshold, Pasternak now deliberately links his name with theirs.[31]

This sense of being part of a larger poetic community permeates the bulk of the work, especially in the sections that appear after Pasternak has moved chronologically through his childhood and then the years when he was occupied largely with music. A poem by the great Symbolist Alexander Blok provides the fulcrum that turns the text, for Pasternak describes the jolt of realization that hit him when he recognized the genius that made Blok's poetry so powerful: Blok renounced artificiality, and as a result his poems seemed to live on their own. This sense of transparency, where the poem itself seems to disappear while its inner world expands to take on the shape of unmediated reality, captivated Pasternak. Blok's ability to observe, to see things that others routinely overlooked, was a revelation. The verbal devices—adjective placement, subjectless predicates, unusual syntax—did not pass unnoticed, but it was Blok's clarity of vision that gave Pasternak the sense that he could see the spiritual depths of Blok's own inner world.

After acknowledging the influence that German poet Rainer Maria Rilke had on him, Pasternak's tribute to his poetic precursors moves on to trace his own earliest steps in poetry. He describes the generosity of poverty-stricken and now forgotten writer Sergei Durylin, who Pasternak here describes as the figure most responsible for helping him make the final shift from music to poetry. He describes—sometimes with a phrase, sometimes with a sentence, sometimes with several paragraphs—the poets and other literary figures who figured in his own development. Pasternak takes particular care in relating his early involvement in various literary groups, then pauses at length to reflect on his relations with Mayakovsky and the points of similarity and difference between them. Then in the midst of his account, Pasternak deliberately breaks off his description of Mayakovsky and turns to the phenomenon of poets who commit suicide, starting with Mayakovsky before moving on to Tsvetaeva, Esenin, Yashvili and finally the very recent suicide of Alexander Fadeev.[32]

Indeed, many of Pasternak's comments about his fellow poets—especially those who died by suicide or other violent means—tend to make *People and Propositions* a near ideal example of the "survivor's text" or "trauma literature" identified by theorists like Robert Lifton and Kali Tal. In Tal's formulation, literature that follows trauma typically contains three main elements: the experience of trauma, the urge to bear witness, and a sense of community.[33] *People and Propositions* resonates brilliantly with all three of the hallmarks Tal describes, especially when Pasternak concludes his deliberate meditation on suicide with the appeal: "All of them suffered indescribable torment, to the point where the feeling of anguish becomes a mental illness. And as we honour their talent and their serene memory, let us also bow in sympathy for their suffering."[34] Here one of the most poignant moments in the text simultaneously identifies trauma, testifies, and invokes a communal response.

Tal's discussion of trauma literature derives from a study of war literature that may seem rather separate from the literary focus of Pasternak's autobiography, but there are a surprising number of convergences. The literary politics of the 1920s and 1930s explicitly depicted the struggle in military terms, and judging by the frequent and only partially metaphorical usage of terms like "battle," "front," and "assault," Pasternak really was part of a war that claimed the lives of many fellow poets. Nadezhda Mandelstam remembers with particular clarity that on the day RAPP was dissolved in 1932 she happened to meet Nikolai Tikhonov and Petr Pavlenko, two important figures in the literary world, and was told by them that "the war in literature has entered a new phase."[35] Pasternak's text shows just how tenuous the divide between metaphor and reality was, and how metaphor eventually became horribly realized as the body count mounted during decades when poets too frequently went missing in action.

People and Propositions also bears the strong imprint of what Lifton calls "survivor psychology," especially in the areas that he describes as "the death imprint" and "death guilt." The death imprint, which Lifton explains as something that calls forth images of actual deaths or of death equivalents, can be found already in *Safe Conduct*, with its close connection to the death of Mayakovsky and its broad pattern of recurring allusions to death and suicide, but it comes through overpoweringly in *People and Propositions*. Here almost all the poets named by Pasternak have already died, many of them violently. Another key feature of the death imprint is the nearly unavoidable "Why did I survive?" question, frequently accompanied by a severe sense of guilt and lingering questions of whether the survivor could have done more to help the deceased.[36] Pasternak certainly fits this profile, especially when it comes to the death of Tsvetaeva. Here his sense of regret and loss is tinged by distinct traces of self-reproach as he thinks of her last weeks and days, alone and without hope.

Discussions of survivor theory show varying psychological outcomes for the survivor, including the temptation to assume the role of hero in a new personal mythology. After dodging death it can be tempting to exult in the realization of having been spared, even to the point of losing one's fear because death no longer carries the same aura of mystery.[37] This approach carried no appeal for Pasternak, who realized that it was no longer possible to know when—or if—the death toll would finally come to an end. His resistance to the role of hero was articulated already in *Safe Conduct* and he returns to this theme in *People and Propositions* by reminding his readers that accepting the hero's mantle carries a price that he refuses to pay: "I love my life and am content with it. I do not need extra gold leaf on it. A life stripped of secrecy and inconspicuousness, life amid the glittering mirrors of a showcase, is something I cannot conceive of."[38] At the same time, Pasternak had no false sense of security and he resisted the temptation to take comfort in his own good fortune at finding himself still alive. In a 1939 conversation with Anatoly Tarasenkov, Pasternak described his determination not to lose focus: "In those terrible, bloody years anyone could have been arrested. We were shuffled around like a deck of cards. And I don't want to rejoice narrow-mindedly that I remain whole while others have perished. Someone must remain to grieve proudly, to wear mourning, to experience life tragically. . . . A living person is needed to bear this sense of tragedy."[39] In *People and Propositions* Pasternak fulfills that responsibility, bearing witness to the spirit and suffering of several generations of Russian poets and even permitting a sense of grief to touch his narrative from time to time.

In 1956 grief could only be hinted at. Stalin's death in 1953 had touched off a new period of ideological and cultural turmoil, but the rehabilitation of purge victims had barely started. Pasternak was actually taking a risk by making so much of his relationships with poets like Tabidze, Yashvili and Tsvetaeva, although the risk was already significantly less than it would have been just five years earlier. Again, this behavior fits the survivor profile established by Lifton, who makes an important distinction between "mourning" and "impaired mourning," suggesting that a survivor's real disease is not grief in its most readily occurring and natural form, but in the distortion of grief ("impaired mourning") that results when circumstances make it impossible to mourn in the way one customarily does.[40] Lifton's immediate subject was the trauma of the Hiroshima nuclear blast, but the same phenomenon characterized Pasternak's experience in the Soviet Union. For years, even decades, these poets not only couldn't be mourned openly, they couldn't even be mentioned openly. It was not just that they had ceased to exist, it was as though they *never had* existed. This was the message communicated by the state's effort to purge history itself, rewriting historical narratives as often as necessary to make sure that the official record contained no references to those who had recently been eliminated and whose deeds, no matter how great, could thus no longer be acknowledged. If someone who fell from favor had been famous enough to merit a place in an important record like the encyclopedia, registered owners of the encyclopedia set would receive a mailing with instructions to cut out a particular page in a specified volume and then paste in the enclosed replacement page. Photographs were airbrushed to remove inconveniently placed figures who had recently ceased to exist. How could one mourn a nonperson? In *People and Propositions* Pasternak can finally begin to mourn by commemorating those who previously couldn't even be named.

Just as there was one poet who stood apart for Pasternak in *Safe Conduct*, so there is one poet in *People and Propositions* who towers above the others. But while in *Safe Conduct* that poet was Mayakovsky and Pasternak's concern was to separate himself from Mayakovsky's consuming presence, here the poet-counterpart is Tsvetaeva and the connection is celebrated, not resisted. Several times Pasternak expresses grief and remorse at her death. He describes some of her works as "enormous in their scope and ideas, vivid, and extraordinarily original," then says: "If I were to start telling, point by point, the story of the shared strivings and interests that united me with Tsvetayeva [Tsvetaeva], I should go far beyond the bounds I have set myself. I should have to devote a whole book to the subject, so much did we live through together." In the relationship between them there is a direct link to *Safe Conduct* and the description of Tsvetaeva as a "kindred soul," a poet of originality who Pasternak sensed was capable of abandoning all in the name of inspiration. In the context of what Pasternak is trying to accomplish in *People and Propositions*, such a kindred spirit is the only appropriate choice for a poetic Other: Pasternak seeks a poet with whom it will be an honor to link his name and his poetic legacy. He predicted that "the very greatest reevaluation and recognition are in store for Tsvetaeva," and would not have been surprised to learn how accurate his prophecy turned out to be.[41]

It is a rare event to have not just one, but two rich and detailed autobiographies by the same poet. In the case of these two works by Pasternak we have the opportunity to compare the self-presentation that he constructed in 1929–1931 with the second one that followed a quarter century later. We can see that both works are strongly influenced by Pasternak's station in life, and by the life-and-death literary world he sees around him. In *Safe Conduct*, his dilemma is to identify a way to live as a poet, to escape the death that seemed determined to engulf him. By the time he came to *People and Propositions*, Pasternak's situation had changed. He accepted the inevitability of physical death, but insisted on the immortality of the artist through art. The task of *People and Propositions* was to put his poetic house in order, to reconstitute his life in the light of immortality.

Mandelstam also wrote more than one account of his life, but *The Noise of Time* and "Fourth Prose" are so different that they are hard to compare. One is a broad retrospective, while the other is very tightly focused on a narrow set of experiences. Where *The Noise of Time* has a historical orientation with an individual flavor and an interest in tracking the literary spirit of his age, "Fourth Prose" shows no broad concern for history; in its place is a vehement defense of the individual poet's right—and responsibility—to rebel against state control. And while Mandelstam, like Pasternak, adopts a very different style in each autobiography, they move in opposite directions. Mandelstam shifts from detached observations to a visceral emotional outpouring; Pasternak abandons flamboyance and verbal bombast in favor of a sparer, more refined style. And finally, Mandelstam makes no attempt to organize his life, to shape a legacy for posterity. Events mitigated against that. He considered himself engaged in battle and even though he may have recognized that death might not be far off, he could not "prepare" for it because he was too engaged in active struggle. There was no opportunity for the kind of purposeful, considered retrospection (even introspection) that we find in Pasternak's *People and Propositions*.

Perhaps this is what makes *People and Propositions* a fitting conclusion for this study. Its reflectiveness and its sense of "fullness" derive in large part from the realization that Pasternak has indeed survived four decades of Soviet rule and can now look back on a relatively long life—very long, if compared to the lives of many of his poet-contemporaries. Here, knowing that he is one of the few still able to tell the story, Pasternak leaves an account that will properly honor the broader community of poets while also establishing his own legacy with poetry at the center.

At the same time, Pasternak ends this autobiography with a reminder that despite the details that he could already include, the account remains incomplete because contemporary life still prohibits him—and everyone writing in the Soviet state—from mourning and commemorating fully. Writing openly about the years that followed the Revolution would require a discussion of Revolution-imposed trials—and that is still impossible, observes Pasternak. Then he concludes with a passage that hints at the stylistic vector of *Safe Conduct*, where Pasternak frequently names something—an event, an object—and then adds a description of the object while claiming to be leaving an unfilled gap. Here Pasternak applies a similar technique when trying to define what this future writing may look like: "It should be written about in words that make the heart falter and the hair stand on end. To write about it as if it were something learnt and familiar, in language that is not shattering, language that is paler than

Gogol's and Dostoyevsky's when they wrote of Petersburg, would be writing not only without sense or purpose: it would be base and shameless. We are still a long way from this ideal."[42] These words bring the text to its conclusion and convey the depth of Pasternak's concern for the future of poets, of literature, even of the country as a whole. There can be no ultimate sense of peace, no finality in a text that ends by reminding the reader that no account—not even the one presently in hand—is yet able to describe these events as they deserve to be remembered. Implicitly, then, Pasternak recognizes and acknowledges that although *People and Propositions* clearly tells the story of a poet's life and frames his life as a literary testament, neither his memory nor the memory of the poets he describes can be adequately conveyed in these pages. Ultimately his legacy should be determined not by this autobiography—which contains the *story* of the poet—but by his poetry, which captures the essential *spirit* of the poet.

Conclusion

When Pasternak offered the bittersweet conclusion in 1956's *People and Propositions* that "we are still far" from the way the era should be remembered, he wrote that any attempt to write "shatteringly," as he put it, would continue to meet resistance in the Soviet Union. Events in his own life soon confirmed the accuracy of this observation. By 1956 Pasternak had been working on his novel *Doctor Zhivago* for nearly a decade and was anxious to find a publisher for it, considering the book his most important achievement as an artist. When he was turned down by the editorial board of the journal *Novy mir*, Pasternak decided on a dangerous course. Rather than simply hoping that some other Soviet publisher would accept the project, he sent the manuscript to Italy for publication in translation. He hadn't forgotten the harsh Soviet response to other writers when they published abroad in the 1920s and 1930s, nor did he think that a new attempt to bypass domestic restrictions would be viewed more charitably. Instead, his determination to see the novel in print outweighed concerns about the consequences. Still, he moved cautiously since there was still hope that a Russian edition might appear through the state publishing house in 1957. After the Hungarian uprising against Soviet authority during the closing months of 1956, though, a conservative backlash within the Soviet Union insured that the novel would not be published in his homeland in the foreseeable future.

After that, events surrounding the story of Pasternak's text and its reception at home and abroad take on an increasing air of unreality. The extraordinary efforts by the Soviet literary establishment to prevent or delay the novel's publication, Pasternak's complicated public and private attempts to see that publication moved forward while minimizing repercussions in the USSR, and the eventual announcement that Pasternak had been awarded the 1958 Nobel Prize for literature are described thoroughly elsewhere.[1] For the present study it is what happened after the Nobel committee's announcement that provides the clearest indication of how accurate Pasternak's sad conclusion had been just two years earlier.

When the initial news about the Nobel Prize reached him on October 23, 1958, Pasternak sent a short telegram that conveyed his acceptance. The Soviet response was rapid and forceful, although it was largely unseen at the time. Denunciations of the Nobel committee's decision and of Pasternak's acceptance flooded the media. An eerie sense of déjà vu wafted through the cultural backrooms as patterns that had characterized the literary inquisitions of the 1930s reappeared with alarming efficiency. Notorious figures like David Zaslavsky, who made his career more than three decades earlier by leading the denunciations of Osip Mandelstam over the Ulenspiegel translation scandal, reappeared as the shrillest voices in the new wave of accusations. On October 27, only four days after he was awarded the prize, Pasternak was expelled from the Writers' Union by a unanimous vote.

Pasternak was extremely upset and so discouraged by this point that he suggested a double suicide to Olga Ivinskaya, his closest companion at the time. But there was worse to come. Expulsion from the Writers' Union had not satisfied the thirst for retribution. On October 31 the writers met again and went a step further, approving a resolution that called for Pasternak to be stripped of Soviet citizenship. When official voices from the Party suggested that he was free to leave the USSR, Pasternak was afraid that he would be forced to depart against his will. In an effort to shift the course of events, he wrote two letters: one was addressed personally to Soviet leader Nikita Khrushchev, but directed more broadly to the government and the Communist Party at large; the other was sent to the editorial offices of *Pravda*.

The letters were published together in *Pravda* and provoked a new round of controversy—but this time the uproar was in the west. In the letter to Khrushchev, Pasternak indicates dismay at finding himself in the center of such a politically motivated controversy and adds that he has informed the Swedish academy of his "voluntary refusal" to accept the Nobel prize. He concludes with the assertion that leaving his homeland would be the same as death for him and entreats Khrushchev not to take "this extreme measure" in relation to him. Pasternak does include a vague reference to "whatever my mistakes and errors may have been" but concludes with a strong assertion that he has been and still could be useful to Soviet literature. In the second letter he writes about the mistaken ways that *Doctor Zhivago* has been interpreted, and suggests that if it had been possible to prevent such misunderstandings of his intentions through partial corrections, he would have done so.

The entire series of events—and the letters in particular—baffled and even angered many of Pasternak's new readers in the west. Even some who knew his work well interpreted the change of heart as shameful capitulation to state pressure. As Lazar Fleishman points out, the scandal laid bare the degree to which western audiences failed to understand the Soviet system: Westerners could not comprehend why the awarding of the world's most prestigious literary award had been denounced angrily in the winner's homeland, much less how his fellow writers could lead the wave of denunciations. And western readers seemed unaware of how much force the state could bring to bear in pressuring a reluctant writer to comply with official dogma. Some criticized Pasternak rather sharply for betraying literature by declining the prize.[2]

This western sense of disillusionment returns us to the question that I raised at the outset: Can a poet stand as a symbol of courage and resistance? And if so, how? Judging by the response of many western readers to the Nobel Prize uproar, this answer not only can but *must* be answered with a resounding "yes"—at least when the poet is drawn into a conflict that extends beyond literature into politics. Pondering the implications of this dual rejection in the Soviet Union and in the west, Pasternak's translator Manya Harari concludes that the western response was connected to the need "felt always and particularly in our time, not only for heroism but for heroic figures—a need to admire and to be assured that no pressure is finally irresistible to the human spirit."[3] And of course, the sense of disappointment in the west emerges from a specific set of expectations: The western readers to which Harari and Fleishman refer seemed to expect a swashbuckling disregard for consequences, a one-against-the-world defiance. They wanted the author of *Doctor Zhivago* to be not just an author but a political symbol, someone who provided at least implicit support for the west in the binary us-versus-them world of the cold war.

But that was not Pasternak's way. He never saw himself as an explicitly political figure, much less a dissident. His entire life in the Soviet system had been lived according to different, less confrontational principles of resistance and flexibility. Perhaps Osip Mandelstam, acting in the ultra-defiant vein that he unveiled in "Fourth Prose," could have provided the flamboyant gesture that western watchers seemed to crave as a defining mark of the hero, but Pasternak weighed his options and chose a subtler approach. Read carefully, his letters show both a resistance to the pressure directed against him and a desire to find a solution that both sides could accept.

The Nobel crisis repeats in real life the same survival strategy that Pasternak sketched out in *Safe Conduct* and *People and Propositions*, where he recorded the frightening specter of death all around him and searched for a way to survive without sacrificing his honor. When writing his letters and when issuing his "voluntary refusal" of the award, he surely did not lose sight of the most important fact: The Prize had indeed been given to him and this decision could not be wiped away and forgotten simply by declining the award. Anders Österling, Permanent Secretary of the Swedish Academy, said as much in the 1958 official Nobel announcement: "As is well known, Pasternak has sent word that he does not wish to accept the distinction. This refusal, of course, in no way alters the validity of the award. There remains only for the Academy . . . to announce with regret that the presentation of the Prize cannot take place."[4] In this crisis, Pasternak's statement of refusal shows a strategic decision to step back from the brink to which he was being pushed by the Writers' Union and the Party itself. After all, the Prize was his and the whole world knew it—and this in itself was a vindication of his decades-long survival strategy. If Pasternak had entered into a more confrontational struggle with the state he would never have lived to write this "one great work," as he called *Doctor Zhivago*, nor would he have survived to defend and commemorate the great poets who perished in the years when so many poets died and poetry itself seemed about to disappear.

Pasternak, Mandelstam and Marina Tsvetaeva shared a passion for poetry and a deep loyalty to the cultural institution of the Russian poet. Even more, the three shared an acute sensitivity to the way poetry was received in the world around them. When poetry was threatened by social or political forces, their prose autobiographies became a means of fighting back. When Mandelstam wrote *The Noise of Time* in the mid-1920s the threat to poetry was still veiled in a hotly contested cultural sphere so he could use the autobiography to find a place for himself within Russian culture while also expressing apprehension about ominous developments in literature. By the end of the decade, though, when poetry was being pushed out of the cultural consciousness by powerful literary forces, autobiographies by Mandelstam and Pasternak show a determination to fight the changes on behalf of poetry and the honor of the genuine poet. Certainly their approaches differed: Mandelstam's irritation at Pasternak's restraint and Pasternak's abhorrence of Mandelstam's seeming death wish are both widely known. In their own ways, though, each traces a clear line of resistance in the autobiographies written at this time, Mandelstam in the intensity of "Fourth Prose" and Pasternak with a more understated but equally compelling voice in *Safe Conduct*.

Marina Tsvetaeva found herself physically removed from the Soviet threat to poetry but still was linked to Mandelstam and Pasternak in a broader concern for poetry's future. Her response came in short installments of autobiographical prose that told a very personal story about her birthright as a poet; the result was not just an individual's assertion of poetic identity, but a depiction of poetry as a force that exists independently, moving and choosing for itself those who are destined to be poets. Poetry, she shows, cannot be crushed or overlooked as long as there are those willing to give themselves to poetry and to the loneliness and loyalty that characterize the true poet's life.

Finally, two decades later Pasternak had one more opportunity to look back on his life and to provide a personal summing up not just of his own artistic legacy, but of the poetic legacy left by his age. By then socialist realism had become entrenched as the official Party-approved approach to art, and didactic, formulaic prose had become the dominant Soviet genre. A poet had little hope of publishing anything outside the narrow version of "reality" allowed to exist in the blinkered vision of socialist realism. In the face of these restrictions Pasternak's tribute to fallen poets never becomes an open challenge to the state but demonstrates his resolve to recognize even those, like Titsian Tabidze and Tsvetaeva, who were still out of favor. Even though poetry as a genre had been pushed largely to the cultural fringe, poetry still dominated his thinking and Pasternak deliberately depicted himself as part of a broad poetic community.

In their own way, each of these three poets showed a personal and artistic integrity that inspired thousands to see them as inspirational and yes, even heroic, figures. It was their unshakeable loyalty to poetry and to the role of the Russian poet that earned them such respect; even when poetry seemed doomed, they stood proudly to announce their identity as poets no matter how unfashionable or risky such a declaration might be. Nadezhda Mandelstam, whose close ties to many poets in these troubled decades gave her ample opportunity to reflect on the traits that mark a "genuine" poet, once made the bold claim that "a real poet is always recognized immediately—by his enemies as well as by his well-wishers. It seems inevitable that a poet should arouse enmity.... Poets can never be indifferent to good and evil, and they can never say that all that exists is rational."[5]

These are powerful claims, to be sure, and reflect Nadezhda Mandelstam's own determination to function as a locus of cultural and especially poetic preservation. But similar sentiment could be found elsewhere and the lasting image of the Russian poet as truth teller survived through decades of repression. From the start, the USSR's cultural watchdogs recognized the potential threat that genuine poets represented and set out to keep poetry—and other arts—within carefully defined boundaries. But poets (and poetry) could never thrive in the restrictive conditions of Soviet socialist realism. Instead, poetry went underground, burrowing into the collective memory and spreading surreptitiously through the self-publishing system known as *samizdat* and through the Russian genius for memorization. Eventually cracks started to appear in the cultural walls, and thanks in large part to the courage of poets like Mandelstam, Tsvetaeva and Pasternak, the cultural thaw of the 1960s revealed a new generation of poets and showed that Russians had not lost their passion for poetry or their respect for the poet. And while these three poets were no longer alive to witness the changes, others were. Their contemporary, poet Anna Akhmatova, lived to see poetry's incredible change of fortune in the 1960s, when thousands of people crowded into concert halls and arenas to hear poets speaking out boldly in a suddenly more tolerant political climate. "I am easy in my mind now," said Akhmatova. "We have seen how durable poetry is."[6]

The resurgence of poetry in the 1960s proved to be an extremely powerful force, and for people like Akhmatova the sense of vindication, of having persevered and conquered, was unmistakable. This was a recovery of Russia's most precious cultural treasure, and they saw poetry as uniquely able to spark a moral and intellectual rebirth. Poetry "is the golden treasury in which our values are preserved," wrote Nadezhda Mandelstam, "it brings people back to life, awakens their conscience, and stirs them to thought. . . . The new awakening is accompanied by the copying out and reading of poetry, which thus plays its part in setting things in motion again and reviving thought."

Poetry not only survived, but blossomed once again. This simple realization was the ultimate tribute to the efforts of Mandelstam, Tsvetaeva, Pasternak and the many other poets who did not abandon their calling. There is a sense of not just satisfaction but even triumph as Nadezhda Mandelstam continues, "The keepers of the flame hid in darkened corners, but the flame did not go out. It is there for all to see."[7]

Endnotes

INTRODUCTION

1. "Letter to the Editor," *The Dial* 1899: 329. History proved the letter-writer wrong, of course, and perhaps it was poetic justice that it was in this same *Dial* that T. S. Eliot's *The Waste Land* made its American debut and eventually went on to achieve broad recognition as one of the twentieth-century's greatest achievements in verse.

2. Nadezhda Mandelstam, *Hope Against Hope*, trans. Max Hayward (New York: Atheneum, 1970), 159.

3. Stephen Spender, *The Thirties and After: Poetry, Politics, People (1933–1970)* (New York: Random House, 1978), 32, 35.

4. The series of events leading up to this decision by the Politburo, including correspondence between Maxim Gorky, People's Commissar for Enlightenment Anatoly Lunacharsky, Lenin and Menzhinsky, was reconstructed by Aleksandr Potapov from letters and other documents that he found in the Russian Center for the Preservation and Study of Documents of Contemporary History (*Rossiiskii tsentr khraneniia i izucheniia dokumentov noveishei istorii*) and the Archive of the President of the Russian Federation (*Arkhiv prezidenta Rossiiskoi Federatsii*). For a fuller description of the documents and of the events that preceded Blok's death in August, 1921 see Aleksandr Potapov, 'Taina smerti Aleksandra Bloka,' *Sovershenno sekretno—versiia v Pitere*, December 9, 2002, http://www.kohkpetho.ru/versia.php?article=169 (May 30, 2005).

5. Tsvetaeva was herself aware of some ways that Pasternak fell under and conformed to Soviet pressure in the 1930s, and looked for ways to understand how the Pasternak she knew could be deciphered in these acts of seeming weakness. For a discussion of Tsvetaeva's response, see Catherine Ciepiela, *The Same Solitude:*

Boris Pasternak and Marina Tsvetaeva (Ithaca, NY: Cornell University Press, 2006), 241–44; and Elena Korkina, "Pushkinskaia tema v sud'be Pasternaka i Tsvetaevoi v 1930-e gody," in *Marina Tsvetaeva: Pesn' zhizni,* ed. Efim Etkind and Veronique Lossky (Paris: YMCA Press, 1996), 102–26. I am grateful to an anonymous reader of my manuscript for drawing the essay by Elena Korkina to my attention.

6. Vitaly Shentalinsky, *Arrested Voices: Resurrecting the Disappeared Writers of the Soviet Regime,* trans. John Crowfoot (New York: The Free Press, 1996), 199.

7. Anna Akhmatova describes a letter in which Klyuev identified the cause of his arrest as "The Blasphemers of Art" [*Khuliteli iskusstva,* or in other versions *Klevetniki iskusstva*], while Vitaly Shentalinsky identifies a letter in which "The Burned Ruins" [*Pogorel'shchina*] was said to be the poem most responsible. See Anna Akhmatova, *Sochineniia* (New York: Interlanguage Literary Associates, 1968), 2:180, and Shentalinsky, *Arrested Voices,* 202.

8. Shentalinsky, *Arrested Voices,* 205.

9. Akhmatova, *Sochineniia,* 1:262. "Час мужества пробил на наших часах. / И мужество нас не покинет. . . . И мы сохраним тебя русская речь, / Великое русское слово. / Свободным и чистым тебя пронесем, / И внукам дадим и от плена спасем / Навеки!"

10. Oleg Kalugin, "Delo KGB na Annu Akhmatovu," in *Gosbezopasnost' i literatura na opyte Rossii i Germanii (SSSR i GDR)* (Moscow: Rudomino, 1994), 76–78.

11. Akhmatova, *Sochineniia,* 2:253.

12. Lydia Ginzburg, *On Psychological Prose,* trans. and ed. Judson Rosengrant (Princeton, NJ: Princeton University Press, 1991), 105. Ginzburg's work appeared in Russian in 1971, and anticipated by more than a decade similar debates over autobiography readership in the west.

Some have argued that Ginzburg's description of autobiography as an "intermediate" or boundary genre is a slight to autobiography, a suggestion that autobiography is not good enough to be "real" fiction. Ginzburg's contrast between the "incomplete" world of autobiography and the "complete" world of fiction can be taken to imply that autobiography lacks something essential. I interpret Ginzburg's comments to be not hierarchical but descriptive, referring to different functions of the text. The autobiography is "incomplete" because the author is not trying to create a closed system that functions entirely within its own frame of reference: autobiography wants and/or needs *another* reference point, which Ginzburg describes as its "orientation to authenticity." Jane Gary Harris has wondered whether Ginzburg really allows for an *aesthetic* response to autobiography, suggesting that Ginzburg "recognizes the essential tension or duality of 'documentary literature,' identifying its 'peculiar dynamics,' [but] she does not consider the esthetic value of that tension. Rather, she opposes it to the esthetic coherence of a fictional text that is said to reveal no connections with 'the plane of the life experience' because it is an autonomous 'second reality.'" I would characterize Ginzburg's approach differently, drawing more attention to the reader's role and expectations: the reader, as I understand Ginzburg, has a different set of expectations when reading fiction than when reading autobiography.

With autobiography, the reader doesn't necessarily *exclude* an aesthetic element, but also doesn't assume that the text is a self-contained aesthetic universe (which is how one tends to approach fiction, even historical fiction); instead, the reader expects a dual orientation that points both to literature and to reality. See Jane Gary Harris, "Autobiographical Theory and the Problem of Esthetic Coherence in Mandelstam's *Noise of Time*," *Essays in Poetics* 9 (1984): 44.

13. Ginzburg, *On Psychological Prose*, 6 (emphasis in original).

14. See Paul de Man, "Autobiography as Defacement," *MLN* 94 (1979): 919–30; Michael Sprinker, "Fictions of the Self: The End of Autobiography," in *Autobiography: Essays Theoretical and Critical*, ed. James Olney (Princeton, NJ: Princeton University Press, 1980), 321–42; William K. Wimsatt and Monroe C. Beardsley, *The Verbal Icon; Studies in the Meaning of Poetry* (Lexington: University of Kentucky Press, 1954).

15. Paul John Eakin, *Touching the World: Reference in Autobiography* (Princeton, NJ: Princeton University Press, 1992), 28–29. Eakin has no quarrel with autobiography's status as an imaginative art, but rather with an emphasis on imagination that ignores referentiality.

16. Paul John Eakin, "Relational Selves, Relational Lives: The Story of the Story," in *True Relations: Essays on Autobiography and the Postmodern, Contributions to the Study of World Literature* 85, ed. G. Thomas Couser and Joseph Fichtelberg (Westport, CT: Greenwood Press, 1998), 63.

CHAPTER ONE

1. B. Ia. Bukhshtab, *A. A. Fet: ocherk zhizni i tvorchestva*, 2nd ed. (Leningrad: Nauka, 1990), 23–24.

2. D. I. Pisarev, *Sochineniia v 4kh tomakh* (Moscow: Khudozhestvennaia literatura, 1955), 2:333.

3. Edward Brown, *The Proletarian Episode in Russian Literature, 1928–1932* (New York: Columbia University Press, 1953), 9–10.

4. Evgeny Dobrenko, *Aesthetics of Alienation: Reassessment of Early Soviet Cultural Theories*, trans. Jesse M. Savage (Evanston, IL: Northwestern University Press, 2005), xvi. In *Aesthetics of Alienation*, Dobrenko provides a welcome new analysis that offers more details about the movements and controversies that are summarized in this chapter.

5. Cited in Brown, *The Proletarian Episode*, 15.

6. P. S. Kogan, *Proletarskaia literatura* (Ivanovo-Voznesensk: Osnova, 1926), 50.

7. Robert Maguire, *Red Virgin Soil: Soviet Literature in the 1920's* (Ithaca, NY: Cornell University Press, 1987), 23.

8. Leon Trotsky, *Literature and Revolution* (New York: Russell and Russell, 1957) 184–89, 192–93.

9. Trotsky, *Literature and Revolution*, 125.

10. Trotsky, *Literature and Revolution*, 201–2, 213.

11. Trotsky, *Literature and Revolution*, 219–21.

12. Trotsky, *Literature and Revolution*, 139.

13. An English translation of the resolution, "On the Policy of the Party in the Field of Belles-Lettres: Resolution of the TsK RKP, July 1, 1925," can be found in Brown, *The Proletarian Episode*, 235–40.

14. Brown, *The Proletarian Episode*, 45.

15. Quoted in Evgeny Dobrenko, *The Making of the State Writer: Social and Aesthetic Origins of Soviet Literary Culture*, trans. Jesse M. Savage (Stanford, CA: Stanford University Press, 2001), 245.

16. H. E. Warner, "Will Poetry Disappear?" *Lippincott's Magazine* 63 (1899): 285.

17. B. M. Volin, ed., *Poeziia rabochikh professii: sbornik rabochikh stikhov* (Moscow: Novaia Moskva, 1924); A. Bezymenskii, ed., *Poeziia gorniatskogo udara: pervaia kniga stikhov gorniakov poetov-rabkorov* (Moscow: Izd. TSK SG, 1929). For a lively discussion of the rise in proletarian poetry, see Dobrenko, *The Making of the State Writer*, 247–77.

18. See B. M. Volin, "Poeziia rabochikh professii," *Na postu* 2–3 (1923): 129. Dobrenko provides additional commentary to these poems, along with partial translations, in *The Making of the State Writer*, 251–52.

19. Brown, *The Proletarian Episode*, 87.

20. Brown, *The Proletarian Episode*, 88.

21. N. F. Chuzhak, "Pisatel'skaia pamiatka," in *Literatura fakta: Pervyi sbornik materialov rabotnikov LEFa*, ed. N. F. Chuzhak (Moscow: Izd. Federatsiia, 1929; repr., Moscow: Zakharov, 2000), 29, 11, 22. Later theoretical discussions of autobiography, biography, and historiography have, of course, pointed out that the notion of an autobiography's "natural plot" is inaccurate, since any selection of some "facts" implies the rejection of many others. As the agent of selection, the author still arranges facts to form the plot.

22. S. Tret'iakov, "Chto novogo," *Novyi LEF* 9 (1928): 4–5.

23. Stephen Spender, *The Thirties and After: Poetry, Politics, People (1933–1970)* (New York: Random House, 1978), 35.

24. Tret'iakov, "Chto Novogo," 5.

25. O. Brik, "Protiv 'tvorcheskoi' lichnosti," in Chuzhak, *Literatura fakta*, 77–79.

26. N. Aseev, "Liricheskii fel'eton," *Novyi LEF* 11 (1928): 3–8.

27. Roman Jakobson, "On a Generation That Squandered Its Poets," in *Twentieth Century Russian Literary Criticism*, ed. Victor Erlich (New Haven, CT: Yale University Press, 1975), 140.

CHAPTER TWO

1. The notorious "Stalin Ode" (written in 1936–1937) seems to be an attempt to show some measure of accommodation on Mandelstam's part, and significantly complicates any attempt to depict Mandelstam as an absolute figure of resistance to the state. Mandelstam's wife Nadezhda devotes considerable attention to an

account of how this ode came to be and argues that Mandelstam described the process of writing it as an "attempt to do violence to himself." She writes that the poem's weakness can be attributed to this internal conflict as a powerful internal resistance sabotaged the conscious attempts to write. As a result, she continues, the "Ode" was "cancelled out" by the genuine poetry that emerged organically as if in opposition to it. See Nadezhda Mandelstam, *Hope Against Hope*, trans. Max Hayward (New York: Atheneum, 1970), 198–201. Nadezhda Mandelstam's memoirs of life with her husband are frequently the only accounts that fill in the details of Osip Mandelstam's life; her determination to memorialize him in these accounts can be inspirational, but also stamps the text with a clear personal bias that must not be disregarded.

2. See Nadezhda Mandelstam, *Hope Abandoned* (New York: Atheneum, 1974), 337; and "Vnutrennie retsenzii i predislovie dlia izdatel'stva 'Vremia,'" *Slovo i sud'ba. Osip Mandel'shtam*, ed. Z. S. Papernyi (Moscow: Nauka, 1991), 9n9.

3. P. Nerler, "Osip Mandel'shtam v Narkomprose v 1918–1919 godakh," *Voprosy literatury* 9 (1989): 275.

4. A. A. Bogdanov, "Chto takoe proletarskaia poeziia?" *Proletarskaia kul'tura* 1 (July 1918): 19.

5. Vladimir Kirillov, *Stikhotvoreniia i poemy* (Moscow: Khudozhestvennaia literatura, 1970), 35–36. "Мы несметные, грозные легионы Труда. / . . . Мы во власти мятежного, страстного хмеля; / Пусть кричат нам: «Вы палачи красоты», / Во имя нашего Завтра—сожжем Рафаэля, / Разрушим музеи, растопчем искусства цветы. // . . . Слезы иссякли в очах наших, нежность убита, / Позабыли мы запахи трав и весенних цветов. / Полюбили мы силу паров и мощь динамита, / Пенье сирен и движенье колес и валов. . . // О, поэты-эстеты, кляните Великого Хама, / Целуйте обломки былого под нашей пятой, / Омойте слезами руины разбитого храма. / Мы вольны, мы смелы, мы дышим иной красотой."

6. "И пятиглавые московские соборы / С их итальянскою и русскою душой / Напоминают мне явление Авроры, / Но с русским именем и в шубке меховой." Osip Mandel'shtam, *Sobranie sochinenii v chetyrekh tomakh* (Moscow: Terra, 1991; New York: Mezhdunarodnoe Literaturnoe Sodruzhestvo, 1969), 1:58. Further references to this text will be designated "OM, *Ss*."

7. Kirillov, *Stikhotvoreniia i poemy*, 41. "Спаситель, земли властелин, / Владыка сил титанических."

8. " Я слово позабыл, что я хотел сказать." OM, *Ss*, 1:81.

9. "Когда Психея-жизнь спускается к теням / В полупрозрачный лес вослед за Персефоной, / Слепая ласточка бросается к ногам / С стигийской нежностью и веткою зеленой." OM, *Ss*, 1:80.

10. Osip Mandelstam, *The Complete Critical Prose and Letters*, ed. Jane Gary Harris, trans. Jane Gary Harris and Constance Link (Ann Arbor, MI: Ardis, 1979), 108; the original Russian text can be found in OM, *Ss*, 3:123. Further references to Mandelstam's *The Complete Critical Prose and Letters* will be designated "OM, *CCPL*."

11. OM, *CCPL*, 108; OM, *Ss*, 3:123–24.

12. Nadezhda Mandelstam, *Hope Abandoned*, 525.

13. The description comes in Mandelstam's November, 1917 poem "When the October favorite prepared for us . . ." (Kogda oktiabr'skii nam gotovil vremenshchik), OM, *Ss*, 1:142.

14. O. M. Smola, "Zametki k teme 'Mandel'shtam i revoliutsiia,'" in *Zhizn' i tvorchestvo O. E. Mandel'shtama*, ed. O. E. Makarova and I. E. Kharitonchik (Voronezh: Izdatel'stvo Voronezhskogo universiteta, 1990), 507, 509, 511.

15. From the reminiscences of Vasilisa Shklovskaya-Kordi in *Osip i Nadezhda Mandel'shtamy v rasskazakh sovremennikov*, comp. O. S. Figurnova and M. V. Figurnova (Moscow: Natalis, 2001), 104–5.

16. Lev Kolodnyi, *Poety i vozhdi. Dokumental'nye ocherki* (Moscow: Golos, 1997), 19.

17. It is Pasternak's account of the meetings that indicates the two recitals took place on the same evening. His version of events has been widely quoted, but Evgeny Pasternak writes that his father is "not quite accurate" in supposing that it was the same evening when he and Mayakovsky arrived too late to prevent a scandal at the Press House. In fact, archival records of Blok's visit to Moscow show that the two events were at least two days apart, since Blok read at the Polytechnical Museum on May 3 and 5, and at the Press house on May 7. See E. B. Pasternak, *Boris Pasternak. Biografiia*, 2nd ed. (Moscow: Izd. Tsitadel', 1997), 333.

18. "Мастера, / а не длинноволосые проповедники / нужны сейчас нам." Vladimir Maiakovskii, *Sobranie sochinenii v vos'mi tomakh*, vol. 2 (Moscow: Izdatel'stvo "Pravda," 1968), 121.

19. OM, *CCPL*, 113, 115; OM, *Ss*, 2:223, 226.

20. Nadezhda Mandelstam, *Hope Abandoned*, 304.

21. See Kolodnyi, *Poety i vozhdi*, 111–12, and Nadezhda Mandelstam, *Hope Against Hope*, 115–16. There is a curious discrepancy between these accounts, which agree in many respects but disagree on the most central question: the identity of the brother who was arrested. Kolodnyi indicates that it was Aleksandr, while Nadezhda Mandelstam says that it was Evgeny.

22. Nadezhda Mandelstam, *Hope Against Hope*, 174.

23. G. Lelevich, "1923 god: literaturnye itogi," *Na postu* 5 (May 1925): 73–75.

24. These include the articles in Kiev's *Russian Art* mentioned above, but may also have included some of his sharp criticism of Marina Tsvetaeva and others in the first of his 1922 "Literary Moscow" articles.

25. Tynianov's "On Literary Evolution" was only published in 1927, but it is likely that he and Mandelstam discussed the concept of evolution in literature much earlier. Mandelstam's comments can be found in OM, *CCPL*, 119; OM, *Ss*, 2:243.

26. OM, *CCPL*, 122; OM, *Ss*, 2:247.

27. OM, *CCPL*, 132; OM, *Ss*, 2:259.

28. OM, *CCPL*, 151–53; OM, *Ss*, 2:334–36. Mandelstam is not completely negative about prose, though, and the title of the essay comes from what Mandelstam sees as prose's only hope: folklore. Some writers, like the Serapion Brothers and those associated with them, were succeeding in prose because their writing was based on folklore, which Mandelstam called "the birth of plot."

29. Nadezhda Mandelstam, *Hope Abandoned*, 119, 121.

30. See "Some Notes on Poetry" and "Storm and Stress," in OM, *CCPL*, 165–69, 170–80; OM, *Ss*, 2:260–65, 339–51.

31. OM, *CCPL*, 181–83; OM, *Ss*, 2:352–54. Nadezhda Mandelstam states that it was his brother's arrest in 1922, and especially his meeting with secret police chief Feliks Dzerzhinsky, that started Mandelstam thinking in these terms: "This meeting gave him much food for thought about the relative value of the 'social structure' and the human personality. The new structure was then only beginning to take shape, but it already promised to be of unprecedented grandeur." See *Hope Against Hope*, 256.

32. Nadezhda Mandelstam, *Hope Abandoned*, 24.

33. Sergei Bobrov, "Rev. of *Tristia*," *Pechat' i revoliutsiia* (June–July, 1923): 259–62.

34. Valerii Briusov, "Rev. of *Vtoraia kniga*," *Pechat' i revoliutsiia* (October, 1923): 63–66. Ironically, Osip Mandelstam and Sergei Bobrov both appear as reviewers elsewhere in the same issue.

35. "Into Whom Is LEF Sinking Its Teeth?" *LEF* 1 (1923): 9.

36. See Boris Kushner, "Organizatory proizvodstva," *LEF* 3 (1923): 103; and Osip Brik, "Tak nazivaemyi formal'nyi metod," *LEF* 1 (1923): 214.

37. G. Lelevich, "Nam nuzhna partiinaia liniia," *Na postu*, no. 1 (1923): 101–108; "Ot redaktsii," *Na postu*, nos. 2–3 (1923): 9. See also Evgeny Dobrenko, *Aesthetics of Alienation: Reassessment of Early Soviet Cultural Theories*, trans. Jesse M. Savage (Evanston, IL: Northwestern University Press, 2005), 39–40.

38. See Veniamin Kaverin, "Vstrechi s Mandel'shtamom," in *Osip Mandel'shtam i ego vremia*, comp. V. Kreid and E. Necheporuk (Moscow: L'Age d'Homme—Nash dom, 1995), 268; and V. Kaverin, "Kak ia ne stal poetom," *Oktiabr'* 10 (1959): 131.

39. This incident appears to have gained broad circulation and evolved into several variants.

Anna Akhmatova records Mandelstam's words somewhat differently: "Did they publish André Chénier? Did they publish Sappho? Did they publish Jesus Christ?" See Semen Lipkin, "Ugl', pylaiushchii ognem; vstrechi i razgovory s Osipom Mandel'shtamom," in Kreid and Necheporuk, *Osip Mandel'shtam i ego vremia*, 301, 296; Anna Akhmatova, "Mandel'shtam (Listki iz dnevnika)," in *Sochineniia* (Washington: Inter-Language Literary Associates, 1968), 2:187.

40. Gregory Freidin, *A Coat of Many Colors: Osip Mandelstam and His Mythologies of Self-Presentation* (Berkeley, CA: University of California Press, 1987), 177.

41. OM, *CCPL*, 192–93; OM, *Ss*, 2:209–11.

42. OM, *CCPL*, 194; OM, *Ss*, 2:212–13.

43. Freidin, *A Coat of Many Colors*, 18, 12.

44. For a good introduction to Mandelstam's historical method and its aesthetic expression, see Gregory Freidin's "The Whisper of History and the Noise of Time," *The Russian Review* 37 (1978): 421–37, and several articles by Jane Gary Harris: "Autobiographical Theory and the Problem of Esthetic Coherence in Mandelstam's *Noise of Time*," *Essays in Poetics* 9 (1984): 33–66; "Autobiography and

History: Osip Mandelstam's *Noise of Time*," in *Autobiographical Statements in Twentieth-Century Russian Literature*, ed. Jane Gary Harris (Princeton, NJ: Princeton University Press, 1990), 99–113; and "Mandel'shtam's Aesthetic of Performance," *Canadian-American Slavic Studies* 19 (1985): 426–42.

45. Viktor Krivulin, "Tri prozy poeta," *Zvezda* 6 (1995): 182.

46. Osip Mandelstam, *The Noise of Time and Other Prose Pieces*, trans. Clarence Brown (London: Quartet Books, 1988), 78, 84, 77; OM, *Ss*, 2:57–58, 66, 55. In further notes, *The Noise of Time* will be identified as "OM, *NT*."

47. OM, *NT*, 86; OM, *Ss*, 2:68–69.

48. OM, *NT*, 84; OM, *Ss*, 2:66.

49. OM, *NT*, 85; OM, *Ss*, 2:66–67.

50. For a different and more positive interpretation of this "babble," see Nancy Pollak's *Mandelstam the Reader* (Baltimore: Johns Hopkins University Press, 1995), 32–34. She links this reference to Mandelstam's poetry from the 1930s to suggest that speechlessness can actually have positive connotations for Mandelstam. My own view is that the poetry of the 1930s has much stronger links to the radical new formulation of the poet's place in society that Mandelstam articulated in the early 1930s, especially in "Fourth Prose" (see chapter 4). In 1923, a lack of language is a definite liability.

51. OM, *NT*, 109–10; OM, *Ss*, 2:99.

52. See Jane Gary Harris's articles "Autobiographical Theory" (p. 37) and "Autobiography and History" (p. 100) for a further discussion of "biography" in Mandelstam's writing.

53. Charles Isenberg, *Substantial Proofs of Being: Osip Mandelstam's Literary Prose* (Columbus, OH: Slavica, 1987), 54.

54. For a broad discussion of the collision between poetry's lyric voice and the social demands for a collective voice, see Mark D. Steinberg, *Proletarian Imagination: Self, Modernity, and the Sacred in Russia, 1910–1925* (Cornell, NY: Cornell University Press, 2002), 102–46. For a discussion of Lebedev-Polyansky, see Steinberg, 141–42.

55. See Steinberg, *Proletarian Imagination*, 129. Some of the sketches were published in A. Ia. Zavolokin, ed., *Sovremennye raboche-krest'ianskie poety v obraztsakh i avtobiografiiakh s portretami* (Ivanovo-Voznesensk: Osnova, 1925).

56. Jerome Bruner, "Self-Making and World-Making," in *Narrative and Identity: Studies in Autobiography, Self and Culture*, ed. Jens Brockmeier and Donal Carbaugh (Amsterdam: John Benjamins Publishing Company, 2001), 28.

57. Steinberg, *Proletarian Imagination*, 125.

58. Various scholars have produced fine analyses of this theme in Mandelstam's poetry. See, for example, Nancy Pollak, *Mandelstam the Reader*, 85–92; Kiril Taranovsky, *Essays on Mandelštam* (Cambridge, MA: Harvard University Press, 1976), 10–15; Omry Ronen, *An Approach to Mandelštam* (Jerusalem: Magnes Press, 1983), 130–33.

59. OM, *NT*, 69, 70, 111–12; OM, *Ss*, 2:45, 46, 100–101.

60. OM, *NT*, 80; OM, *Ss*, 2:60.

61. OM, *NT*, 107; OM, *Ss*, 2:95–96.

62. Nadezhda Mandelstam, *Hope Abandoned*, 186. Also added later were four sections grouped under the title "Theodosia." Early reviewers noted that they seemed more like an appendix to the main work, and Mandelstam's reasons for adding them are not clear. After the first edition, they were removed from the main text and set apart as a separate work. Scholarly consensus thus considers the last chapter of *The Noise of Time* to be "In a Fur Coat Above One's Station," and I follow that consensus here.

63. OM, *CCPL*, 202; OM, *Ss*, 2:228–29.

64. B. Sarnov, "Defending the Privilege to Write Badly," in *Literature and the New Thinking* (Moscow: Nauka Publishers, 1989), 151–54.

CHAPTER THREE

1. For more on the work's title and its implications, see Christopher J. Barnes, *Boris Pasternak: A Literary Biography*, 2 vols. (Cambridge: Cambridge University Press, 1989–1998), 2:32; Lazar' Fleishman, *Boris Pasternak v dvadtsatye gody* (Munich: Wilhelm Fink Verlag, 1981); and Michel Aucouturier, "Ob odnom kliuche k 'Okhrannoi gramote,'" in *Boris Pasternak, 1890–1960: colloque de Cerisy-la-Salle, 11–14 septembre 1975* (Paris: Institut d'études slaves, 1979), 337–49.

2. For more on how Pasternak accomplished this, see Barnes, *Boris Pasternak: A Literary Biography*, 1:322–23; and Fleishman, *Boris Pasternak v dvadtsatye gody*, 34.

3. See Catherine Ciepiela, *The Same Solitude: Boris Pasternak and Marina Tsvetaeva* (Ithaca, NY: Cornell University Press, 2006), 134–44.

4. Still, *New LEF* continued to list him as a contributor through the fifth issue of 1927. See E. B. Pasternak, *Boris Pasternak: Biografiia*, 2nd ed. (Moscow: Izd. Tsitadel', 1997), 401.

5. S. Tret'iakov, "Novyi Lev Tolstoi," in *Literatura fakta: pervyi sbornik materialov rabotnikov LEFa*, ed. N. F. Chuzhak (Moscow: Izd. Federatsiia, 1929), 31–32, 33. See also Evgeny Dobrenko, *Aesthetics of Alienation: Reassessment of Early Soviet Cultural Theories*, trans. Jesse M. Savage (Evanston, IL: Northwestern University Press, 2005), 60–69.

6. N. F. Chuzhak, "Pisatel'skaia pamiatka," in Chuzhak, *Literatura fakta*, 21.

7. Chuzhak, "Pisatel'skaia pamiatka," 15; N. F. Chuzhak, "Literatura zhiznestroeniia," in Chuzhak, *Literatura fakta*, 66.

8. Chuzhak, "Literatura zhiznestroeniia," 66; V. Trenin, "Rabkor i belletrist," in Chuzhak, *Literatura fakta*, 216.

9. S. Tret'iakov, "Chto novogo," *Novyi LEF* 9 (1928): 4–5.

10. Nikolai Aseev, "Sobstvennye pominki," *Novyi LEF* 3 (1928): 40.

11. By this I mean that *Novyi LEF* publishes no more individual poems. On several occasions, verse fragments appear as illustrations in prose articles.

12. S. Tret'iakov, "S novym godom! S 'Novym LEFom'!" *Novyi LEF* 1 (1928): 2–3.

13. N. Aseev, "Liricheskii fel'eton," *Novyi LEF* 11 (1928): 5.

14. See Lazar' Fleishman, *Boris Pasternak v tridtsatye gody* (Jerusalem: Magnes Press, 1984), 55.

15. For a full discussion of this meeting, see Fleishman, *Boris Pasternak v tridtsatye gody* 58–65.

16. Lazar' Fleishman, *Boris Pasternak v dvadtsatye gody*, 186.

17. Boris Pasternak, *Safe Conduct*, in *The Voice of Prose: Early Prose and Autobiography*, ed. Christopher Barnes (Edinburgh: Polygon, 1986), 22, 23, my emphasis; the original Russian text can be found in Boris Pasternak, *Sobranie sochinenii v piati tomakh* (Moscow: Khudozhestvennaia literatura, 1991), 4: 150, 151. Further references to *Safe Conduct* will be designated "BP, *SC*" and references to Pasternak's Russian texts will be designated "BP, *Ss*."

18. Paul John Eakin, *Touching the World: Reference in Autobiography* (Princeton, NJ: Princeton University Press, 1992), 36.

19. BP, *SC*, 30; BP, *Ss*, 4:158–59.

20. Dmitri Segal, "Pro domo sua: The Case of Boris Pasternak," *Slavica Hierosolymitana* 1 (1977): 204, 201.

21. "О, знал бы я, что так бывает, / Когда пускался на дебют, / Что строчки с кровью—убивают, / Нахлынут горлом и убьют! // От шуток с этой подоплёкой / Я б отказался наотрез. / Начало было так далёко, / Так робок первый интерес." BP, *Ss*, 1:412. Andrew Reynolds suggests that some of the more ominous lines in this poem are Pasternak's response to a new, more combative note in Mandelstam's poetry, "raising the stakes and making poetry a matter of life and death." See "'Komu ne nadoeli liubov' i krov'": The Uses of Intertextuality in Mandelstam's 'Za gremuchuiu doblest' griadushchikh vekov'," in *Stoletie Mandel'shtama: materialy simposiuma/Mandelstam Centenary Conference*, ed. Robin Aizlewood and Diana Myers (Tenafly, NJ: Hermitage Publishers, 1994), 140. For more on the relationship between the two poets, see chapter 4 of this study, "Fighting For Breath."

22. Quoted in Fleishman, *Boris Pasternak v dvadtsatye gody*, 300.

23. BP, *SC*, 21; BP, *Ss*, 4:149. On a more prosaic level, Rilke's Austrian dialect may have contributed to Pasternak's sense of confusion here.

24. BP, *SC*, 23, 28; BP, *Ss*, 4:151, 156.

25. Christopher Barnes, "Biography, Autobiography and 'Sister Life': Some Problems in Chronicling Pasternak's Earlier Years," *Irish Slavonic Studies* 4 (1983): 55.

26. Jens Brockmeier, "From the End to the Beginning: Retrospective Teleology in Autobiography," in *Narrative and Identity: Studies in Autobiography, Self and Culture*, ed. Jens Brockmeier and Donal Carbaugh (Amsterdam: John Benjamins Publishing Company, 2001), 252, 270.

27. BP, *SC*, 29; BP, *Ss*, 4:157.

28. BP, *SC*, 32, 36; BP, *Ss*, 4:160, 165.

29. BP, *SC*, 60, 61, 55; BP, *Ss*, 4:189–90, 184.

30. BP, *SC*, 53; BP, *Ss*, 4:182.

31. The tremendous importance that Pasternak attaches to this encounter with the embodiment (or metonymy, his favorite trope) of Philosophy, and the similar importance earlier ascribed to his encounter with the embodiment of Music (Scriabin), recalls Pushkin's description of his own encounter with Derzhavin (the embodiment of Poetry at the time). In each case the great figure serves as a touchstone to gauge

the worthiness of the younger figure; with music and philosophy, the test has revealed Pasternak's incompatibility—but not unworthiness—with these activities.

32. BP, *SC*, 63–64; BP, *Ss*, 4:192–93.
33. BP, *SC*, 64; BP, *Ss*, 4:193.
34. BP, *SC*, 51, ellipsis in the original; BP, *Ss*, 4:180.
35. BP, *SC*, 52; BP, *Ss*, 4:181.
36. BP, *SC*, 53–54; BP, *Ss*, 4:182–83.
37. Fleishman, *Boris Pasternak v dvadtsatye gody*, 248.
38. Barnes, *Boris Pasternak: A Literary Biography*, 1:137.
39. Boris Pasternak, *Selected Poems*, trans. Jon Stallworthy and Peter France (New York: W. W. Norton, 1982), 57. "Я вздрагивал. Я загорался и гас. / Я трясся. Я сделал сейчас предложение,— / Но поздно, я сдрейфил, и вот мне—отказ. / Как жаль ее слез! Я святого блаженней. // Я вышел на площадь. Я мог быть сочтен / Вторично родившимся." BP, *Ss*, 1:106.
40. BP, *SC*, 66, 68, ellipsis in the original; BP, *Ss*, 4:195, 198. The biblical account can be found in Mark 14: 41–42. There are other allusions to the crucifixion story in *Safe Conduct* as well. Pasternak begins this short chapter by hinting at the stations of the cross ("And so came station after station after station" [*Itk—stantsii, stantsii, stantsii.*]). He mentions the village of St. Gothard, a verbal echo of Gethsemane where Simon Peter was sleeping. And finally, when the train has a stopover in Milan, the only impression left by the city in Pasternak's memory is of the cathedral, which "successively reveals itself" as he wanders the city until he finally finds himself at its base. From there, his eyes are drawn up to the cathedral's peak. Left unsaid is what Pasternak saw there, but since he has deliberately called on readers to fill in important blanks in the text, readers would have no trouble filling this one in—a cross.
41. Fleishman, *Boris Pasternak: The Poet and His Politics* (Cambridge, MA: Harvard University Press, 1990), 159.
42. Lazar' Fleishman discusses Pasternak's LEF-related comments in much more detail; see *Boris Pasternak v dvadtsatye gody*, 256–59.
43. BP, *SC*, 75; BP, *Ss*, 4:206.
44. BP, *SC*, 75, 66; BP, *Ss*, 4:206, 196.
45. BP, *SC*, 76; BP, *Ss*, 4:207.
46. BP, *SC*, 76; BP, *Ss*, 4:207.
47. BP, *SC*, 71, 79; BP, *Ss*, 4:201, 210.
48. BP, *SC*, 85–86; BP, *Ss*, 4:216–17.
49. BP, *SC*, 89, 90; BP, *Ss*, 4:220, 221.
50. BP, *SC*, 96; BP, *Ss*, 4:227.
51. Barnes, *Boris Pasternak: A Literary Biography*, 1:188
52. BP, *SC*, 86; BP, *Ss.*, 4:217.
53. Ciepiela, *The Same Solitude*, 215–16.
54. Richard K. Sanderson, "Relational Deaths: Narratives of Suicide Survivorship," in *True Relations: Essays on Autobiography and the Postmodern*, Contributions to the Study of World Literature 85, ed. G. Thomas Couser and Joseph Fichtelberg (Westport, CT: Greenwood Press, 1998), 36.

55. BP, *SC*, 23, 26, 28, 29; BP, *Ss*, 4:151, 154, 155–57. Olga Hughes points out that Pasternak himself compared his breaks with music and philosophy to suicide. See Ol'ga Raevskaia Khiuz, "O samoubiistve Vladimira Maiakovskogo v *Okhrannoi gramote* Borisa Pasternaka," in *Boris Pasternak and His Times*, ed. Lazar Fleishman (Berkeley, CA: Berkeley Slavic Specialties, 1989), 147.

56. BP, *SC*, 63–65, 51, 52; BP, *Ss*, 4:192–95, 180, 181.

57. Angela Livingstone, "Commentary," in *Pasternak on Art and Creativity*, by Boris Pasternak, ed. Angela Livingstone (Cambridge: Cambridge University Press, 1985), 8.

58. In his own life, Pasternak did what he could to avoid being drawn down this same path. Olga Hughes notes that Pasternak's refusal to give many public recitals of his poetry "was not only an expression of his personal predilection, but also a conscious resistance to the official practice of utilizing the popular romantic view of the poet for the purposes of the party." See Olga Raevsky Hughes, *The Poetic World of Boris Pasternak* (Princeton, NJ: Princeton University Press, 1974), 136.

59. BP, *SC*, 92–93; BP, *Ss*, 4:224.

60. BP, *SC*, 95, 89; BP, *Ss*, 4:226, 220, my emphasis.

61. "Уважаемые / товарищи потомки! / Роясь / в сегодняшнем / окаменевшем г, , , / наших дней изучая потемки, / вы, / возможно, / спросите и обо мне. / . . . Но я / себя / смирял, / становясь / на горло / собственной песне. / Слушайте, / товарищи потомки, / агитатора, / горлана-главаря. / Заглуша / поэзии потоки, / я шагну / через лирические томики, / как живой / с живыми говоря. . . . Мой стих дойдет / через хребты веков / и через головы / поэтов и правительств." Vladimir Maiakovskii, *Sobranie sochinenii v vos'mi tomakh* (Moscow: Izdatel'stvo "Pravda," 1968), 8:182, 184.

62. BP, *Ss*, 1:226.

63. Barnes, *Boris Pasternak: A Literary Biography*, 1:339.

64. "Zametki o peresechenii biografii Osipa Mandel'shtama i Borisa Pasternaka," *Pamiat'* 4 (1979): 316.

65. Boris Pasternak, *Selected Writings and Letters*, trans. Catherine Judelson, comp. Galina Dzubenko (Moscow: Progress Publishers, 1990), 342. For more information about Pasternak's suicide attempts, see his 1932 letter to Ol'ga Friedenberg in BP, *Ss*, 5:322, and Fleishman, *Boris Pasternak v tridtsatye gody*, 57, 64.

CHAPTER FOUR

1. Viktor Krivulin, "Tri prozy poeta," *Zvezda* 6 (1995): 188.

2. Anna Akhmatova, "Mandel'shtam (Listki iz dnevnika)," *Sochineniia* (Washington, DC: Inter-Language Literary Associates, 1968), 2:181.

3. Nadezhda Mandelstam, *Hope Against Hope*, trans. Max Hayward (New York: Atheneum, 1970), 177–78.

4. Boris Gasparov is quite right when he points out that the trip to Armenia itself, which Mandelstam used as the basis for "Journey to Armenia" in prose and which generated an entire cycle of poems in late 1930, played an important part in

Mandelstam's "restoration" and his return to poetry. My point here is only to emphasize that the psychological or spiritual turning point that shaped his new poetic trajectory came when he decided to resist the forces massed against him rather than capitulate to their demands. "Fourth Prose" describes this new orientation, and the trip to Armenia became the further catalyst for Mandelstam's renewed communion with his muse. For an excellent discussion of "Journey to Armenia," Mandelstam's philosophy, and his poetry of the early 1930s, see Boris Gasparov, "The Iron Age of the 1930s: The Centennial Return in Mandelstam" in *Rereading Russian Poetry*, ed. Stephanie Sandler (New Haven, CT: Yale University Press, 1999), 78–103.

5. See "Mandel'shtam v arkhive P.N. Luknitskogo," in *Slovo i sud'ba. Osip Mandel'shtam: Issledovaniia i materialy*, ed. Z. S. Papernyi (Moscow: Nauka, 1991), 128, for a reproduction of Mandelstam's application.

6. "Mandel'shtam v arkhive P. N. Luknitskogo," in *Slovo i sud'ba. Osip Mandel'shtam: Issledovaniia i materialy*, ed. Z. S. Papernyi (Moscow: Nauka, 1991), 131–42.

7. *Krasnaia vecherniaia gazeta* 338, November 28, 1928.

8. *Vecherniaia Moskva* 288, 1928. Cited in Osip Mandelstam, *The Complete Critical Prose and Letters*, ed. Jane Gary Harris, trans. Jane Gary Harris and Constance Link (Ann Arbor, MI: Ardis, 1979), 328. Further references to Mandelstam's *The Complete Critical Prose and Letters* will be designated "OM, CCPL."

9. OM, *CCPL*, 283; the original Russian text can be found in O. E. Mandel'shtam, *Sobranie sochinenii v chetyrekh tomakh*, ed. G. P. Struve and B. A. Filipoff, 2nd ed. (Moscow: Terra, 1991; New York: Mezhdunarodnoe Literaturnoe Sodruzhestvo, 1969), 2:425. Further references to Mandelstam's Russian texts will be to this edition and will be designated as "OM, *Ss*."

10. The clearest statement by Mandelstam indicating his belief that FOSP masterminded the series of attacks on him comes in his "Open Letter to Soviet Writers" (Otkrytoe pis'mo sovetskim pisateliam). In this letter he opens with a direct accusation that FOSP has been harassing him with unheard of methods, using deceptions and concealing facts, falsifying documents and using the services of known slanderers to build their case against him. See Mandel'shtam, OM, *Ss*, 4:544 ff.

11. "Mandel'shtam v arkhive P. N. Luknitskogo," 139.

12. OM, *CCPL*, 291; OM, *Ss*, 2:434.

13. OM, *CCPL*, 545; see also 542–44; OM, *Ss*, 3:262.

14. See A. Ustinov, "1929 god v biografii Mandel'shtama," *Novoe literaturnoe obozrenie* 6 (2002): 123–26.

15. OM, *Ss*, 4:544.

16. The precise date of composition remains unclear, since even Nadezhda Mandelstam's record is not consistent. In *Hope Abandoned* (New York: Atheneum, 1974) she indicates that Mandelstam started to dictate "Fourth Prose" in December 1929 "or thereabouts" (p. 526); in *Hope Against Hope* she gives the date of composition as 1931 (p. 177), but also indicates that she did not want to take the only finished copy of the work with them to Armenia in 1930 (p. 270). It seems most likely that the work was largely composed in early 1930, and that it may have been modified as late as 1931 after their return from Armenia.

17. David M. Bethea, *Joseph Brodsky and the Creation of Exile* (Princeton, NJ: Princeton University Press, 1994), 153.

18. Nadezhda Mandel'shtam, *Vtoraia kniga* (Paris: YMCA Press, 1972), 128. *Hope Abandoned* is to a great extent a translation of this work, but there are some passages (including this one) that are not included in the English-language text.

19. Gregory Freidin, *A Coat of Many Colors: Osip Mandelstam and His Mythologies of Self-Presentation* (Berkeley, CA: University of California Press, 1987), 110.

20. OM, *CCPL*, 192–93; OM, *Ss*, 2:209–10.

21. A. N. Robinson, "Avvakum: lichnost' i tvorchestvo," in *Zhitie Avvakuma i drugie ego sochineniia* (Moscow: Sovetskaia Rossiia, 1991), 11, 10.

22. Osip Mandelstam, "Fourth Prose," in *The Noise of Time and Other Prose Pieces*, trans. Clarence Brown (London: Quartet Books, 1988), 181 (hereafter "OM, 'FP'"); OM, *Ss*, 2:228.

23. Mandelstam, *Hope Against Hope*, 170.

24. OM, *Ss*, 4:544.

25. OM, "FP," 185; OM, *Ss*, 2:187, ellipses in original.

26. Mandelstam, *Hope Against Hope*, 170.

27. Here there is a definite overlap between the narrator and Mandelstam's real-life ideas, according to Nadezhda Mandelstam. She writes: "Many of [my contemporaries] had awaited the Revolution all their lives, but at the sight of what it meant in terms of everyday life, they were horrified and looked away. Then there were others who were frightened of their own fears and were terrified of not seeing the woods for the trees. Among these was M. Not realizing the extent to which he had believed in revolution, people who knew him less well had an oversimplified picture of his life and dismissed as insignificant a major component of his way of thinking. Without this 'revolutionary' element he would not have been so concerned to understand the course of events, or to weigh them on the scales of his values." *Hope Against Hope*, 171.

28. My translation; a slightly different English version can be found in OM, "FP," 189; OM, *Ss*, 2:191.

29. A. I. Gertsen, *Byloe i dumy*, 2nd ed. (Moscow: Academia, 1932), 1:151.

30. OM, *CCPL*, 197, 399; OM, *Ss*, 2:215, 365.

31. OM, *CCPL*, 442 (my emphasis); OM, *Ss*, 2:412–13. As I noted previously when discussing the way the theme of sound production appears in *The Noise of Time*, fine studies of Mandelstam's use of this theme in his poetry have been made by Nancy Pollak, *Mandelstam the Reader* (Baltimore: Johns Hopkins University Press, 1995), 85–92; Kiril Taranovsky, *Essays on Mandelštam* (Cambridge, MA: Harvard University Press, 1976), 10–15; Omry Ronen, *An Approach to Mandelštam* (Jerusalem: Magnes Press, 1983), 130–33, and others.

32. Quoted in Clarence Brown, *Mandelstam* (Cambridge: Cambridge University Press, 1973), 129.

33. OM, *CCPL*, 166, 116, 196; OM, *Ss*, 2:262, 226–27, 215.

34. OM, *CCPL*, 68, 70; OM, *Ss*, 2:234, 237.

35. Iu. I. Levin et al, "Russkaia semanticheskaia poetika kak potentsial'naia

kul'turnaia paradigma," *Russian Literature* 7/8 (1974): 61.

36. S. Tret'iakov, "Novyi Lev Tolstoi," in *Literatura fakta: pervyi sbornik materialov rabotnikov LEFa*, ed. N. F. Chuzhak (Moscow: Izd. Federatsiia, 1929), 31–32, 33.

37. OM, *CCPL*, 129, 121; OM, *Ss*, 2:255, 246.

38. OM, *CCPL*, 115, 407; OM, *Ss*, 2:226, 374–75.

39. Mandelstam's insistence on the word's freedom from automatic association has drawn numerous comparisons to Saussure, whose lectures were published several years before Mandelstam wrote "The Word and Culture" (1921) and "On the Nature of the Word" (1922). In *Mandel'shtam i Pasternak: Popytka kontrastivnoi poetiki* (Tallin: Aleksandra, n.d.), Mikhail Lotman underlines the sophistication of Mandelstam's approach, and remarks on the similarities between Mandelstam and Saussure (pp. 106–8). See also Freidin, *A Coat of Many Colors*, 170–74, for an excellent discussion of how Mandelstam's philosophy of the word relates to Saussure's; Freidin also mentions that Mandelstam was aware of Roman Jakobson's work from the early 1920s.

40. Nathan Rotenstreich, *Alienation: The Concept and Its Reception* (Leiden/New York: E.J. Brill, 1989), 101–2.

41. Lee Upton, *The Muse of Abandonment: Origin, Identity, Mastery in Five American Poets* (Lewisburg, PA: Bucknell University Press, 1998), 49.

42. Charles Isenberg, *Substantial Proofs of Being: Osip Mandelstam's Literary Prose* (Columbus, OH: Slavica, 1987), 151; Jane Gary Harris, "The Impulse and the Text," in OM, *CCPL*, 31.

43. Freidin, *A Coat of Many Colors*, 292.

44. Clare Cavanagh, *Osip Mandelstam and the Modernist Creation of Tradition* (Princeton, NJ: Princeton University Press, 1994), 202.

45. Mandelstam scornful reference here is to the collection of critical articles that A. G. Gornfel'd published under the title *Torments of the Word* [Muki slova] (St. Petersburg: Tipolitografiia A.E. Vineke, 1906).

46. OM, "FP," 184, 180; OM, *Ss*, 2:185, 180–81.

47. My translation; for the translation by Clarence Brown, see OM, "FP," 186; OM, *Ss*, 2:186.

48. Cavanagh, *Osip Mandelstam*, 202.

49. The prophecy about the divided kingdom is found in I Kings 11. The story of the divided kingdoms is told from I Kings 11 to 2 Kings 17.

50. OM, *CCPL*, 113; OM, *Ss*, 2:223.

51. OM, "FP," 185–86; OM, *Ss*, 2:187.

52. OM, "FP," 186; OM, *Ss*, 2:188.

53. Mandelstam appears to have had no illusions about who was working against him. In an unpublished "open letter" he comments on the masterminds who directed the entire Ulenspiegel affair: "The situation was evidently persecution on a rather large scale, and from beginning to end was an affair in the hands of FOSP [the Writers' Federation] itself." See OM, *Ss*, 4:550.

54. The relationship between Mandelstam and Pasternak, and their crucial differences over the path of the poet, has been examined from a variety of perspec-

tives and sometimes in considerable depth. Examples of excellent studies include: Pollak, *Mandelstam the Reader*, 40–42, 86–117; Mikhail Lotman, *Mandel'shtam i Pasternak*; "Zametki o peresechenii biografii Osipa Mandel'shtama i Borisa Pasternaka," *Pamiat'* 4 (1979): 282–337; Andrew Reynolds, "'Komu ne nadoeli liubov' i krov": The Uses of Intertextuality in Mandelstam's 'Za gremuchuiu doblest' griadushchikh vekov,'" in *Stoletie Mandel'shtama: materialy simposiuma/Mandelstam Centenary Conference*, ed. Robin Aizlewood and Diana Myers (Tenafly, NJ: Hermitage Publishers, 1994), 139–41.

55. OM, "FP," 183; OM, *Ss*, 2:184. Anna Akhmatova recalled once saying something uncomplimentary about Esenin, and Mandelstam replied that he "could forgive Esenin virtually anything" for this one line of verse. See Akhmatova, "Mandel'shtam (Listki iz dnevnika)," 180.

56. OM, "FP," 181; OM, *Ss*, 2:182.

57. OM, *CCPL*, 115; OM, *Ss*, 2:226.

58. Even this seemingly final solution isn't sufficient to silence a poet, Mandelstam writes in some of his poems from 1935, where he argues that the poet's voice will conquer death itself. See OM, *Ss*, 1:214; excerpts from two of these poems are cited in the final paragraphs of this chapter.

59. See Boris Pasternak, "Safe Conduct," in *The Voice of Prose: Early Prose and Autobiography*, ed. Christopher Barnes (Edinburgh: Polygon, 1986), 75–77; for a discussion of Pasternak's observations, see chapter 3 above, and Lazar' Fleishman, *Boris Pasternak v dvadtsatye gody* (Munich: Wilhelm Fink Verlag, 1981).

60. Cavanagh, *Osip Mandelstam*, 208. Cavanagh notes that Gorodetsky was especially negative, but Vladimir Markov and Yuly Margolin were also critical.

61. See Cavanagh, *Osip Mandelstam*, 208–9, for further discussion of Mandelstam's flamboyantly "impermissible" style.

62. Krivulin, "Tri prozy poeta," 189.

63. OM, "FP," 189; OM, *Ss*, 2:191.

64. OM, "FP," 189; OM, *Ss*, 2:192.

65. See Isenberg, *Substantial Proofs of Being*, 152.

66. A poem written two years later hints that Mandelstam saw the wind as this kind of unpredictable, potentially liberating air. In "Tell Me, Draftsman of the Desert" (Skazhi mne, chertezhnik pustyni), one of the "Octaves," Nancy Pollak associates the "blowing wind" with breath or spirit, and suggests that since this cycle as a whole describes the poet's work, it is the "circling of the wind" that is the model for this poetic creation. See Pollak, *Mandelstam the Reader* (Baltimore: Johns Hopkins University Press, 1995), 60.

I recently learned much more about Mandelstam's curious final phrase after a chance conversation with Aleksey Tikhomirov, a native of Armavir, led to a discussion of Mandelstam's puzzling reference to the city. When Aleksey and his mother, Valentina Tikhomirova, visited Armavir in the summer of 2007, they decided to investigate. Meetings with local scholars Roman Zasukhin, Nikolai Krizhanovsky and Sergei Ktitorov in Armavir's university and city museum revealed that: (a) Armavir had no coat of arms before 1975, (b) there is no evidence that Mandelstam ever visited the city, and (c) none of the local nobility had a coat of arms that matches Mandelstam's description. Sergei Ktitorov suggests that perhaps the closest explanation is that Mandelstam either passed through the city or heard about it during his time in the region and remembered it as a city "known for its intrigues, full of gossip." I am most grateful to each person who helped with the inquiry, and especially to Aleksey Tikhomirov for the intellectual curiosity and generosity that led him to take up this question with such thoroughness.

67. Akhmatova, "Mandel'shtam (Listki iz dnevnika)," 181; Stanislav Rassadin, *Ochen' prostoi Mandel'shtam* (Moscow: Izd. Knizhnyi sad, 1994), 93–95.

68. See Freidin, *A Coat of Many Colors*, 228–29, 250–71.

69. For an excellent discussion of the poems that express the differences between Mandelstam and Pasternak at this time, see Pollak, *Mandelstam the Reader*, 40–43.

70. OM, *Ss*, 1:241.

71. OM, *Ss*, 1:250.

72. Cavanagh, *Osip Mandelstam*, 248–49.

73. "Да, я лежу в земле, губами шевеля, / Но то, что я скажу, заучит каждый школьник." OM, *Ss*, 1:214.

74. "Лишив меня морей, разбега и разлета / И дав стопе упор насильственной земли, / Чего добились вы? Блестящего расчета: / Губ шевелящихся отнять вы не могли." OM, *Ss*, 1:214.

CHAPTER FIVE

1. Joseph Brodsky, "A Poet and Prose," in *Less Than One* (New York: Farrar, Straus, Giroux, 1986), 184.

2. Marina Tsvetaeva, *Sobranie sochinenii v semi tomakh*, ed., comp., and annot. Anna Saakiants and Lev Mnukhin (Moscow: Terra, 1997), 6.2:78–79. Unless otherwise indicated, further references to Tsvetaeva's Russian texts will be to this edition and will be designated as "MTs, *Ss*."

3. Viktoria Schweitzer, *Tsvetaeva*, trans. Robert Chandler, H. T. Willetts, and Peter Norman, ed. Angela Livingstone (London: Harvill, 1992), 214.

4. Tsvetaeva spent much of her adult life moving from one complicated relationship to another. The effect of these affairs on her poetry has been examined by many of Tsvetaeva's best readers, including Viktoria Schweitzer, *Tsvetaeva*, and Lily Feiler, *Marina Tsvetaeva: The Double Beat of Heaven and Hell* (Durham, NC: Duke University Press, 1994).

5. Schweitzer, *Tsvetaeva*, 252.

6. Marina Tsvetaeva, "The Poet on the Critic," in *Art in the Light of Conscience: Eight Essays on Poetry by Marina Tsvetaeva*, trans. and ed. Angela Livingstone (Cambridge, MA: Harvard University Press, 1992), 51, 52, 61–62; MTs, *Ss*, 5.1:285, 286, 295.

7. Feiler, *Marina Tsvetaeva*, 166–67.

8. MTs, *Ss*, 6.2:18.

9. For examples of Tsvetaeva's description of her domestic circumstances and loneliness, see Tsvetaeva's letters to Anna Tesková in MTs, Ss, 6.2:62, 67, 70, 84–85, 109.

10. Elena Izvol'skaia, in *Marina Tsvetaeva v vospominaniiakh sovremennikov. Gody emigratsii*, comp. L. A. Mnukhin and L. M. Turchinskii (Moscow: Agraf, 2002), 223–24.

11. MTs, Ss, 6.1:98, 101.

12. MTs, Ss, 6.1:70–71.

13. Tsvetaeva, "Epic and Lyric of Contemporary Russia," in *Art in the Light of Conscience*, 120; MTs, Ss, 5.2:66. Tsvetaeva, "The Poet and Time," in *Art in the Light of Conscience*, 93; MTs, Ss, 5.2:13.

14. Quoted in Viktoria Shveitser, *Byt´ i bytie Mariny Tsvetaevoi* (Fontenay-aux-Roses: Syntaxis, 1988), 316.

15. "The Poet and Time," 92, emphasis in the translated version; MTs, Ss, 5.2:12.

16. Michael Wachtel, *The Development of Russian Verse* (Cambridge: Cambridge University Press, 1998), 2.

17. "Art in the Light of Conscience," in *Art in the Light of Conscience*, 174; MTs, Ss, 5.2:45.

18. "The Poet and Time," 92; MTs, Ss, 5.2:12.

19. "The Poet and Time," 93; MTs, Ss, 5.2:12.

20. Simon Karlinsky, *Marina Tsvetaeva: The Woman, Her World, and Her Poetry* (Cambridge: Cambridge University Press, 1985), 178.

21. See the commentary on Tsvetaeva's poem "To Mayakovsky" (Maiakovskomu) for a brief summary of these events: MTs, Ss, 2:497.

22. Marina Tsvetaeva, "Mother and Music," *A Captive Spirit: Selected Prose*, ed. and trans. J. Marin King (Ann Arbor, MI: Ardis Publishers, 1994), 172; MTs, Ss, 5.1:10. All further references to English translations of Tsvetaeva's autobiographical prose will be to this edition of *A Captive Spirit* and will be designated "MTs, CS."

23. This interest in one's mother is not the only key feature of women's autobiographies, of course, and Heldt notes that other dominant themes include public life versus private life, and the woman's emergence as a writer. Barbara Heldt, *Terrible Perfection: Women and Russian Literature* (Bloomington, IN: Indiana University Press, 1987), 77, 65.

24. Bella Brodzki, "Mothers, Displacement, and Language in the Autobiographies of Nathalie Sarraute and Christa Wolf," in *Life/Lines: Theorizing Women's Autobiography*, ed. Bella Brodzki and Celeste Schenk (Ithaca, NY: Cornell University Press, 1988), 491. This topic has generated considerable interest in recent years; see also Nancy Miller, "Mothers, Daughters, and Autobiography: Maternal Legacies and Cultural Criticism," in *Mothers in Law: Feminist Theory and the Legal Regulation of Motherhood*, ed. Martha Albertson Fineman and Isabel Karpin (New York: Columbia University Press, 1995), 3–26.

25. Beth Holmgren, "For the Good of the Cause: Russian Women's Autobiography in the Twentieth Century," in *Women Writers in Russian Literature*, ed. Toby W. Clyman and Diana Greene (Westport, CT: Greenwood Press, 1994), 140; Natasha Kolchevska, "Mothers and Daughters: Variations on Family Themes in Tsvetae-

va's *The House at Old Pimen*," in *Engendering Slavic Literatures*, ed. Pamela Chester and Sibelan Forrester (Bloomington, IN: Indiana University Press, 1996), 135–57; Stephanie Sandler, "Embodied Words: Gender in Cvetaeva's Reading of Puškin," *Slavic and East European Journal* 34 (1990): 139–57.

26. MTs, *CS*, 229; MTs, *Ss*, 5.1:85.
27. MTs, *CS*, 175; MTs, *Ss*, 5.1:14.
28. MTs, *CS*, 159; MTs, *Ss*, 5.1:126.
29. Tsvetaeva, "O poezii i proze," *Zvezda* 10 (1992): 4. Tsvetaeva's linkage of poets and prophets was not uncommon, but it does raise another gender-based problem since terms like "prophet" and "priest" are typically associated with males. The issues that this compartmentalization posed for Tsvetaeva cannot be discussed here, but a western manifestation of this paradigm has been examined by Sandra M. Gilbert and Susan Gubar in "Gender, Creativity, and the Woman Poet," in *Shakespeare's Sisters: Feminist Essays on Women Poets*, ed. Gilbert and Gubar (Bloomington, IN: Indiana University Press, 1979).
30. For an example of how Tsvetaeva's autobiographical writing has been grouped and described by critics, see J. Marin King's discussion in the notes to Marina Tsvetaeva, *A Captive Spirit*, 298–99, and the analysis in Donald Loewen, "Life Beyond the Lyric: The Autobiographical Prose of Russian Poets" (Ph.D. diss., University of Wisconsin, 2001), 228–32.
31. "И как могу / Не лгать,—раз голос мой нежнее,— / Когда я лгу . . ." MTs, *Ss*, 1.1:234; Jane A. Taubman, *A Life Through Poetry: Marina Tsvetaeva's Lyric Diary* (Columbus, OH: Slavica Publishers, 1988), 4.
32. Marina Tsvetaeva, *Neizdannye pis'ma* (Paris: YMCA Press, 1972), 428, 434.
33. MTs, *CS*, 195; MTs, *Ss*, 5.1:145.
34. The following works are only some of the excellent studies that examine Tsvetaeva's mythmaking: Pamela Chester, "Engaging sexual demons in Marina Tsvetaeva's Devil: the body and the genesis of the woman poet," *Slavic Review* 53 (1994): 1025–45; Alyssa W. Dinega, *A Russian Psyche: The Poetic Mind of Marina Tsvetaeva* (Madison: University of Wisconsin Press, 2001); Olga Raevsky Hughes, "'Avtobiografiia' v proze Tsvetaevoi, Remizova i Pasternaka," in *Marina Tsvetaeva: Trudy 1go mezhdunarodnogo simpoziuma (Lozanna, 30 VI– 3 VII 1982)* (Bern: Peter Lang, 1991), 146–59; Zbignev Matseevskii, "Priem mifizatsii personazhei i ego funktsiia v avtobiograficheskoi proze Tsvetaevoi," in *Marina Tsvetaeva: Trudy 1go mezhdunarodnogo simpoziuma*, 131–41; M. V. Serova, "Avtobiograficheskaia proza v obshchem kontekste poeticheskogo samoopredeleniia Mandel'shtama i Tsvetaevoi," in *"Vse v grudi slilos' i spelos.'" Piataia tsvetaevskaia mezhdunarodnaia nauchno-tematicheskaia konferentsiia (9–11 oktiabria 1997 goda)* (Moscow: Dom-muzei Mariny Tsvetaevoi, 1998), 175–86.
35. Feiler, *Marina Tsvetaeva*, 160.
36. MTs, *CS*, 172, 186; MTs, *Ss*, 5.1:10, 30.
37. Literally to bet the entire bank in a game; MTs, *CS*, 175; MTs, *Ss*, 5.1:14.
38. MTs, *CS*, 180, 178; MTs, *Ss*, 5.1:20, 18.
39. MTs, *CS*, 184; MTs, *Ss*, 5.1:28.

40. MTs, *CS*, 172, 173; MTs, *Ss*, 5.1:10, 11.
41. MTs, *CS*, 183, 176, 184, 185; MTs, *Ss*, 5.1:26, 16, 28, 29.
42. MTs, *CS*, 180–81; MTs, *Ss*, 5.1:20, 21.
43. MTs, *CS*, 181; MTs, *Ss*, 5.1:21.
44. MTs, *CS*, 177–78; MTs, *Ss*, 5.1:17–18.
45. MTs, *Ss*, 6:415, 410, 415–16.
46. MTs, *CS*, 188; MTs, *Ss*, 5.1:33. Pamela Chester has examined the devil's appearance and its place in the autobiographical prose in "Engaging sexual demons in Marina Tsvetaeva's 'Devil,'" 1027–28. See also Sibelan Forrester for further discussion of the devil's appearance and its connection to Tsvetaeva's grandfather: "Where the Dog Is Buried: Clues to the Ancestry of Tsvetaeva's Canine 'Devil,'" *Canadian Slavonic Papers* 44, nos. 1–2 (2002): 3–17. Svetlana Elnitsky (El'nitskaia) treats these themes as well in "Tsvetaeva i chert," *Russian Language Journal*, 40, no. 136–37 (1986): 75–93.
47. MTs, *CS*, 189, 190; MTs, *Ss*, 5.1:34. Tsvetaeva's account of the devil appearing in her life as a powerful, liberating force certainly relates to her poem "On the Red Steed" (Na krasnom kone). For good discussions of this poem see David M. Bethea, *Joseph Brodsky and the Creation of Exile* (Princeton, NJ: Princeton University Press, 1994), 180–87, and Dinega, *A Russian Psyche*, 71–89.
48. See MTs, *CS*, 313n1.
49. MTs, *CS* 192; MTs, *Ss*, 5.1:37.
50. MTs, *CS*, 190; MTs, *Ss*, 5.1:34–35.
51. MTs, *CS*, 193; MTs, *Ss*, 5.1:38–39.
52. MTs, *CS*, 192; MTs, *Ss*, 5.1:37.
53. MTs, *Ss*, 5.1:56.
54. MTs, *CS*, 195; MTs, *Ss*, 5.1:41.
55. MTs, *CS*, 214, my emphasis; MTs, *Ss*, 5.1:69.
56. "Father" is a volatile concept in Tsvetaeva's writing, and "My Pushkin" is no exception. While Pushkin becomes a poetic father who encourages creativity and risk-taking, the real-life fathers in this work are much more controlling. We need not look any farther than Tsvetaeva's maternal grandfather, who forbids his daughter from following her heart in pursuit of true love.
57. See Dinega, *A Russian Psyche*, 90–128 for more on Tsvetaeva's "creation" of Pasternak.
58. MTs, *Ss*, 6:393–94.
59. MTs, *Ss*, 6:221.
60. "The Poet and Time," 97–98; MTs, *Ss*, 5.2:17.
61. "The Poet and Time," 103; MTs, *Ss*, 5.2:22–23.
62. Tsvetaeva, "Epic and Lyric of Contemporary Russia," in Art in the Light of Conscience, 120; MTs, SS, 5.2:66.
63. "Epic and Lyric of Contemporary Russia," 120, 122, 125; MTs, *Ss*, 5.2:66, 68, 71. For further discussion of how Tsvetaeva accounted for Pasternak's signs of weakness, see Catherine Ciepiela, *The Same Solitude: Boris Pasternak and Marina Tsvetaeva* (Ithaca, NY: Cornell University Press, 2006), 241–44; Elena Korkina,

"Pushkinskaia tema v sud'be Pasternaka i Tsvetaevoi v 1930-e gody," in *Marina Tsvetaeva: pesn' zhizni*, ed. Efim Etkind and Veronique Lossky (Paris: YMCA Press, 1996), 102–26; and Irina Shevelenko, *Literaturnyi put' Tsvetaevoi* (Moscow: Novoe literaturnoe obozrenie, 2002), 399–400.

64. MTs, *Ss*, 5.2:51; Shevelenko, *Literaturnyi put'*, 410–13.

65. The scant details that I have provided as a summary here cannot do more than hint at the depths and complexity of the relationship between Pasternak and Tsvetaeva. Catherine Ciepiela's *The Same Solitude: Boris Pasternak and Marina Tsvetaeva* provides the most comprehensive examination to date of their interaction in letters, of the intertextual dialogue that they carried on through their poems, and of the way they imagined each other in relation to real and created figures. See also Shevelenko, *Literaturnyi put'*, 381–425, for a careful look at the relationship especially in the late 1920s and early 1930s.

66. MTs, *CS*, 210, 215; MTs, *Ss*, 5.1:64, 69.

67. MTs, *CS*, 205; MTs, *Ss*, 5.1:58, 59. Tsvetaeva's mother kept a copy of A. A. Naumov's painting "The Duel of A. S. Pushkin with d'Anthés" (1884) in her bedroom; in the early paragraphs of "My Pushkin," Tsvetaeva reflects in considerable detail on how this painting affected her early thoughts about Pushkin and the mortality of the poet.

68. MTs, *CS*, 215–16; MTs, *Ss*, 5.1:70.

69. MTs, *CS*, 217; MTs, *Ss*, 5.1:72.

70. Barbara Heldt and Stephanie Sandler see more of an attempt to raise the status of women in the text; for their analysis, see Heldt, *Terrible Perfection: Women and Russian Literature*, 99, and Sandler, "Embodied Words: Gender in Cvetaeva's Reading of Puškin," 142. For a wide-ranging discussion of Tsvetaeva's attempt to dissolve gender separation in her poetry, see Dinega, *A Russian Psyche*.

71. MTs, *CS*, 229, translation slightly modified; MTs, *Ss*, 5.1:85.

72. Shevelenko, *Literaturnyi put'*, 134–40, especially 136–37. For Tsvetaeva's notebook entries, see Marina Tsvetaeva, *Zapisnye knizhki: v dvukh tomakh* (Moscow: Ellis Lak, 2000–2001), 1:268. Catherine Ciepiela sees a similar retreat from corporeal sexuality but argues that a primary impetus for this shift can be traced to the death of Tsvetaeva's daughter Irina; see *The Same Solitude*, 30–32.

73. Dinega, *A Russian Psyche*, 4.

74. MTs, *CS*, 205; MTs, *Ss*, 5.1:58–59.

75. "Жизнь—это место, где жить нельзя: / Ев—рейский квартал . . . // Так не достойнее ль во сто крат / Стать Вечным Жидом? / Ибо для каждого, кто не гад, / Ев—рейский погром—[. . . .] Гетто избранничеств! Вал и ров. / По—щады не жди! / В сём христианнейшем из миров / Поэты—жиды!" MTs, *Ss*, 3.1:48.

76. MTs, *CS*, 218, 220; MTs, *Ss*, 5.1:73–74, 76.

77. Tsvetaeva would surely bring her own 1926 poem "From the Sea" (S moria) into this dramatic encounter linking her, Pasternak and Pushkin. For an excellent discussion of this poem and its connections to Pasternak, see Ciepiela, *The Same Solitude*, 179–89.

78. MTs, *CS*, 218, 234; MTs, *Ss*, 5.1:73, 91.

CHAPTER SIX

1. Lazar Fleishman, *Boris Pasternak: The Poet and His Politics* (Cambridge, MA: Harvard University Press, 1990), 163. It was Fleishman's series of works on Pasternak which prompted me to look much more closely at the events that influenced Russian poets in the 1920s and 1930s; readers who would like more information about the way events in those decades influenced Pasternak will find Fleishman's series of books on Pasternak extremely rewarding. See *Boris Pasternak: The Poet and His Politics*; *Boris Pasternak v dvadtsatye gody* (Munich: Wilhelm Fink Verlag, 1981); and *Boris Pasternak v tridtsatye gody* (Jerusalem: Magnes Press, 1984).
2. Fleishman, *Boris Pasternak: The Poet and His Politics*, 163.
3. See Fleishman, *Boris Pasternak: The Poet and His Politics*, 166.
4. See Pasternak's 1932 letter to Ol'ga Friedenberg in Boris Pasternak, *Sobranie sochinenii v piati tomakh*, vol. 5 (Moscow: Khudozhestvennaia literatura, 1991), 322; further references to this edition will be designated "BP, *Ss*"; see also Lazar' Fleishman, *Boris Pasternak v tridtsatye gody*, 57, 64, for more on this suicide attempt.
5. Fleishman, *Boris Pasternak: The Poet and His Politics*, 176.
6. There are many surviving versions of this phone call and the entire set of circumstances surrounding Mandelstam's poem and his arrests. For one account of the arrest and phone call, as well as a discussion of the relations between Pasternak and Mandelstam, see Nadezhda Mandelstam, *Hope Against Hope* (New York: Atheneum Publishers, 1970) 3–33, 145–55.
7. Fleishman, *Boris Pasternak: The Poet and His Politics*, 204; Christopher Barnes, *Boris Pasternak: A Literary Biography* (Cambridge: Cambridge University Press, 1998), 2:134.
8. Donald Rayfield, "The Death of Paolo Iashvili," *The Slavonic and East European Review* 68, no. 4 (1990): 660.
9. Rayfield, "The Death of Paolo Iashvili," 633n5.
10. Donald Rayfield, "Unicorns and Gazelles: Pasternak, Rilke and the Georgian Poets," *Forum for Modern Language Studies* 26, no. 4 (October 1990): 380.
11. Letter to N. P. Smirnov, April 5, 1955, BP, *Ss*, 5:537, 536; letter to N. A. Tabidze, December 10, 1955, BP, *Ss*, 5:541.
12. Letter to N. P. Smirnov, April 28, 1955, *Russkie novosti* 1041 (May 28, 1965): 5.
13. Letter to M. G. Batagin, December 15, 1955, BP, *Ss*, 5:542–43.
14. Quoted in Olga Carlisle, *Poets on Street Corners* (New York: Vintage Books, 1970), 88–89, 84.
15. Barnes, *Boris Pasternak: A Literary Biography*, 2:305.
16. Angela Livingstone in Boris Pasternak, *Pasternak on Art and Creativity*, ed. Angela Livingstone (Cambridge: Cambridge University Press, 1985), 204.
17. Victor Erlich, "Boris Pasternak and Russian Poetic Culture of His Time," in *Boris Pasternak and His Times*, ed. Lazar Fleishman (Berkeley, CA: Berkeley Slavic Specialties, 1989), 41–43.
18. Barnes, *Boris Pasternak: A Literary Biography*, 2:305–6.
19. Boris Pasternak, *People and Propositions*, ed. Christopher Barnes (Edinburgh:

Polygon, 1990), 26; the Russian original can be found in BP, *Ss*, 4:296. Further references to *People and Propositions* will be designated "BP, *PP*."

20. Boris Pasternak, *Safe Conduct* in *The Voice of Prose: Early Prose and Autobiography*, ed. Christopher Barnes (Edinburgh: Polygon, 1986), 85–86; BP, *Ss*, 4:217.

21. BP, *PP*, 67–68; BP, *Ss*, 4:333–34.

22. *Safe Conduct*, 59; BP, *Ss*, 4:188. BP, *PP*, 53; BP, *Ss*, 4:320–21.

23. This *samokritika* would certainly have been a welcome sight to the forces of literary orthodoxy that were already becoming aware that *Doctor Zhivago* would soon be published in Italy. The presence of these confessions in *People and Propositions*, though, is determined by their function in the text: they are there to show Pasternak's integrity in not glossing over his own errors and problems. If Pasternak wants the reader to accept his account, he has to prove that he can be trusted.

24. BP, *PP*, 37–38, 64, 65, 45, 44, 59–60; BP, *Ss*, 4:306–7, 330–31, 313, 312, 326–27.

25. BP, *PP*, 26; BP, *Ss*, 4:296.

26. Olav Severijnen, "The Renaissance of a Genre: Autobiography and Modernism," *New Comparison: A Journal of Comparative and General Literary Studies* 9 (1990): 43, 44.

27. BP, *PP*, 44; BP, *Ss*, 4:312.

28. BP, *PP*, 312n73.

29. BP, *PP*, 52–53; BP, *Ss*, 4:320.

30. BP, *PP*, 55, 71; BP, *Ss*, 4:322, 337. *Safe Conduct*, 89; BP, *Ss*, 4:220.

31. Khlebnikov, referred to twice in *Safe Conduct* as someone whose poetry Pasternak simply couldn't appreciate, is here identified as a poet whose work Pasternak underestimated for many years. BP, *PP*, 77; BP, *Ss*, 4:339.

32. Fadeev is somewhat out of place here, since he was never known for poetry; it is most likely that Pasternak includes him because Fadeev had taken his life so recently. Some of the suicides that Pasternak mentions are now the subject of intense debate. In Pasternak's day, of course, no one publicly questioned the official explanations for any of these deaths—that came later, when the opening of archives and other records started to cast doubt on some of the official verdicts of suicide. I mention this detail here not to argue one way or the other on the contested cases but merely to point out how subsequent events sometimes underline in unexpected ways that our assessments or speculations—like Pasternak's speculative explanations of suicidal motivation, for example—often say more about our own psychological states or value systems than they can ultimately say about the ostensible subject of our conversation. It is worth remembering that by 1956 Pasternak had seriously contemplated suicide on at least two occasions, and attempted it at least once. Another suicide drama followed only two years later at the height of the Nobel Prize scandal.

The controversy in the present instance relates to the deaths of Esenin and to a lesser degree Mayakovsky. Since 1989, when Edward Khlystalov published an article called "The Secret of the Hotel Angleterre" in the July issue of the journal *Moskva*, a flood of articles and even a high-budget television series have debated whether Esenin's death was really a political murder or a suicide. Mayakovsky's case has not been the focus of such intense scrutiny yet, so I was surprised to find even Russian literary scholars acknowledging almost offhandedly their suspicion that Mayakovsky's fatal gunshot wound was not self-inflicted. Indeed, even one of the forensic specialists who argues that Esenin really did hang himself points out that Mayakovsky's case presents a more complicated and contradictory case than Esenin's; see "Smert' Esenina: ubiistvo ili samoubiistvo?" *Komsomol'skaia pravda* (November 19, 2005) http://www.kp.ru/daily/23609.3/46548/ (August 3, 2006).

33. Kali Tal, "Speaking the Language of Pain: Vietnam War Literature in the Context of the Literature of Trauma," in *Fourteen Landing Zones: Approaches to Vietnam War Literature*, ed. Philip Jason (Iowa City: University of Iowa Press, 1991), 217–18.

34. BP, *PP*, 67; BP, *Ss*, 4:333.

35. Nadezhda Mandelstam, *Hope Against Hope*, 233.

36. Robert Jay Lifton, *The Broken Connection: On Death and the Continuity of Life* (Washington, DC: American Psychiatric Press, 1979), 169, 171. For a more detailed discussion of the same concepts, see Lifton's *Death in Life* (New York: Random House, 1967), 480–84.

37. See Lifton, *Death in Life*, 482–83.

38. BP, *PP*, 73; BP, *Ss*, 4:338.

39. A. K. Tarasenkov, "Pasternak. Chernovye zapisi. 1930–1939," in *Vospominaniia o Borise Pasternake*, ed. E. V. Pasternak and M. I. Feinberg (Moscow: Slovo, 1993), 173.

40. Lifton, *Death in Life*, 484.

41. BP, *PP*, 78–79; BP, *Ss*, 4:340–41. Catherine Ciepiela sees greater ambivalence here and describes Pasternak's remarks as an "objective if not wholly accepting portrait of [Tsvetaeva] and her writing as hysterical—as miming masculine force in works of exceptional power." See Catherine Ciepiela, *The Same Solitude: Boris Pasternak and Marina Tsvetaeva* (Ithaca, NY: Cornell University Press, 2006), 245.

42. BP, *PP*, 85–86; BP, *Ss*, 4:346.

CONCLUSION

1. Lazar Fleishman, *Boris Pasternak: The Poet and His Politics* (Cambridge, MA: Harvard University Press, 1990), 281. For a more detailed account of these events, see 280–97, and Christopher Barnes, *Boris Pasternak: A Literary Biography* (Cambridge: Cambridge University Press, 1998), 2:312–51.

2. Fleishman lists Jules Romains and Serge Lifar as two prominent examples of people who deplored Pasternak's apparent weakness (*Boris Pasternak: The Poet and His Politics*, 290, 302).

3. Manya Harari, "Pasternak," *The Twentieth Century* 164 (December 1958): 527.

4. "Nobel Prize in Literature 1958—Announcement," The Nobel Foundation.

http://nobelprize.org/nobel_prizes/literature/laureates/1958/press.html (August 20, 2006).

5. Nadezhda Mandelstam, *Hope Against Hope*, trans. Max Hayward (New York: Atheneum, 1970), 225–26.

6. Quoted in Mandelstam, *Hope Against Hope*, 222.

7. Mandelstam, *Hope Against Hope*, 333.

Bibliography

Akhmatova, Anna. "Mandel'shtam. (Listki iz dnevnika)." In *Sochineniia*, vol. 2. Washington, DC: Inter-Language Literary Associates, 1968.
———. *Sochineniia*. 2 vols. New York: Interlanguage Literary Associates, 1968.
Aseev, N. "Liricheskii fel'eton." *Novyi LEF* 11 (1928): 3–8.
———. "Sobstvennye pominki." *Novyi LEF* 3 (1928): 37–40.
Aucouturier, Michel. "Ob odnom kliuche k 'Okhrannoi gramote.'" Pp. 337–49 in *Boris Pasternak, 1890–1960: colloque de Cerisy-la-Salle, 11–14 septembre 1975*, edited by Michel Aucouturier. Paris: Institut d'études slaves, 1979.
———. "Biography, Autobiography and 'Sister Life': Some Problems in Chronicling Pasternak's Earlier Years." *Irish Slavonic Studies* 4 (1983): 48–58.
Barnes, Christopher J. *Boris Pasternak: A Literary Biography*. 2 vols. Cambridge: Cambridge University Press, 1989–1998.
Bethea, David M. *Joseph Brodsky and the Creation of Exile*. Princeton, NJ: Princeton University Press, 1994.
Bezymenskii, A., ed. *Poeziia gorniatskogo udara: pervaia kniga stikhov gorniakov poetov-rabkorov*. Moscow: Izd. TSK SG, 1929.
Bobrov, Sergei. "Rev. of *Tristia*." *Pechat' i revoliutsiia* 6 (1923): 259–62.
Bogdanov, A. A. "Chto takoe proletarskaia poeziia?" *Proletarskaia kul'tura* 1 (July 1918): 12–22.
Borsobin, Vladimir. "Smert' Esenina: ubiistvo ili samoubiistvo?" *Komsomol'skaia pravda* (November 19, 2005) http://www.kp.ru/daily/23609.3/46548/ (August 3, 2006).
Brik, Osip. "Protiv 'tvorcheskoi' lichnosti." Pp. 76–79 in *Literatura fakta: pervyi sbornik materialov rabotnikov LEFa*, edited by N. F. Chuzhak. Moscow: Izd. Federatsiia, 1929. Reprint, Moscow: Zakharov, 2000.

———. "Tak nazivaemyi formal'nyi metod," *LEF* 1 (1923): 213–15.
Briusov, Valerii. "Review of *Vtoraia kniga.*" *Pechat' i revoliutsiia* 6 (1923): 63–66.
Brodsky, Joseph. "A Poet and Prose." Pp. 176–94 in *Less Than One*, by Joseph Brodsky. New York: Farrar, Straus, Giroux, 1986.
Brodzki, Bella. "Mothers, Displacement, and Language in the Autobiographies of Nathalie Sarraute and Christa Wolf." Pp. 243–59 in *Life/Lines: Theorizing Women's Autobiography*, edited by Bella Brodzki and Celeste Schenk. Ithaca, NY: Cornell University Press, 1988.
Brown, Clarence. *Mandelstam*. Cambridge: Cambridge University Press, 1973.
Brown, Edward. *The Proletarian Episode in Russian Literature, 1928–1932*. Studies of the Russian Institute. New York: Columbia University Press, 1953.
Bruner, Jerome. "Self-Making and World-Making." Pp. 22–37 in *Narrative and Identity: Studies in Autobiography, Self and Culture*, edited by Jens Brockmeier and Donal Carbaugh. Amsterdam: John Benjamins Publishing Company, 2001.
Bukhshtab, B. Ia. *A. A. Fet: ocherk zhizni i tvorchestva*. 2nd ed. Leningrad: Nauka, 1990.
Carlisle, Olga. *Poets on Street Corners*. New York: Vintage Books, 1970.
Cavanagh, Clare. *Osip Mandelstam and the Modernist Creation of Tradition*. Princeton, NJ: Princeton University Press, 1994.
Chester, Pamela. "Engaging Sexual Demons in Marina Tsvetaeva's 'Devil': The Body and the Genesis of the Woman Poet." *Slavic Review* 53 (1994): 1025-45.
Chuzhak, N. F., ed. *Literatura fakta: pervyi sbornik materialov rabotnikov LEFa*. Moscow: Izd. Federatsiia, 1929. Reprint, Moscow: Zakharov, 2000.
———. "Literatura zhiznestroeniia." Pp. 34–67 in *Literatura fakta: pervyi sbornik materialov rabotnikov LEFa*.
———. "Pisatel'skaia pamiatka." Pp. 9–28 in *Literatura fakta*.
Ciepiela, Catherine. *The Same Solitude: Boris Pasternak and Marina Tsvetaeva*. Ithaca, NY: Cornell University Press, 2006.
de Man, Paul. "Autobiography as Defacement." *MLN* 94 (1979): 919–30.
———. Letter to the Editor."*Dial*" 1899: 329.
Dinega, Alyssa W. *A Russian Psyche: The Poetic Mind of Marina Tsvetaeva*. Madison: University of Wisconsin Press, 2001.
Dobrenko, Evgeny. *Aesthetics of Alienation: Reassessment of Early Soviet Cultural Theories*. Trans. Jesse M. Savage. Evanston, Ill.: Northwestern University Press, 2005.
———. *The Making of the State Writer: Social and Aesthetic Origins of Soviet Literary Culture*. Trans. by Jesse M. Savage. Stanford, CA: Stanford University Press, 2001.
Eakin, Paul John. *Touching the World: Reference in Autobiography*. Princeton, NJ: Princeton University Press, 1992.
———. "Relational Selves, Relational Lives: The Story of the Story." Pp. 63–82 in *True Relations: Essays on Autobiography and the Postmodern*. Contributions to the Study of World Literature 85, edited by G. Thomas Couser and Joseph Fichtelberg. Westport, CT: Greenwood Press, 1998.

Elnitsky (El'nitskaia), Svetlana. "Tsvetaeva i chert." *Russian Language Journal* 40, nos. 136–37 (1986): 75–93.

Erlich, Victor. "Boris Pasternak and Russian Poetic Culture of His Time." Pp. 32–45 in *Boris Pasternak and His Times*, edited by Lazar Fleishman. Berkley, CA: Berkley Slavic Specialties, 1989.

Feiler, Lily. *Marina Tsvetaeva: The Double Beat of Heaven and Hell*. Durham, NC: Duke University Press, 1994.

Figurnova, O. S., and M. V. Figurnova, comp. *Osip i Nadezhda Mandel'shtamy v rasskazakh sovremennikov*. Moscow: Natalis, 2001.

Fleishman, Lazar, ed. *Boris Pasternak and His Times*. Berkeley, CA: Berkeley Slavic Specialties, 1989.

———. *Boris Pasternak: The Poet and His Politics*. Cambridge, MA: Harvard University Press, 1990.

———. *Boris Pasternak v dvadtsatye gody*. Munich: Wilhelm Fink Verlag, 1981.

———. *Boris Pasternak v tridtsatye gody*. Jerusalem: Magnes Press, 1984.

Forrester, Sibelan. "Where the Dog Is Buried: Clues to the Ancestry of Tsvetaeva's Canine 'Devil.'" *Canadian Slavonic Papers* 44, nos. 1–2 (2002): 3–17.

Freidin, Gregory. *A Coat of Many Colors: Osip Mandelstam and His Mythologies of Self-Presentation*. Berkeley, CA: University of California Press, 1987.

———. "The Whisper of History and the Noise of Time." *Russian Review* 37 (1978): 421–37.

Gasparov, Boris. "The Iron Age of the 1930s: The Centennial Return in Mandelstam." Pp. 78–103 in *Rereading Russian Poetry*, edited by Stephanie Sandler. New Haven, CT: Yale University Press, 1999.

Gertsen, A. I. *Byloe i dumy*. 2nd ed. Moscow: Academia, 1932.

Gilbert, Sandra M., and Susan Gubar. "Gender, Creativity, and the Woman Poet." Pp. xv–xxvi in *Shakespeare's Sisters: Feminist Essays on Women Poets*, edited by Sandra M. Gilbert and Susan Gubar. Bloomington: Indiana University Press, 1979.

Ginzburg, Lydia. *On Psychological Prose*. Translated and edited by Judson Rosengrant. Princeton, NJ: Princeton University Press, 1991.

Gornfel'd, A. G. *Muki slova*. St. Petersburg: Tipolitografiia A.E. Vineke, 1906.

Hall, Donald. *Death to the Death of Poetry: Essays, Reviews, Notes, Interviews*. Ann Arbor: University of Michigan Press, 1994.

Harari, Manya. "Pasternak." *Twentieth Century* 164 (Dec 1958): 527.

Harris, Jane Gary. "Autobiographical Theory and the Problem of Esthetic Coherence in Mandelstam's *Noise of Time*." *Essays in Poetics* 9 (1984): 33–66.

———. "Autobiography and History: Osip Mandelstam's *Noise of Time*." Pp. 99–113 in *Autobiographical Statements in Twentieth-Century Russian Literature*, edited by Jane Gary Harris. Princeton, NJ: Princeton University Press, 1990.

———. "Introduction: The Impulse and the Text." Pp. 3–49 in Mandelstam, *The Complete Critical Prose and Letters*, edited by Jane Gary Harris, translated by Jane Gary Harris and Constance Link. Ann Arbor, Mich.: Ardis, 1979.

———. "Mandel'shtam's Aesthetic of Performance." *Canadian-American Slavic Studies* 19, no. 4 (1985): 426–42.

Heldt, Barbara. *Terrible Perfection: Women and Russian Literature.* Bloomington: Indiana University Press, 1987.

Holmgren, Beth. "For the Good of the Cause: Russian Women's Autobiography in the Twentieth Century." Pp. 127–48 in *Women Writers in Russian Literature*, edited by Toby W. Clyman and Diana Greene. Westport, CT: Greenwood Press, 1994.

Hughes, Olga Raevsky. (See also Khiuz, Ol'ga Raevskaia.) "'Avtobiografiia' v proze Tsvetaevoi, Remizova i Pasternaka." Pp. 146–59 in *Marina Tsvetaeva: Trudy 1go mezhdunarodnogo simpoziuma*.

———. *The Poetic World of Boris Pasternak.* Princeton, NJ: Princeton University Press, 1974.

Isenberg, Charles. *Substantial Proofs of Being: Osip Mandelstam's Literary Prose.* Columbus, OH: Slavica, 1987.

Izvol'skaia, Elena, ed. *Gody emigratsii.* Vol. 2 of *Marina Tsvetaeva v vospominaniiakh sovremennikov*, compiled by L. A. Mnukhin and L. M. Turchinskii. Moscow: Agraf, 2002.

Jakobson, Roman. "On a Generation That Squandered Its Poets." Pp. 138–66 in *Twentieth Century Russian Literary Criticism*, edited by Victor Erlich. New Haven, CT: Yale University Press, 1975.

Karlinsky, Simon. *Marina Tsvetaeva: The Woman, Her World, and Her Poetry.* Cambridge: Cambridge University Press, 1985.

Kaverin, Veniamin. "Kak ia ne stal poetom." *Oktiabr'* 10 (1959): 131.

———. "Vstrechi s Mandel'shtamom." Pp. 268–272 in *Osip Mandel'shtam i ego vremia*. Compiled by V. Kreid and E. Necheporuk. Moscow: L'Age d'Homme–Nash dom, 1995.

Kemball, Robin, ed. *Marina Tsvetaeva: Trudy 1go mezhdunarodnogo simpoziuma (Lozanna, 30 VI–3 VII 1982).* Bern: Peter Lang, 1991.

Khiuz, Ol'ga Raevskaia. (See also Hughes, Olga Raevsky.) "O samoubiistve Vladimira Maiakovskogo v *Okhrannoi gramote* Borisa Pasternaka." Pp. 141–52 in *Boris Pasternak and His Times*, edited by Lazar Fleishman. Berkeley, CA: Berkeley Slavic Specialties, 1989.

Kirillov, Vladimir. *Stikhotvoreniia i poemy.* Moscow: Khudozhestvennaia literatura, 1970.

Kogan, P. S. *Proletarskaia literatura.* Ivanovo-Voznesensk: Osnova, 1926.

Kolchevska, Natasha. "Mothers and Daughters: Variations on Family Themes in Tsvetaeva's *The House at Old Pimen*." Pp. 135–57 in *Engendering Slavic Literatures*, edited by Pamela Chester and Sibelan Forrester. Bloomington: Indiana University Press, 1996.

Kolodnyi, Lev. *Poety i vozhdi. Dokumental'nye ocherki.* Moscow: Golos, 1997.

Krivulin, Viktor. "Tri prozy poeta." *Zvezda* 6 (1995): 182.

Kushner, Boris. "Organizatory proizvodstva." *LEF* 3 (1923): 97–103.

Lelevich, G. "1923 god: literaturnye itogi." *Na postu* 5 (May 1925): 73–102.

———. "Nam nuzhna partiinaia liniia." *Na postu* 1 (1923): 101–8.
Levin, Iu. I., et al. "Russkaia semanticheskaia poetika kak potentsial'naia kul'turnaia paradigma." *Russian Literature* 7–8 (1974): 47–83.
Lifton, Robert Jay. *The Broken Connection: On Death and the Continuity of Life.* Washington, DC: American Psychiatric Press, 1979.
———. *Death in Life.* New York: Random House, 1967.
Lipkin, Semen. "Ugl', pylaiushchii ognem; vstrechi i razgovory s Osipom Mandel'shtamom." Pp. 294–311 in *Osip Mandel'shtam i ego vremia*, comp. V. Kreid and E. Necheporuk Moscow: L'Age d'Homme–Nash dom, 1995.
Livingstone, Angela. "Commentary." In *Pasternak on Art and Creativity*, by Boris Pasternak, edited by Angela Livingstone. Cambridge: Cambridge University Press, 1985.
Loewen, Donald. "Life Beyond the Lyric: The Autobiographical Prose of Russian Poets." Ph.D. diss., University of Wisconsin, 2001.
Lotman, Mikhail. *Mandel'shtam i Pasternak: popytka kontrastivnoi poetiki.* Tallinn: Aleksandra, n.d.
Maguire, Robert. *Red Virgin Soil: Soviet Literature in the 1920's.* Ithaca, NY: Cornell University Press, 1987.
Maiakovskii, Vladimir. *Sobranie sochinenii v vos'mi tomakh.* 8 vols. Moscow: Izdatel'stvo Pravda, 1968.
Mandel'shtam, Nadezhda. (See also Mandelstam, Nadezhda.) *Vtoraia kniga.* Paris: YMCA Press, 1972.
"Mandel'shtam v arkhive P. N. Luknitskogo." In *Slovo i sud'ba. Osip Mandel'shtam: Issledovaniia i materialy*, edited by Z. S. Papernyi. Moscow: Nauka, 1991.
Mandel'shtam, Osip. (See also Mandelstam, Osip.) *Sobranie sochinenii v chetyrekh tomakh.* New York: Mezhdunarodnoe Literaturnoe Sodruzhestvo, 1969. Reprint Moscow: Terra, 1991.
Mandelstam, Nadezhda. (See also Mandel'shtam, Nadezhda.) *Hope Abandoned.* New York: Atheneum, 1974.
———. *Hope Against Hope.* Translated by Max Hayward. New York: Atheneum, 1970.
Mandelstam, Osip. (See also Mandel'shtam, Osip.) *The Complete Critical Prose and Letters.* Edited by Jane Gary Harris. Translated by Jane Gary Harris and Constance Link. Ann Arbor, MI: Ardis, 1979.
———. *The Noise of Time and Other Prose Pieces.* Translated by Clarence Brown. London: Quartet Books, 1988.
Matseevskii, Zbignev. "Priem mifizatsii personazhei i ego funktsiia v avtobiograficheskoi proze Tsvetaevoi." Pp. 131–41 in *Marina Tsvetaeva: Trudy 1go mezhdunarodnogo simpoziuma (Lozanna, 30 VI–3 VII 1982)*, edited by Robin Kemball. Bern: Peter Lang, 1991.
Miller, Nancy. "Mothers, Daughters, and Autobiography: Maternal Legacies and Cultural Criticism." Pp. 3–26 in *Mothers in Law: Feminist Theory and the Legal Regulation of Motherhood*, edited by Martha Albertson Fineman and Isabel Kar-

pin. New York: Columbia University Press, 1995.

Nerler, P. "Osip Mandel'shtam v Narkomprose v 1918–1919 godakh." *Voprosy literatury* 9 (1989): 275–79.

The Nobel Foundation. "Nobel Prize in Literature 1958—Announcement." http://nobelprize.org/nobel_prizes/literature/laureates/1958/press.html (August 20, 2006).

Kalugin, Oleg. "Delo KGB na Annu Akhmatovu." In *Gosbezopasnost' i literatura na opyte Rossii i Germanii (SSSR i GDR)*. Moscow: Rudomino, 1994.

Pasternak, Boris. *Sobranie sochinenii v piati tomakh*. Moscow: Khudozhestvennaia literatura, 1991.

———. *Selected Writings and Letters*. Translated by Catherine Judelson. Compiled by Galina Dzubenko. Moscow: Progress Publishers, 1990.

———. "Letter to N. P. Smirnov, April 28, 1955." *Russkie novosti* 1041 (May 28, 1965): 5.

———. *Safe Conduct*. Pp. 21–108 in *The Voice of Prose: Early Prose and Autobiography*, vol. 1, by Boris Pasternak, edited and translated by Christopher Barnes. Edinburgh: Polygon, 1986.

———. "People and Propositions." Pp. 26–86 in *People and Propositions*, vol. 2 of *The Voice of Prose*, by Boris Pasternak, edited by Christopher Barnes. Edinburgh: Polygon, 1990.

Pasternak, E. B. *Boris Pasternak. Biografiia*. 2nd ed. Moscow: Izdatel'stvo Tsitadel', 1997.

Pisarev, D. I. *Sochineniia v 4kh tomakh*. 4 vols. Moscow: Khudozhestvennaia literatura, 1955.

Pollak, Nancy. *Mandelstam the Reader*. Baltimore: Johns Hopkins University Press, 1995.

Potapov, Aleksandr. "Taina smerti Aleksandra Bloka." *Sovershenno sekretno—versiia v Pitere* (December 9, 2002), http://www.kohkpetho.ru/versia.php?article=169 (May 30, 2005).

Rassadin, Stanislav. *Ochen' prostoi Mandel'shtam*. Moscow: Izd. Knizhnyi sad, 1994.

Rayfield, Donald. "Unicorns and Gazelles: Pasternak, Rilke and the Georgian Poets." *Forum For Modern Language Studies* 26, no. 4 (1990): 370–81.

———. "The Death of Paolo Iashvili." *Slavonic and East European Review* 68, no. 4 (1990): 631–64.

Reynolds, Andrew. "'Komu ne nadoeli liubov' i krov": The Uses of Intertextuality in Mandelstam's 'Za gremuchuiu doblest' griadushchikh vekov'." Pp. 136–54 in *Stoletie Mandel'shtama: materialy simposiuma/Mandelstam Centenary Conference*, edited by Robin Aizlewood and Diana Myers. Tenafly, NJ: Hermitage Publishers, 1994.

Robinson, A. N. "Avvakum: lichnost' i tvorchestvo." Pp. 5–26 in *Zhitie Avvakuma i drugie ego sochineniia*, by Avvakum Petrovich. Moscow: Sovetskaia Rossiia, 1991.

Ronen, Omry. *An Approach to Mandelštam*. Jerusalem: Magnes Press, 1983.

Rotenstreich, Nathan. *Alienation: The Concept and Its Reception*. Leiden: E. J. Brill, 1989.

Sanderson, Richard K. "Relational Deaths: Narratives of Suicide Survivorship." Pp. 33–50 in *True Relations: Essays on Autobiography and the Postmodern*. Contributions to the Study of World Literature 85, edited by G. Thomas Couser and Joseph Fichtelberg. Westport, CT: Greenwood Press, 1998.

Sandler, Stephanie. "Embodied Words: Gender in Cvetaeva's Reading of Puškin." *Slavic and East European Journal* 34 (1990): 139–57.

Sarnov, B. "Defending the Privilege to Write Badly." Pp. 149–69 in *Literature and the New Thinking. History of the USSR: New Research 9*, compiled by I. A. Dedkov. Moscow: Nauka, 1989.

Schweitzer, Viktoria. (See also Shveitser, Viktoria.) *Tsvetaeva*. Translated by Robert Chandler, H. T. Willetts, and Peter Norman. Edited by Angela Livingstone. London: Harvill, 1992.

Segal, Dmitri. "Pro domo sua: The Case of Boris Pasternak." *Slavica Hierosolymitana* 1 (1977): 199–250.

Serova, M. V. "Avtobiograficheskaia proza v obshchem kontekste poeticheskogo samoopredeleniia Mandel'shtama i Tsvetaevoi." Pp. 175–86 in *"Vse v grudi slilos' i spelos'"*. *Piataia tsvetaevskaia mezhdunarodnaia nauchno-tematicheskaia konferentsiia (9–11 oktiabria 1997 goda)*, compiled and edited by N. I. Kataeva-Lytkina, E. S. Krasovskaia, and O. G. Revzina. Moscow: Dom-muzei Mariny Tsvetaevoi, 1998.

Severijnen, Olav. "The Renaissance of a Genre: Autobiography and Modernism." *New Comparison: A Journal of Comparative and General Literary Studies* 9 (1990): 41–59.

Shentalinsky, Vitaly. *Arrested Voices: Resurrecting the Disappeared Writers of the Soviet Regime*. Translated by John Crowfoot. New York: The Free Press, 1996.

Shevelenko, Irina. *Literaturnyi put' Tsvetaevoi*. Moscow: Novoe literaturnoe obozrenie, 2002.

Shveitser, Viktoria. (See also Schweitzer, Viktoria.) *Byt i bytie Mariny Tsvetaevoi*. Fontenay-aux-Roses: Syntaxis, 1988.

Smola, O. M. "Zametki k teme 'Mandel'shtam i revoliutsiia'." Pp. 506–14 in *Zhizn' i tvorchestvo O. E. Mandel'shtama*, edited by O. E. Makarova and I. E. Kharitonchik. Voronezh: Izdatel'stvo Voronezhskogo universiteta, 1990.

Spender, Stephen. *The Thirties and After: Poetry, Politics, People (1933–1970)*. New York: Random House, 1978.

Sprinker, Michael. "Fictions of the Self: The End of Autobiography." Pp. 321–42 in *Autobiography: Essays Theoretical and Critical*, edited by James Olney. Princeton, NJ: Princeton University Press, 1980.

Steinberg, Mark D. *Proletarian Imagination: Self, Modernity, and the Sacred in Russia, 1910–1925*. Cornell, NY: Cornell University Press, 2002.

Tal, Kali. "Speaking the Language of Pain: Vietnam War Literature in the Context of the Literature of Trauma." Pp. 217–48 in *Fourteen Landing Zones: Approaches* to *Vietnam War Literature*, edited by Philip Jason. Iowa City: University of Iowa Press, 1991.

Taranovsky, Kiril. *Essays on Mandelštam*. Cambridge, MA: Harvard University Press, 1976.

Tarasenkov, A. K. "Pasternak. Chernovye zapisi. 1930–1939." Pp. 150–74 in *Vospominaniia o Borise Pasternake*, edited by E. V. Pasternak and M. I. Feinberg. Moscow: Slovo, 1993.

Trenin, V. "Rabkor i belletrist." Pp. 213–16 in Chuzhak, *Literatura fakta: pervyi sbornik materialov rabotnikov LEFa*. edited by N.F. Chuzak. Moscow:Izd. Federatsiia, 1929. Reprint, Moscow: Zakharov, 2000.

Tret'iakov, S. "Chto novogo." *Novyi LEF* no. 9 (1928): 1–5.

———. "Novyi Lev Tolstoi." Pp. 29–33 in *Literatura fakta: pervyi sbornik materialov rabotnikov LEFa*, edited by N. F. Chuzak. Moscow: Izd. Federatsiia, 1929. Reprint, Moscow: Zakharov, 2000.

———. "S novym godom! S 'Novym LEFom'!" *Novyi LEF* 1 (1928): 1–3.

Trotsky, Leon. *Literature and Revolution*. New York: Russell and Russell, 1957.

Tsvetaeva, Marina. *Art in the Light of Conscience: Eight Essays on Poetry by Marina Tsvetaeva*. Trans. and ed. Angela Livingstone. Cambridge, MA: Harvard University Press, 1992.

———. *A Captive Spirit: Selected Prose*. Edited and translated by J. Marin King. Ann Arbor, MI: Ardis Publishers, 1994.

———. *Neizdannye pis'ma*. Paris: YMCA Press, 1972.

———. "O poezii i proze." *Zvezda* 10 (1992): 4.

———. *Sobranie sochinenii v semi tomakh*. Edited, compiled, and annotated by Anna Saakiants and Lev Mnukhin. Moscow: Terra, 1997.

———. *Zapisnye knizhki: v dvukh tomakh*. Moscow: Ellis Lak, 2000–2001.

Upton, Lee. *The Muse of Abandonment: Origin, Identity, Mastery in Five American Poets*. Lewisburg, PA: Bucknell University Press, 1998.

Ustinov, A. "1929 god v biografii Mandel'shtama." *Novoe literaturnoe obozrenie* 6 (2002): 123–126.

"V kogo vgryzaetsia LEF?" *LEF* 1 (1923): 8–9.

"Vnutrennie retsenzii i predislovie dlia izdatel'stva 'Vremia.'" In *Slovo i sud'ba. Osip Mandel'shtam*, edited by Z. S. Papernyi. Moscow: Nauka, 1991.

Volin, B. M. "Poeziia rabochikh professii." *Na postu* 2–3 (1923): 129.

———, ed. *Poeziia rabochikh professii: sbornik rabochikh stikhov*. Moscow: Novaia Moskva, 1924.

Wachtel, Michael. *The Development of Russian Verse*. Cambridge: Cambridge University Press, 1998.

Warner, H. E. "Will Poetry Disappear?" *Lippincott's Magazine* 63 (1899): 282–88.

Wimsatt, William K., and Monroe C. Beardsley. *The Verbal Icon; Studies in the Meaning of Poetry*. Lexington: University of Kentucky Press, 1954.

"Zametki o peresechenii biografii Osipa Mandel'shtama i Borisa Pasternaka." *Pamiat'* 4 (1979): 282–337.

Index

Acmeism, Russian, 17, 35, 37, 40, 107
Akhmatova, Anna, 17, 91, 118, 157, 184, 191n39; and autobiography, 8; campaign against, 7–9, 164; "Courage" (*Muzhestvo*), 8; defends Osip Mandelstam, 97; Mandelstam's criticism of, 37; *Poem Without a Hero* (*Poema bez geroia*), 9; *Requiem* (*Rekviem*), 9; temporary rehabilitation of, 164
Aseev, Nikolai, 27, 64, 65
Averbakh, Leopold, 63, 163
Avvakum (Archpriest Avvakum Petrov). *See also* Mandelstam, Osip

Balmont, Konstantin, 81, 127
Bannikov, Nikolai, 168
Barnes, Christopher, 70, 75, 83, 88, 163, 167, 168
Bedny, Demyan: ideal poet for the state, 21
Bely, Andrey (Boris Bugaev), 81, 82
Beria, Lavrenty, 161, 163
Bethea, David, 98
Bezymensky, Alexander, 19
Blok, Alexander, 7, 16, 27, 52, 53, 127, 173; as model for Pasternak, 173; poetry readings in Moscow, 35, 190n17; relationship to Soviet state, 4, 27, 127, 185n4; "The Twelve" (*Dvenadtsat'*), 21
Bobrov, Sergei, 40, 81
Bogdanov, Alexander, 33; influence on Bolshevik literary policy, 18, 32, 48–49
Brik, Osip, 61; attack on "creative" personalities, 27; and relationship of technology to poetry, 41
Brodsky, Joseph, 121, 154
Brown, Edward, 22, 25
Bruner, Jerome, 50
Bryusov, Valery, 40, 41
Bukharin, Nikolai, 54, 163; assists Mandelstam, 37, 92

Carlisle, Olga, 166
Cavanagh, Claire, 109, 110, 120
Chester, Pamela, 203n45
Chuzhak, N. (N. F. Nasimovich): against "creative" literature, 25–26, 62–63
Ciepiela, Catherine, 61, 83, 204n63
Cohen, Hermann, 69, 75, 84; mentor for Pasternak, 72, 73

Communist Party: 1925 statement on literature, 22, 23, 24, 63, 93; 1932 decree instituting control of literary groups, 160; 1934 Writers' Congress, 161–62; attitude towards literature, 8–9, 18–25, 42, 50, 54, 63, 93, 126–27, 164, 183; pressure on Pasternak, 180–82

cultural and literary organizations: disputes among, 17–27, 37–40, 42; FOSP (Federation of Organizations of Soviet Writers), 25, 92, 97–99, 101, 197n10; LEF (Left Front of the Arts), 20, 25, 26, 37–39, 41, 44, 45, 50, 54, 60–65, 77–80, 93, 106; and "literature of fact," 10, 25, 62–63, 66, 67, 71, 78, 80, 106, 132; Narkompros (People's Commissariat for Enlightenment), 30, 32, 33; October, 18, 19, 37–38, 42, 44, 45, 50, 54; Proletkult (Proletarian Cultural and Educational Organization), 19, 31, 107; RAPP (Russian Association of Proletarian Writers), 25, 65, 160, 163, 174; the Smithy (Kuznitsa), 19, 21; VAPP (All-Russian Association of Proletarian Writers), 19–22, 25

cummings, e. e., 3

Dante Alighieri, 98, 99, 104–6, 119
Derzhavin, Gavrila, 12, 86, 132, 167
Dinega, Alyssa, 152
Dobrenko, Evgeny, 18
Dzerzhinsky, Felix, 30, 37, 190n31

Eakin, Paul John, 67; and autobiography's relationship to reality, 13; and relational autobiography, 14
Efron, Sergei, 122, 123, 125
Eikhenbaum, Boris, 34; defends Osip Mandelstam, 97
Eliot, T. S., 3
Erlich, Victor, 168
Esenin, Sergei, 7, 27, 54, 81, 108, 173; as inspiration for Mandelstam, 115,

200n55; dispute about suicide of, 207n32

Fadeev, Alexander, 173
Feiler, Lily, 124, 133
Fet, Afanasy, 15, 16, 55, 132; and collapse of poetry, 15–16
Fleishman, Lazar, 66, 75, 77, 78, 158, 160, 161, 163, 181
Formalism, 78, 107; and philosophy of artistic creation, 34–35, 38, 41
Forrester, Sibelan, 203n45
FOSP. *See* cultural and literary organizations
Freidin, Gregory, 43, 44, 98, 108, 118
Frost, Robert, 3, 56, 170
Futurism, Russian, 17, 35, 36, 38, 39, 60, 78–81, 86, 98, 107

Gasparov, Boris, 196n4
Gide, André, 163
Ginzburg, Lydia, 12; and autobiography's relationship to reality, 12–13, 132, 143, 186n12
Gippius, V. V., 55, 56, 59, 96
Gorky, Maxim, 20, 162, 170
Gornfeld, A.G.: role in Ulenspiegel scandal, 92, 95, 96, 109, 113
Gumilyov, Nikolai, 17, 27, 37, 54, 108

Hall, Donald, 5
Harari, Manya, 181
Harris, Jane Gary, 108, 110, 186n12
Herzen, Alexander: and *The Noise of Time*, 31, 36, 45, 46; and "Fourth Prose," 98, 99, 101–3, 113
Herzen House: headquarters for literary associations, 36, 101–2, 113; residence for Osip Mandelstam, 31, 36
Holmgren, Beth, 129, 130

Isenberg, Charles, 49, 108, 110, 117

Jakobson, Roman, 27

Karlinsky, Simon, 128
Kaverin, Veniamin, 42

Khlebnikov, Velimir (Victor), 27, 39, 81;
Mandelstam attempts to help, 36;
Mandelstam's opinion of, 36, 39;
Pasternak's opinion of, 207n31
Khlystalov, Edward: disputes suicide
of Sergei Esenin, 207n32
Khrushchev, Nikita, 180
King, J. Marin, 110, 111, 140
Kirillov, Vladimir: and technology-
oriented poetry, 32, 33
Klyuev, Nikolai, 7; and threats to
poets, 27
Kolchevska, Natasha, 129
Krivulin, Viktor, 45, 91, 117
Kushner, Boris, 41, 118
Kuznetsov, Nikolai, 27

Lebedev-Polyansky, Pavel, 50
LEF. *See* cultural and literary
organizations
Lelevich, G. (Labory Gilelevich
Kalmanson), 37, 39
Lenin, Vladimir, 127; and the nature
of poets, 4; involved in literary
disputes, 18, 19
Lezhnev, I. G., 30, 31
Lifton, Robert, 174, 175
literary journals: disputes among,
20–21, 25–26, 36, 41–43, 62–64; *New
LEF* (*Novyi LEF*), 25, 61, 62, 64, 65,
93; *Novy mir*, 179; *On Guard* (*Na
postu*), 20, 39, 42, 50, 54; *Red Virgin
Soil* (*Krasnaia nov'*), 20–22, 25, 60,
65, 159; *Russia* (*Rossiia*), 30; *The Star*
(*Zvezda*), 60
"literature of fact." *See also* cultural
and literary organizations
Livingstone, Angela, 85, 168
the Literary Gazette (*Literaturnaia
gazeta*): controversy about
Mandelstam in, 96–97
Loks, Konstantin, 68, 89
Lotman, Mikhail: on connection
between Mandelstam and Saussure,
199n39
Lunacharsky, Anatoly: as leader of
Narkompros, 25, 30, 32, 185n4; as

theorist on literature, 18, 54

Mandelstam, Alexander, 30–31
Mandelstam, Nadezhda, 4, 29–31, 34,
36, 37, 39, 40, 54, 91–94, 98, 101, 102,
174; and Anna Akhmatova, 184; as
memoirist, 29, 183, 188n1, 198n27
Mandelstam, Osip, 2–4, 6, 7, 9–13, 15,
17, 27, 29–57, 59, 67–69, 83, 88, 89,
91–121, 123, 124, 126, 128–32, 148,
153, 158, 161, 164, 174, 177, 180–84;
and Acmeism, 17, 37, 40–41; and
alienation of the poet, 98–100,
106–9, 111; appeals to Dzerzhinsky,
30, 37; and Archpriest Avvakum,
98–101, 104, 109, 111, 116, 117; and
Armavir, 200n66; attitude towards
language, 34, 36, 38, 43, 46–48, 104–
6, 116–18, 198n39; on composing
poetry, 104–5, 106–7, 115–16, 118;
and Dante, 104–6, 119; and Herzen,
44–46, 98, 99, 101–3, 113; and
Jewishness, 46–48, 108–13, 120;
and literary establishment, 30–45,
94–98, 101, 109, 111–14; place in
Russian culture, 30, 33, 45–48, 107,
110, 111, 114, 120; and the poet's
voice, 34, 52–56, 103–5, 114–18;
travels after the Revolution, 30–32,
34, 36–37; and Ulenspiegel affair 92,
94–97, 99, 109, 113, 115, 180, 197n10
199n53; working in Narkompros,
32–33. *See also* Pasternak, Boris
Works: "An Army of Poets"
(*Armiia poetov*), 42, 43, 104, 105, 124;
"Birth of Plot" (*Rozhdenie fabuly*),
38; "Conversation About Dante"
(*Razgovor o Dante*), 99, 104–6,
119; "Fourth Prose" (*Chetvertaia
proza*), 3, 11, 91–93, 95, 98–104,
107–21, 126, 128, 129, 153, 177, 181,
182; "Government and Rhythm"
(*Gosudarstvo i ritm*), 33; "Hagia
Sophia" (*Aiia–Sofiia*), 32; "Having
deprived me of seas" (*Lishiv
menia morei*), 120; "Humanism
and the Present" (*Gumanism i*

sovremennost'), 39; "I hear, I hear the early ice" (*Slyshu, slyshu, rannii led*), 119; "I sing while my larynx is moist and my soul is dry" (*Poiu, kogda gortan' syra, dusha sukha*), 119; "I wince from the cold" (*Ia vzdragivaiu ot kholoda*), 52; "In the Discordance of the Maidens' Choir" (*V raznogolositse devicheskogo khora*), 33; *The Noise of Time* (*Shum vremeni*), 9, 10, 13, 30, 31, 39, 44–46, 48–50, 52–56, 59, 67, 69, 92, 93, 96, 98–101, 104, 107, 108, 110, 111, 113, 115, 116, 120, 128, 131, 153, 177, 182; "On the Addressee" (*O sobesednike*), 52, 105; "On the Nature of the Word" (*O prirode slova*), 38, 43; "On Translations" (*O perevodakh*), 97, 98; "Out of the evil and miry pool" (*Iz omuta zlogo i viazkogo*), 52; "Silentium," 52; "The Slump" (*Vypad*), 54; "Stalin Ode" (*Oda*), 93, 118, 188n1; "Stifling gloom covers the river bed" (*Dushnyi sumrak kroet lozhe*), 52; "The Swallow" (*Lastochka*), 33; "Torrents of Hackwork" (*Potoki khaltury*), 96, 98; "The Twilight of Freedom" (*Sumerki svobody*), 34; "We live without sensing the land underfoot" (*My zhivem pod soboiu ne chuia strany*), 93, 120; "The Word and Culture" (*Slovo i kul'tura*), 35, 43, 105, 106, 111; "Yes, I lie in the ground" (*Da, ia lezhu v zemle*), 120

Mayakovsky, Vladimir, 35, 39, 54, 76, 77, 114, 127, 128, 145, 147, 148, 157, 162, 169, 170, 172–74, 176; "A Slap in the Face of Public Taste" (*Poshchechina obshchestvennomu vkusu*), 17; *At the Top of My Voice* (*Vo ves' golos*), 86, 172; leader of Futurists, 35, 64, 81; "Order No. 2 to the Army of Art" (*Prikaz No. 2 Armii iskusstva*), 35; "state poet," 82–83, 85–89; suicide of, 10, 27, 60, 68, 84, 85, 173, 174, 207n32; *Vladimir Mayakovsky* (*Vladimir Maiakovskii*), 82; "War and the World" (*Voina i mir*), 86. *See also* Tsvetaeva, Marina; *see also* Pasternak, Boris

Narkompros. *See* cultural and literary organizations
Nadson, Semyon, 53
New LEF (*Novyi LEF*). *See* literary journals

October. *See* cultural and literary organizations
On Guard (*Na postu*). *See* literary journals
Opoyaz. *See* Society for the Study of Poetic Language.

Pasternak, Boris, 2, 3, 6, 7, 9–13, 15, 27, 35, 39, 59–62, 65–89, 91, 93, 94, 114, 116, 118, 120, 121, 128, 131, 132, 135, 145–49, 153, 154, 157–84; and "authorized" art, 77–80; association with Centrifuge, 81, 171; attitudes towards language, 68–70, 74, 158, 165–66, 168; condemned by literary groups, 65, 66, 162, 160, 165, 180; and Georgia, 148, 159, 160, 161, 162, 168; and Mandelstam, 68, 69, 88–89, 114, 118, 158, 161, 164, 174, 177; and Mayakovsky, 81–87 89 162, 169, 170, 172–74, 176; and political trials, 162–63, 166; relationship with LEF, 60–64, 77–80; and suicide, 6, 60, 66, 68, 84–85, 88, 89, 158, 160, 161, 163, 164, 173, 174, 180, 195n55; and survivor theory, 84, 173–76; and the Nobel prize, 180–82; Works: "A century and a bit" (*Stolet'e s lishnim*), 159; "Death of a Poet" (*Smert' poeta*), 68; *Doctor Zhivago* (*Doktor Zhivago*), 165–68, 179–82; *Lieutenant Schmidt* (*Leitenant Shmidt*), 61, 62, 147; "Marburg," 75–76; *My Sister, Life* (*Sestra, moia—zhizn'*), 61, 145; *People and Propositions* (*Liudi i*

polozheniia), 12, 157, 165–79, 181;
Safe Conduct (*Okhrannaia gramota*),
9–13, 59–89, 114, 116, 128, 131, 153,
157–60, 165, 167–72, 174–77, 181,
182; *Second Birth* (*Vtoroe rozhdenie*),
68, 160; *Sublime Malady* (*Vysokaia bolezn'*), 61; "To a Friend" (*Drugu*)
87, 159; "To Boris Pilnyak" (*Borisu Pilniaku*), 87, 159; *Twin in the Clouds*,
(*Bliznets v tuchakh*), 68, 171; *The Year 1905* (*1805 god*), 61, 147. See also
Tsvetaeva, MarinaPavlenko, Petr,
174
Pertsov, V., 65
Petrov, Archpriest Avvakum. See
Mandelstam, Osip
Pilnyak, Boris, 54, 87, 159, 163
Pisarev, Dmitry, 16
Poetry and science, 18–20, 24, 34–35,
38, 40–42, 61–65
Pollak, Nancy, 192n50
Proletkult. *See* cultural and literary
organizations
Pushkin, Alexander, 12, 15, 16, 17, 48,
67, 81, 108, 109, 133, 145, 149–54,
159, 167; monument to, 144; *Eugene Onegin* (*Evgenii Onegin*), 151; as
Marina Tsvetaeva's "father," 149,
151; *The Mermaid* (*Rusalka*), 151;
"The Poet and the Crowd" (*Poet i tolpa*), 150; *Poltava* (*Poltava*),
153; "To the Sea" (*K moriu*), 154;
"Stanzas" (*Stansy*), 159

Radek, Karl, 161
RAPP. *See* cultural and literary
organizations
Red Virgin Soil (*Krasnaia nov'*). *See*
literary journals
Rilke, Rainer Maria, 60, 66, 69, 75, 80,
82, 84, 173
Rotenstreich, Nathn: on psychology of
isolation, 107
Russia (*Rossiia*). *See* literary journals

Sandler, Stephanie, 129
Schweitzer, Viktoria, 122, 123

Scriabin, Alexander: influence on Boris
Pasternak, 69, 70, 72, 84
Severijnen, Olav, 171
Shevelenko, Irina, 148, 152, 204n63
Shklovsky, Victor, 31, 34, 38, 96;
friendship with Osip Mandelstam,
31, 34, 96; and Society for the Study
of Poetic Language (Opoyaz), 34
Shklvoskaya-Kordi, Vasilisa, 31, 34
Shostakovich , Dmitry: persecution of,
162
Smirnov, Nikolai, 165, 166
the Smithy (*Kuznitsa*). *See* cultural and
literary organizations
Smola, O. P., 34
Society for the Study of Poetic
Language (Opoyaz), 34
Spender, Stephen, 4, 26
Sprinker, Michael, 13
Stalin, Joseph, 2, 3, 6, 11, 12, 25, 29, 62,
88, 93, 114, 118, 119, 148, 157–59,
161–63, 175
Mandelstam's criticism of, 88, 93, 161;
praises Mayakovsky, 162; subject
of poems, 6, 93, 118, 148, 161,
163; telephone conversation with
Pasternak, 161, 205n6
The Star (*Zvezda*). *See* literary journals
Steinberg, Mark, 50
Stevens, Wallace, 153
Struve, Alexander: attacks Alexander
Blok, 35
Symbolism, Russian, 16, 17, 21, 35, 52,
53, 78, 81, 98, 105, 107, 171–73

Tabidze, Nina, 165
Tabidze, Titsian, 158, 159, 162–65,
175, 183; death of, 163, 164; and
Georgian writers' association, 164;
friendship with Boris Pasternak,
159, 162
Tal, Kali, 174
Tarasenkov, Anatoly, 175
Taubman, Jane, 132
Tesková, Anna: correspondence with
Marina Tsvetaeva, 122, 124, 125,
139, 144, 145

Tikhonov, Nikolai, 174
Tolstoy, Leo (Lev), 16, 17; death of, 171–72
Tretyakov, Sergei, 26, 27, 62–64
Trotsky, Leon (Lev Bronstein), 20–22; on genuine proletarian culture, 20–21; on poets who support the Revolution, 21; and Party policy concerning the arts, 21–22
Tsvetaeva, Maria Aleksandrovna, 60, 133–36, 138–40, 142, 149, 151, 173
Tsvetaeva, Marina, 2, 3, 6, 7, 9, 11, 12, 15, 27, 75, 81, 83, 120–55, 158, 162, 164, 173–76, 182–184; and Alexander Pushkin, 131, 133, 141, 144, 145, 149–54; and Boris Pasternak, 81–92, 128, 131, 132, 135, 145–49, 153, 154 158, 162, 164, 173–76, 182–84, 185n5; compares Vladimir Mayakovsky and Boris Pasternak, 147–48; in emigration, 122–28; and music, 135–38; philosophy of poet as outsider, 124–26, 128, 142–44, 152–54; and politics, 124, 126, 127, 128, 145–47, 153–54; relationship with mother, 129–30, 133–42, 149, 151–52; and sexual politics, 129–31, 145, 151–52, 202n29; suicide of, 2, 6, 164, 173; and Vladimir Mayakovsky, 127, 128, 145, 147, 148; Works: "The Devil" (*Chert*), 75, 131, 133, 139–42, 144, 145; "Epic and Lyric in Contemporary Russia" (*Epos i lirika v sovremennoi Rossii*), 125, 147; "The House at Old Pimen" (*Dom u Starogo Pimena*), 130, 131, 141; "Mother and Music" (*Mat' i muzyka*), 129, 131, 133, 135, 138–41; "My Pushkin" (*Moi Pushkin*), 131, 141, 144, 145, 149, 151, 152, 153, 154; "Perekop" (*Perekop*), 127; "Poem of the End" (*Poema kontsa*), 120, 153; "The Poet and Time" (*Poet i vremia*), 125, 127, 145, 146; "The Poet on the Critic" (*Poet o kritike*), 123
Tynyanov, Yury, 34; and literary evolution, 38; defends Osip Mandelstam, 97

Ulenspiegel affair. *See under* Mandelstam, Osip

VAPP. *See* cultural and literary organizations
Voronsky, A. K., 20
Vysotskaya, Ida: romance with Pasternak, 74–76, 85

Yashvili, Paolo, 158, 173, 175; hymn to Stalin, 163; Pasternak's friendship with, 159; suicide of, 163–64

Zaslavsky, David: attacks Mandelstam, 96, 97; attacks Pasternak, 180
Zhdanov, Andrei: attacks Anna Akhmatova, 8–9, 164; institutes literary crackdown, 164
Zoshchenko, Mikhail, 54, 164

About the Author

Donald Loewen is associate professor of Russian in the Department of German, Russian, and East Asian Languages at Binghamton University (State University of New York). He has published numerous articles on the autobiographical prose of Russian poets.